Silent Witnesses

Edward Hopper, *Automat,* 1927
Oil on canvas, 28 1/8 x 36 in.
Purchased with funds from the Edmundson Art Foundation, Inc.;
Des Moines Art Center Permanent Collections, 1958.2

Silent Witnesses:
Representations of Working-Class Women in the United States

Jacqueline Ellis

Bowling Green State University Popular Press
Bowling Green, OH 43403

Copyright 1998 © Bowling Green State University Popular Press

Library of Congress Cataloging-in-Publication Data
Ellis, Jacqueline, 1969-
    Silent witnesses : representations of working-class women in the
United States / Jacqueline Ellis.
        p.   cm.
    Includes bibliographical references and index.
    ISBN 0-87972-743-8 (cloth). -- ISBN 0-87972-744-6 (pbk.)
    1. Working class women--United States--History--20th century.
2. Working class women--United States--Pictorial works.   3. Working class women in art.   4. Working class women in literature.
    HD6058.E44   1997
    305.4'0973--DC21   97-3115
                                                                          CIP

Cover design by Dumm Art

To my parents,
Patricia and Trevor Ellis

Contents

Acknowledgments

I began this book as an undergraduate in the American Studies department at the University of Hull, England. The classes I took there helped me start thinking about 1930s culture, feminism, literature, and working-class identity in the United States. In particular, I was inspired by John Osborne who encouraged me to formulate, value, and question my opinions, and who gave me the confidence I needed to begin writing.

I was fortunate to receive a three-year fellowship from the British Academy. An additional grant from the Academy also gave me the means to conduct research in the United States. In this respect, I am grateful to the American Studies program at the University of Massachusetts, Amherst, where I was a visiting scholar for one year. I am especially thankful to Judith Davidov, who provoked my interest in photography and offered challenging and insightful readings of my work.

My research into FSA photography would not have been possible without the help of the prints and photographs division at the Library of Congress, the collections at Oakland Museum, and the Roy Stryker Archives at the University of Kentucky, Louisville. I am also grateful to the staff of the libraries at the University of Massachusetts and the University of Hull. I am indebted to the *Feminist Review* collective and the *History of Photography,* who published my work on Esther Bubley, and offered helpful suggestions in the process. The editors Pat Browne and Barbara Solosy at Popular Press were invaluable as I prepared various drafts of the manuscript. Thanks also to Diana Roberts who proofread a draft.

This book was inspired by some of my working-class heroes: Tillie Olsen, Dorothy Allison, Carolyn Chute, Michael Moore, Roseanne, John Lennon and Billy Bragg. Especially Deirdre Murphy, who, in long conversations over beer and chips, reminded me that there was a point to this project.

Above all, I am grateful to my parents and to my husband, Steven, without whom I would never have begun or finished this book.

Introduction

Describing the difference between documentary photography and straightforward photojournalism, Dorothea Lange noted that documentary meant going "in over your head, not just up to your neck."[1] In her introduction to *Calling Home*, an anthology of writing by working-class women, Janet Zandy responded to Lange's comment: "to dare to write about working-class literature in a culture where the working-class itself is denied a name, never mind a literary category, is to plunge in over one's head."[2] Extending from these analogies, to begin a critical analysis of photographic and literary representations of working-class women in American culture, particularly as somebody from a country where class identity is named and discussed at length, could be considered an especially perilous pursuit.[3] Nevertheless, I began this project with a clear conviction: that working-class experiences and working-class identity are fundamental to American consciousness however much this has been denied and disguised by history, politics, popular culture, national mythology, in theories about gender and race, and even by people whose economic situations might indicate their working-class status.

Even though class difference is "America's dirty little secret," official statistics and government surveys do not deny the existence of poverty.[4] According to recent evidence, 15% of all Americans have incomes under the poverty line. This figure is compounded when one notes that the official poverty level is only $15,150 per year for a family of four. Poverty rates are highest among families of color. Estimates have shown that 46% of African-American and 41% of Latino children live below the poverty line. Figures also show that levels of poverty are especially high for women. In 1991, almost half of all women workers earned less than the minimum sufficiency wage of $6.67 per hour. Moreover, the rate of poverty has been increasing since the 1970s, a process exacerbated by conservative welfare policies coupled with an increase in levels of corporate "welfare." Statistics show that corporate taxes make up only 10% of all federal tax revenue. Tax breaks, together with downsizing, low wages and fewer regulations, have all benefited shareholders and directors but have also increased the differential between rich and poor in the United States.[5]

1

Statistical evidence is compounded with personal testimony. In 1993 Michael Frisch conducted a series of interviews to illustrate Milton Rogovin's photographic investigation of declining steel industries in Buffalo, New York. In the course of these discussions, Frisch discovered that workers who had previously taken pride in their "middle-class" status, were becoming increasingly disillusioned after the security offered by relatively high wages and mostly regular employment became less dependable.[6] For example, Ralph and Rose Wils describe their lifestyle as comfortable. They own their own house, take regular holidays in Florida, and always have plenty of food on the table. Even though they could not afford to send their children to college, they still consider themselves middle class. After the Shenango plant closed down and the Wilses' income became less regular, however, they became less confident that they would be able to avoid the kind of absolute poverty that they associated with being working class. Their concern was especially concentrated on the future of their children:

Ralph: They're not going to be able to do some of the things that I think a kid should be able to do because with these service jobs, three, four dollars an hour, they're not going to be able to afford to do it. They're going to exist; that's all.[7]

The Wilses' trepidation is echoed by almost all of Frisch's interviewees. Mark and Lynn Cieslica had also been sure of their status as middle-class Americans; but industrial decline meant that the family's connection to the accouterments of an archetypically American middle-class lifestyle became increasingly tenuous:

LC: Now we're at a point in America where the middle-class, I think, it's going to be real hard for us to hang on to and to see our children hang on to this type of living that we had made for ourselves. You can't take life for granted anymore. It's a definite struggle. I mean America was always the melting pot, there were so many different opportunities that everybody could find a focus. Everybody could find something out there for them. But now it's not a line anymore, now it's become like a crater between the two ["middle-class" and "upper-class" Americans]—you either have to be making an awful lot of money or you have to be on the edge wondering, "Can I keep a roof over my head or am I going to be living in my car tomorrow?"[8]

These experiences testify to the existence of a significant difference between those whose economic position allows them a measure of personal freedom—not simply in terms of the things they can afford to buy—but according to the kind of choices they are able to make: as employees, homeowners, parents, and citizens; and those for whom such choices are circumscribed by their material status. The delineation might not always be evident during times of national prosperity. Before the 1970s, the workers at the Buffalo steel plants enjoyed lifestyles that would have been unimaginable for their parents and grandparents. Frisch notes that until the steelworks began closing and employees were gradually laid off or fired, there was not an immediately obvious difference between the lifestyles of the steel workers and those with more typically middle-class occupations:

In the old days, working-class often meant people whose lives were totally different from, let's say, the middle-class. But then in the period you're growing up in, you're moving to the suburbs, you know, in fact out here you had a boat and working-class people have televisions and their kitchens look like anybody else's kitchen, you know, it's not that big a divide.[9]

Nevertheless, in periods of economic decline—in this case, when manufacturing industry was being replaced with service and technical work—it was the people whose connection to material wealth was most expendable that were inevitably excluded from economic progression. According to one of the former steelworkers, William Douglass Jr., this was a continuum that had existed throughout the history of American labor: "Maybe it is a natural evolution that we go from the dust bowl to the rust bowls to high tech. But it would be a shame to lose all those skills and all that knowledge and in the future find that we need it."[10] For the purposes of this study, Douglass's description sets out the historical and economic contexts that inform my definition of working-class identity in America.

Douglass's perspective also helped determine my choice of artists who worked to represent working-class people between 1933 and 1945. In particular, I chose not to include the most famous woman photographer of that period, Margaret Bourke-White. Coincidentally, Bourke-White began her career documenting the steel-making process at the Otis Mill in Cleveland, Ohio. Her images are beautifully composed, concentrating on the imposing elegance of the machinery and the abstracted shapes of the manufacturing process. Bourke-White was artistically transfixed by what she perceived as the "drama" of industrial production. She focused on "the rush of flowing metal, the dying sparks, the clouds of smoke, the heat, the traveling cranes clanging back and forth."[11] Her perspective reflected a belief that manufacturing industry was the most fundamental component of art and human identity. She noted that: "art that springs from industry should have real flesh and blood because industry is the vital force of this great age."[12] Indeed, Bourke-White was so enamored with the physicality of the steel industry that her images rendered human participation in steel making almost obsolete. There were very few workers depicted in her photographs, and those shown appear as something of an aberration in what Bourke-White would have considered an otherwise perfect image. Her irritation was clearly expressed in one comment: "Posing American workers for photographs is often very difficult. . . . The minute an American worker sees a camera he becomes self conscious. Often I have to work over every detail of his posture, changing the slope of his back, the attitude of his head, the position of every finger."[13] Significantly, the absence of workers in Bourke-White's photography was especially appealing to the corporate heads of the steel industry. Consequently, she was regularly employed by several manufacturing companies during her career. The president of Otis Steel gave her $100 per image for her first project. His enthusiasm was matched by her earnings for subsequent work at Republic Steel and Chrysler Incorporated.

Bourke-White's dehumanized photographic approach to the steel industry was reflected in later documentary projects. In collaboration with writer Erskine Caldwell, she produced *You Have Seen Their Faces*, a documentary book depicting the people most affected by the Depression.[14] In general, her images were sensationalized, manipulative and one dimensional. The impact of her photography was enforced by a text in which Caldwell used extensive poetic license to record the words of their subjects. Working-class identity was reduced to insignificance in a series of impressions summed up in Bourke-White's own words:

Occasionally we found an interesting condition—a mother who didn't want people to see how poor things were—had lived in better houses and was ashamed. In many cases they felt it was a good thing to take their pictures—to show the world just how bad things were. But usually we encountered plain apathy. Most of the people we photographed were way too ignorant to know what it was all about. . . . In many cases people did not have the least vestiges of pride.[15]

The aim of this book is to examine the dimensions of working-class identity that were so steadfastly ignored in the work of artists like Bourke-White. In the process I want to examine how working-class identity has been defined in American culture, for what purpose and for whose benefit. Ultimately, my aim is to suggest how working-class people might have arrived at the social and economic point identified by those interviewed in *Portraits in Steel*. I have concentrated on the period between 1933 and 1945 because this was one of the rare instances in American history where economic deprivation was recorded and made visible to middle-class—that is, financially more secure—Americans. Indeed, the photographs taken for the Historical Section of the Farm Security Agency offer a comprehensive survey of poverty during the 1930s and early 1940s. In images made by Dorothea Lange, for example, the desperate circumstances of those portrayed are very clear. In the liberal context of New Deal politics, it would have been difficult for a viewer of FSA photographs to argue that migrant workers or tenant farmers did not require financial assistance. Sympathy was elicited, concern was voiced, and the American people who were not the focus of FSA images responded to the need that was displayed before them. The central message contained in FSA images was clear: that poverty was not an acceptable part of American society and therefore must be eased—if not eradicated—for the mutual benefit of both the subject and the viewer of government photography. FSA documentary seemed to serve a practical purpose in the 1930s, not only in making visible and attempting to resolve the problems of economic and social deprivation, but in apparently bridging the psychological distance between poverty and security through the visual dynamic of documentary photography. In so doing, the government could claim that even despite the factual evidence represented in the images, the economic difference between subject and viewer was secondary to the metaphoric equality evoked by the photographs. The construction of this ideological facade is particularly relevant to the way working-class identity was represented to a middle-class audience in official images.

Alongside Walker Evans, Dorothea Lange is perhaps the best known of the FSA photographers. Certainly, her "Migrant Mother" image is probably the best known photograph from the era. Moreover, it is clear in the many assessments made of her work that Lange's depictions of working-class subjects were more politically sympathetic than those of Margaret Bourke-White. Lange's photographic skills, coupled with her meticulous investigation of the social and economic histories that informed her empathetic relationship with her subjects, built her reputation as a superlative documentary photographer. Nevertheless, by examining Lange's work according to the political imperatives of FSA photography, it becomes clear that her images were so successful because they could be easily adapted to the ideological purposes of the New Deal. This is not to say that Lange—unlike Bourke-White—did not attempt to construct a complex individual context for each of her images. Rather, she approached and arranged her subjects in such a way that they conformed to notions of equality, individuality, and self-identity that were defined from the perspective of the economically privileged viewer rather than the materially deprived subject. As such, a photograph like "Migrant Mother" gives the impression of mutuality between the working-class woman who is depicted and a sympathetic middle-class point of view. At the same time, however, that sense of equality is dependent on Lange's manipulating her subject to fit moral values, aesthetic tastes, and political opinions that are abstracted away from the individual self-identity of the woman portrayed. Consequently, while the image shows that the woman's material circumstances are manifestly unequal to that of the middle-class viewer, that difference appears to be irrelevant since Lange had adapted her subject to fit a middle-class perspective, more politically sensitive than Bourke-White's, but nonetheless equally as imposing.

My analysis of Lange's images shows that poverty was depicted in a way that appropriated the perspective of the economically deprived subject for a political purpose that served the interests of the viewer. This is not to suggest that if the subjects of Lange's images could speak for themselves they would necessarily express an archetypically Marxist agenda. Or that if they were politically more conservative than the viewers of FSA photographs—as they probably were—that they were expressing a false consciousness. Rather, even though the rural poor were so frequently the subjects of photographic investigation, their visibility was dependent on their silence. This inequality is a fundamental constituent of my definition of working-class identity, in relation to what I would call a middle-class point of view in the 1930s. Exemplified in the context of FSA photography, it is the difference between being defined by someone else and being able to define oneself according to one's individual experience.

Marion Post Wolcott's photographs for the FSA differ from Lange's most obviously because they were taken in a prewar context rather than as representations of the Depression. Post Wolcott's images were also significant because they appeared to be less easily adaptable to the ideological machinations of New Deal policy. The fact that Post Wolcott's work was not widely published in the 1930s, and that she is not often analyzed by contemporary critics, also suggests a certain political incongruity in her images compared with other FSA photographers. Post Wolcott's photographs are particularly suited to the purposes of this study because she approached her FSA work from a perspective that was more explicitly radical than that of Lange. Moreover, her work contained an implicit feminist impulse that often intersected with her analysis of class difference. She portrayed the landscape as being fundamentally rejuvenative and symbolically expressive of a woman's body. This approach extended into her portraits of working-class people. She focused on what she perceived to be their strong sexual impulses, and portrayed their physicality as a radical force that could undermine the materially privileged perspective of the viewer. For Post Wolcott, human sexuality—especially in women—was a positive energy that had been weakened and commodified by capitalism. As such, her images highlight another way in which working-class identity was defined in opposition to material privilege. By representing working-class subjects as physically pure and inspirationally uncorrupted by consumer capitalism, economic disempowerment was apparently transformed into political power. At the same time, however, Post Wolcott depicted working-class identity as innately physical, irrational, emotional and sexually driven, in relation to a middle-class perspective that she presented as intellectual, objective, and central to the political and economic processes from which working-class subjects were inevitably excluded.

In both Lange's and Post Wolcott's photographs, then, the identity of economically deprived subjects is portrayed as being one dimensional, uncomplicated, and politically fixed according to the perspective of the middle-class viewer. In contrast, Esther Bubley portrayed socially marginalized subjects so that their perspective was less easily defined and therefore represented in more complex ways. At the same time, her photographs were taken as America entered the Second World War, when government photography began to concentrate on the nation's wealth, on the wide availability of consumer products and, as a result—rather than focusing on poverty and deprivation—represented the population as being homogeneously middle class. In this way, Bubley's work captures a point in American history when economic inequality was increasingly disguised, since consumer products—radios, fashionable clothes, lipstick, movies, and cheap magazines—could be purchased by a wider section of the population. As such, her images of smartly dressed young women provide a visual context for the attitudes of consecutive generations of working-class people who defensively assumed middle-class identities.

Nevertheless, Bubley photographed this emergent consumerism in order to reveal economic and social inequalities that remained constant, despite the increased purchasing power of her subjects. To this end, Bubley utilized the rhetoric of propaganda campaigns in order to highlight how economically and socially deprived people had been left out of popular images of wartime America, or else struggled to maintain an appearance of material equality. More important, Bubley also created a visual means that allowed her subjects to undermine the perspective of materially privileged viewers. Consequently, while government campaigns emphasized national identity and community spirit, Bubley concentrated on separation, self-involvement, and individual thought. By assigning these qualities to working-class subjects, she artfully subverted widely disseminated images that promoted a safely middle-class future for all Americans.

Having discovered a more complicated image of working-class identity in Bubley's photographs, I then wanted to compare her perspective with representations that claimed to express an identifiably working-class point of view. In the 1930s, radical politics and proletarian literature apparently provided a nurturing context for writing by and about working-class experiences. The movement defined itself in opposition to what it considered to be "bourgeois" writing; a term that seemed to cover any work that had preceded the 1930s and did not feature a strike, a mining accident, or a battle with police at some point in the narrative. Instead, proletarian writing was concerned with the immediacy of action, with solidarity between workers, and with the sensual romanticism of direct conflict. At the same time, its dogmatic agenda eschewed literary experimentation, narrative objectivity, introspective characterization, or any form of expression that might be interpreted as being middle class and, in relation to a working-class identity that was portrayed as distinctively macho, pejoratively effeminate. The gender oppositions in proletarian literature were particularly relevant for female radical writers, especially those from middle-class backgrounds. Consequently, their marginalized position has been the central focus of critical investigations that have attempted to exhume a subtextual feminist position beneath the literary machismo of proletarian writing.

At this point, my ideas about working-class identity collided with a feminist perspective that I wanted to be integral to my argument. I had purposefully chosen women photographers and writers because I thought they would be more politically sensitive to the marginalized position of their deprived subjects. At the same time, I wanted to use contemporary feminist theory to highlight the experiences of working-class women. Not surprisingly, I found that a particular photographer's or writer's ability to represent a complicated context from which to begin examining working-class identity in the 1930s, had nothing whatsoever to do with their gender. More problematic, however, was the realization that feminist politics and critical theory did not provide a means for analyzing economic differences between women. More often, these interpretations presented an antagonistic counterpoint to my examination of class, while simultaneously valorizing what I found to be a totalizing middle-class perspective. The political inadequacy of feminist analysis was most evident in relation to the two radical women writers I studied: Meridel Le Sueur and Tillie Olsen.

As active members of the Communist party and the proletarian literary movement, Le Sueur and Olsen began writing about working-class subjects in a context that was politically opposed to most other woman-authored works of the 1930s. Despite their ideological differences however, Le Sueur's work in particular bears some significant resemblance to Marjorie Kinnan Rawlings's Pulitzer Prize–winning novel, *The Yearling* (1939). Rawlings's novel was the result of an extensive period spent living with people she labeled "Florida cracker folk." According to Rawlings, this was a population who lived simply, while expressing no other conscious thought except "to buy their excellent corn liquor and to hunt."[16] Rather than echoing Margaret Bourke-White's disdainful pity for such apparent ignorance, Rawlings found herself so enamored by the "moonshiners" lifestyle that she felt "in danger of losing all sophistication and perspective."[17] As a result, Rawlings's writing produced a romanticized, pastoral, and ultimately patronizing image of working-class life in Florida. Consequently, her work was apolitical in a way that opposed the dictates of proletarianism, but that nonetheless echoed Meridel Le Sueur's representations of inherently feminist and naturally socialist working-class women.

In opposition to Rawlings, however, both Le Sueur and Olsen were emblematic of the intersection between class and gender identity in radical writing, since both women began writing in the 1930s from a self-consciously proletarian position. Furthermore, although their writing about women was often subsumed by male-centered radical politics, in the 1970s both Le Sueur and Olsen were rediscovered by the emergent feminist movement. Le Sueur's work was especially suited to a developing feminist perspective that concentrated on women's reproductive capabilities as a basis from which to establish a difference between politically powerful, socially oppressive, and naturally aggressive men, and women who had been systematically repressed, devalued, and attacked throughout history. More recent feminist criticism detracts from the biological essentialism in Le Sueur's writing, and has attempted to show how her representations of working-class women allowed her to express her own perspective as a middle-class woman in a literary context that often denied female experiences. At the same time, other analyses of Le Sueur's work have suggested that her writing about working-class women subverted definitions of an exclusively male proletariat, by concentrating on the biological processes of the female body in opposition to industrial production that was presented as peculiarly male labor. Nevertheless, in all these cases, Le Sueur's writing about women depended on a one-dimensional representation of working-class identity. As a middle-class woman, Le Sueur identified with an image of working-class experience that in proletarian terms was defined as being reactive, communally identified, unself-conscious, and naturally antagonistic, in relation to an image of "bourgeois" identity that was intellectual, individualized, and articulate. Moreover, I found that none of the recent feminist analyses of Le Sueur's work attempted to complicate this simplistic dialectic. Instead, they either tried to integrate a female perspective within this opposition while ignoring the class bias of its construction; or else they seemed to completely accept the proletarian image of working-class identity as being fundamentally gender opposed, rather than an expression of an economic hierarchy that did not easily include the perspective of the working-class subjects portrayed in their writings. In this way Le Sueur—and her contemporary critics—repeated the methods of Lange and Post Wolcott's photographs, where economic deprivation and social marginalization was represented according to the definitions of the middle-class viewer, or in this case author, reader, and critic.

Tillie Olsen's writing has also been analyzed as an expression of female experiences within a literary context defined from an essentially male point of view. Nevertheless, while it seemed clear that Le Sueur's writing conformed to proletarian definitions of class identity even while she complicated definitions of gender, Olsen's work from the 1930s was less easily adapted to that dichotomous context. In the same way, because contemporary examinations of radical women authors emphasized their gender identity rather than interpreting their writing about class, Olsen's complicated representation of working-class identity meant that she was also often misread and only partially understood as a feminist writer. Consequently, I found that Olsen's writing about working-class women became the critical text that framed and illuminated the whole of my investigation. Her work attested to the absence of working-class identity in official and radical representation in the 1930s. Moreover, her focus on female experience as an extension of material circumstances complicated feminist theory, which consistently refused to investigate economic differences between women, preferring instead to repeat the class, race, gender mantra as if each were a separate and exclusive category.

My intention in this book is to examine the intersection between these politicized identities. As such, when I describe a perspective as being working class, I do not only mean poor white, or African-American, or single mother, or tenant farmer, or low-paid office worker; I mean a position that is disempowered—economically, socially, and politically—in relation to the institutionalized power of those who claim to represent and speak for it; and disempowered in comparison with the sections of American society for whom that image or speech is intended to be received. In relation to FSA photography, the difference is clear. The government was interested in promoting images that would reconstitute the ideological tenets of the American Dream. As such, official photographs were made for the benefit of the middle-class Americans who represented a revitalized political mandate for the Democratic Party. Thus, although the rural poor were sometimes temporarily helped by legislative reforms, in relation to the rest of the population their economic position was unaltered. Consequently, in the early 1940s—and into the following decades—the appearance of being working class changed, but the economic hierarchy that ensured their social marginalization remained the same. As a result, while an increased number of Americans could afford consumer items, were able to send their children to minor institutions of higher education, and even occasionally acquired the means with which to escape their material circumstances, the experience of being working-class has remained a constant facet of American culture.[18]

Tillie Olsen has stated that "class remains the great unexamined factor" in analyses of why certain sections of American society are prevented from expressing themselves creatively.[19] As a response to Olsen's observation, this investigation is intended to reveal how working-class people have been misrepresented, manipulated, and silenced in order to fit the expectations of a middle-class audience. At the same time, however, my aim is to show that it is possible to represent working-class identity in ways that allow for a potential for self-expression. Nevertheless, it is telling that apart from Olsen, all of the artists in this book are from middle-class backgrounds and that none of them are women of color. This dualistic absence attests to a vital intersection between economic status and racial identity in American culture.

It will become clear in the course of this book that working-class identity was represented one-dimensionally in FSA photography and in proletarian writing. It is equally obvious that despite the political and social limitations of such representations, the images of working-class subjects that were published, analyzed, and disseminated in popular magazines, radical journals, museum exhibitions, and government reports, were almost exclusively white. Reflecting this, in his analysis of images made of African Americans for the FSA, Nicholas Natanson discovered that while they were relatively well represented in the files, photographs of black tenant farmers and sharecroppers were generally considered unsuitable for publication and display. Official excuses made for this exclusion reflected the government's passive acceptance of racism in the 1930s. Roy Stryker's seemingly reasonable advice to Dorothea

Lange is a perfect example of official acquiescence to this issue: "Regarding the tenancy pictures . . . I would suggest that you take both black and white, but place the emphasis on white tenants, since we know that these will receive much wider attention."[20] Natanson notes that black subjects were usually represented as if they were an intrinsic part of the land; consequently individuals were not named. Moreover, if they were identified, African-American subjects were mentioned at the bottom of a descending list that began with machinery, cattle, and mules. Otherwise, most published images of African Americans conformed entirely to white prejudices. Photographs showed congregations of wide-eyed, ecstatic worshipers, or focused on black workers sleeping or relaxing. In Natanson's words, black people were represented in official images as "comfortably predictable in an unpredictable age, enviably happy in an unhappy age, consistently entertaining in a mortifying age."[21]

Racial imbalance in FSA images might have been redressed by the arrival in 1942 of a black photographer, Gordon Parks. Parks joined the agency despite Stryker's reservations and in the face of open hostility from the darkroom technicians.[22] Even though he had confronted racism throughout his upbringing in Minnesota, Parks was nevertheless outraged by the extent of bigotry in segregated Washington, D.C.[23] His response was to produce a series of documentary portraits that sensitively depicted black people as proud and accomplished American citizens. Given the personal restrictions that must have affected Parks as a black photographer working in an intrinsically and extrinsically racist institution, it is perhaps inevitable that his photographic approach was generally aggrandizing rather than incisive, broadly symbolic instead of individually detailed, and circumspect rather than challenging in relation to the racist status quo. As a result, for the purposes of this book, Parks's images of African-American subjects are less interesting than Esther Bubley's complex investigations of the individualized effects of segregation and discrimination. Parks's photographs are limited by an element of didacticism that detracts from the self-identity of the subjects portrayed. This is made clear in his description of taking his most famous photograph, a portrait of Ella Watson, a black woman posed with a mop and broom in the style of Andrew Wyeth's "American Gothic."

There was a huge American flag hanging from a standard near the wall. I asked her to stand before it, then placed the mop in one hand and the broom in the other. "Now think of what you just told me and look straight into this camera." Eagerly I began clicking the shutter. It was done and I went home to supper. Washington could now have a conversation with her portrait.[24]

Despite the limitations of his work, Parks's presence in the FSA highlights a complex interconnection between race and class identity that was not comprehensively investigated in the photographs produced by the agency. Added to this, Parks's work also reveals the relevance of gender in relation to representations of working-class subjects. This point is investigated in Jeanne Montaussamy-Ashe's chronicle of African-American women photographers, *Viewfinders*. She shows that many black women made a living from photography in the 1930s and 1940s. Most, like Winifred Hall Allen, worked as portrait photographers.[25] Some, such as Billie Louise Barbour-Davies, experimented with landscape and abstract images.[26] Vera Jackson was a famous photographer in the black press, illustrating articles about celebrities such as Lena Horne and Dorothy Dandridge with superlative portraits.[27] Most of the women identified in *Viewfinders* were from middle-class backgrounds and found their work in relatively wealthy black communities. In this context, African-American women from working-class backgrounds faced a triple exclusion. Nevertheless, a few were able to develop photographic careers. In particular, Elizabeth "Tex" Williams worked for the U.S Army during World War II. Williams took pictures of operations, military maneuvers, and everyday activities in segregated barracks. Williams's success was achieved despite the fact that African-Americans were barred from army photo-schools and government training programs.[28] More usual photographic experience for working-class black women (and presumably for white working-class women also) was to be employed as a "camera girl" taking pictures for sale to couples in nightclubs. This work required women not only to be fast and skillful but also to be able to charm potential customers into buying their portraits.[29] Despite the instances documented in *Viewfinders*, black women photographers in the 1930s and 1940s were limited by the restrictions placed on them as women, as African Americans, and as working-class people. Consequently, no black women were employed by the FSA. Nevertheless, particular images by Lange, Post Wolcott, and especially Esther Bubley, provide serious and complicated analyses of black female identity, some of which I have included in this book.

The centrality of race as part of working-class identity in America was also avoided in radical literature written in the 1930s and 1940s. The proletarian movement, like the FSA, demurred from directly confronting racism as a political issue, adhering instead to Marxist dogma that defined race rather like gender, as a secondary result of working-class emancipation. Consequently, even writers like Richard Wright, who were initially supportive of communism, eventually became frustrated with the Party's racial equivocations.[30] In opposition to the exclusivity of proletarianism, some black writers represented African Americans as a population entirely divorced from any defining economic context. In particular, Zora Neale Hurston's *Their Eyes Were Watching God* (1937) portrays black female identity in a romanticized setting somewhat removed from the vestiges of white racism and economic deprivation. Hurston prefers instead to present the black population as a "metaphorical folk" viewed from a perspective of middle-class privilege.[31]

Given the ambiguous relationship of African-American writing to the proletarian movement in the 1930s, the simple explanation for the absence of black authors in this book would be that there were no radical black women writers examining working-class female subjects between 1933 and 1945. Although that fact explains the absence of black women writers from the parameters of my investigation, I think that further clarification is necessary. In his investigation of black images in FSA photography, Nicholas Natanson highlights a few instances when black and white working-class people were photographed side by side. In some of these images miners are shown working together, collecting their pay together and shopping at the same company stores. It is clear that their economic status is identical in a conventionally Marxist sense. Despite the background of equivalency, however, black and white workers segregate themselves within situations that might connote their working-class communality. As Natanson states "the tone of racial convention appears as strong as ever," in images of black and white workers.[32]

The focus on racial division over economic communality is echoed in *Their Eyes Were Watching God*. Janie has grown up playing with the middle-class children of the white family who employ her grandmother. Interestingly, she first recognizes her racial difference from them after seeing a photograph. Noticing her blackness, she cries: "Aw, aw! Ah'm colored! . . . before Ah seen de picture Ah thought Ah wuz just like de rest."[33] Janie's African-American identity is framed by photographic evidence and the course of her narrative is determined as racially separated from white culture at that moment. Nevertheless, Hurston defines Janie's economic ambitions in relation to the middle-class definitions of her white childhood companions. Consequently, Janie values individual material wealth and economic independence, which she achieves in an all-black town with a thriving capitalist economy. Significantly, in terms of gender, race, and working-class identity, Janie only rejects her middle-class status in favor of an occasionally violent, and ultimately doomed romance, which eventually leads to her personal fulfillment and inner peace.

The uplifting conclusion of *Their Eyes Were Watching God* is a testimony to Hurston's poetic skill, but it is extraordinarily nihilistic in its portrayal of African-American identity in 1937. Hurston's complete rejection of class analysis, despite the economic plight of the vast majority of black people in the 1930s and 1940s, shows that given the inherent racism of the proletarian movement, it was far easier for black writers to imagine racial rebellion than economic revolution. Furthermore, given the sexism of class politics in the 1930s (and perhaps the machismo of black politics and cultural expression at that time) Hurston also envisioned an intrinsically feminist conclusion to her book.[34] As a result, the narrative trajectory of *Their Eyes Were Watching God* reflects a dialectic progression that diffuses and fragments working-class identity into multifluous configurations of race and gender experience.

I hope that in the course of this book, my unraveling of working-class female identities from the middle-class perspectives that defined them in American culture between 1933 and 1945 will lead to a protracted analysis of why materially deprived people so value their gender, race, and ethnic differences over their economic similarities. The predominance of middle-class and white artists in the FSA, in the proletarian movement, and in this book, attests to the fundamental necessity of articulating any potential for common ground. The same economic hierarchies that defined working-class identity between 1933 and 1945 allowed Zora Neale Hurston to express her vision of a black female utopia—albeit to a limited audience—in 1937, and prevented Tillie Olsen from completing or publishing *Yonnondio* until 1973. In the same way, the racial exclusivity of the feminist movement in the 1970s nurtured Olsen and Le Sueur while neglecting Hurston. Moreover, writing by the majority of working-class women was often not even begun (if it was begun at all) until the generation after the Depression, especially if they happened to be African American.[35] Finally, middle-class ignorance of working-class identity has allowed investigation of its aspects: women's studies, African-American studies, muticultural studies, labor history, etc., while deriding its whole. As a result, minority literatures and histories are marginalized, Marxists ignore white working-class racism, middle-class feminists ignore female culpability in working-class oppression, economically deprived people of all races are increasingly excluded from higher education, and it is still considered acceptable to ridicule working-class people as rednecks or white trash.[36] These facts demand that systems of representation that have been constructed to the exclusion of women, racial minorities, and poor people be open to, and nurturing of, working-class identity. For these reasons, I would like this book to contribute to a continuing process of writing and thinking about working-class experiences in the United States.

Part I

Representing Working-Class Women

Introduction to Part I

The house seemed empty. "Else, Ben," she called softly. No-one answered. Slowly she pulled herself up and edging along the wall, pushed open the door into the front room. It lay in shadow, and out of an old enlarged photo, a very young Anna with a baby Will in her arms smiled down upon her. Her face contorted. Quickly she closed the door.[1]

In *Camera Lucida*, Roland Barthes follows an emotional photographic track in an attempt to come to terms with his mother's death. In so doing, he identifies two elements that form an individual reaction to a particular image. "Studium" connotes a general cultural response: a provocation of historical sympathy, a political commitment, or enthusiasm for a certain event or particular set of poses. Within this, what one might call a rational response, Barthes identifies the concept of "punctum": a reaction he describes as the element "which rises from the scene, shoots out of it like an arrow and pierces."[2] Punctum disturbs contemplation with an injection of irrationality, an interruption that designates the unfixable emotion of the image. Punctum signifies that element in photography that made Dorothea Lange uncomfortable with classification of her work as factual or merely documentary: "that magical power . . . that makes people look at it again and again and find new truths with each looking."[3]

As Barthes searched through many photographs of his mother, his general response was one of studium. He recognized her reproduced image, but he "missed her being"—the element of punctum.[4] At last, in one photograph of her, taken when she was a child in a winter garden in 1898, Barthes found what, for him, was the "truth" of his mother's image. He does not reproduce the Winter Garden picture in *Camera Lucida*; the element of punctum exists only for himself, as the son of the young girl portrayed, now dead. For the general readership, Barthes's mother exists only in the realm of studium where, he concludes, there can be "no wound."[5] *Camera Lucida* only briefly touches on the political implications of studium and punctum. The book is more of an introspective meditation than a critical work concerning theories of representation. However, its referents are a useful way of illuminating my own position within the body of theory and criticism examining photography for the United States Government between 1935 and 1943.

19

The passage that begins this discussion is from Tillie Olsen's novel *Yonnondio: From the Thirties*. Olsen's book is a useful illustration of Barthes's theory, widening his view beyond individual reactions to specific images, into a response that identifies the relationship of photography to capitalist ideology and its prescriptive notions of class and gender identity. In the novel, Anna, a working-class mother of four children, is struggling to survive in the Depression. Her existence has become engulfed by community pressures and the social demands of motherhood. For Anna, motherhood is a day-to-day battle in which any sense of her self-identity has been destroyed. Her only recognition of her own individuality comes when she collapses from exhaustion and consequently has time for self-reflection. She is reminded of the demanding necessities of her role by a photograph of herself as a young woman with one of her babies. The immediacy of this image—its element of punctum—forces her to resume the arduous task "of making a better life for her children to which her being was bound."[6]

Unlike Anna, while Barthes looks at his mother's picture he can begin a reverie of personal self-signification. In contrast, Anna's brief sense of self-awareness is suffocated as she faces her reproduced image: the act of recognition initiates a negative response. Anna's economic circumstances, and the demands of motherhood, engulf the drift of consciousness that would contextualize punctum into studium. Looking at the picture, she is not reminded of happier times. She does not see her child's smile or her own youth. She does not respond with nostalgia or with regret that time has taken its toll and her hopes have not been fulfilled. In this sense, the photograph and Anna's relationship to it, do not comment directly on the political and economic circumstances that have ensured her oppression. Rather, the photograph enshrines Anna's insignificance. It is a manifest denial of her need for self-expression and self-definition. The photograph does not engage Anna. In her deprived social context she is repelled by the element of punctum. Within the politics of representation she does not exist. As a working-class woman she can only ever be a subject.

I hesitate to draw too emphatic a conclusion from this comparison, since *Yonnondio* is a work of fiction and therefore no less problematic as a form of representation than a photograph. However, it is legitimate to use Olsen's work as a starting point since it provides a rare image of a working-class woman in the position of the viewer rather than as the framed subject (in this case she is both). It is this perspective that I have found absent from critical examinations of documentary photography. Moreover, this is an absence that is politically pertinent since the majority of government photographs from the 1930s and 1940s depict working-class people, and the social and economic upheavals that have come to represent their subjectivity.

Critical inquiry into FSA images has centered on undermining the notion of photographic truth. Accepting that a photograph is "realistic" allows the relationship between the depicted subject and the viewer to be clearly defined. Questioning this idea introduces a more complicated scenario. For example, William Stott highlights a distinct ideological purpose behind FSA photography. In most images, the working-class person—tenant farmer or migrant worker, preferably with toothless wife and scrawny children—is portrayed, as "helpless, guiltless . . . and though helpless, yet unvanquished by the implacable wrath of nature."[7] These simplistic depictions were designed to arouse enough guilt and pity in the viewer to induce a sufficient parting with tax dollars in support of FSA policies. More tellingly, the unequal relationship between subject and audience reconfirms middle-class superiority. The photographs do not show anger, nor do they present a threat to the viewer. Instead, the photographs imply a simple gratitude at Christian generosity, which in some cases was compounded by an assuring caption: "I will work for five dollars a month if I have to." As Maren Stange suggests, "[T]he documentary mode testified both to the existence of painful social facts and the reformers' expertise in ameliorating them, thus reassuring a liberal middle class that social oversight was both its duty and its right."[8] In short, critical interest has emphatically discovered the ideological construct that was barely concealed by the pathetic dignity of FSA photography. From this beginning, distinct but related lines of investigation have emerged.

First, insightful examinations of the contexts in which FSA images were created and used have exposed their ideological purpose. Such investigation frees the image—but not the subject—from its imposed meaning. To this end, Stange has meticulously investigated the FSA file and the specific contexts that led to its conception. In so doing, she has revealed the ways in which each image was captioned, cropped, and published, and how and why particular types of image were taken. She discusses these issues as reflections of the political ethos of Roy Stryker, the head of the Historical Section of the Resettlement Administration, the Farm Security Administration, and the Office of War Information; and also of Rexford Tugwell, the director of the RA. Stange contends that both men sought to advance the idea of a technocratic, capitalist economy, which would eliminate class distinctions and create social equilibrium. "Economic efficiency" and "technical progress" were the watchwords of RA policy, ironically undermining the agrarian mythologies captured in the photographs. Stange highlights how political incongruity was transformed into ideological clarity that was made concrete by the ways the FSA photographs were used. From this she is able to interpret the images in ways that undermine the narratives of New Deal ideology. Consequently, Stange concludes, what is left out of the images—forms of independent protest, unionization etc.—becomes significant, and criticism of FSA policy is revealed in images previously interpreted as illustrations of its success.

Stange's discussion is typical of a critical approach to documentary photography from the 1930s, made from the perspective of the image so as to uncover the manipulation of both framed subject and viewer. From the same perspective, Sally Stein has read particular images for the ways in which ideological monoliths are undermined. For example, she has examined photographs made by Marion Post Wolcott that depict economic stratification and racial inequality during the Depression.[9] Stein argues that—notwithstanding Stange's insistence on specific contextuality—radical representation is possible as long as the viewer knows what to look for.

Alternatively, other critics have examined the FSA file from the perspective of the viewer as a construct of ideology.[10] This position shows how the discursive process of history has decontextualized the meaning of FSA images and transformed them into cultural icons. As a result, the file itself has reconstituted historical fact into mythologized narrative. Ironically, such investigation has resulted in a double appropriation where the past is transformed into aestheticism, where the photographers' social purpose is devalued, and where the perspective of the framed subject is—as Martha Rosler suggests—"shaded over into combinations of exoticism, tourism, and voyeurism, psychologism and metaphysics, trophy hunting and careerism."[11]

My purpose here is not to create a false dichotomy between two perspectives that are closely related. Nor do I want to arrive at an essentialist definition of either working-class or middle-class identity. Rather, my argument is that in the many and various examinations of documentary photographs from the 1930s and 40s, the possibility of representing a working-class perspective beyond framed subjecthood has been circumvented. Critics have shown how and why working-class experience has been misrepresented to a middle-class audience, and how this misrepresentation has become mythologized into historical discourse. Arguments have also been made to explain how the position of viewer has been ideologically constructed to maintain hierarchical oppositions of otherness. Middle-class audiences have been urged to consider contextuality in their ways of seeing; to note the interaction of composition, text, captions, and usage, which can either dislodge or reinforce the monolithic concept of photographic realism. In these ways critics have freed working-class subjectivity—but only within the context of representation. They have assumed that politically enlightened seeing of a carefully contextualized image somehow constitutes material equality. There has been no consideration of the social and economic circumstances that provide the physical and psychological freedoms required for self-recognition, creativity, political empowerment, and the ability to see oneself beyond representation. A comparison of a passage from John Berger's text in *Another Way of Telling* with another excerpt from *Yonnondio*, perfectly illustrates this critical oversight:

One can lie on the ground and look up at the almost infinite number of stars in the night sky, but in order to tell stories about those stars they need to be seen as constellations, the invisible lines which connect them need to be assumed.[12]

"Stars," she began "what are they now? Splinters offn the moon I've heard it said."
He laughed then he told how the stars seemed dancing . . . the Greeks who had named these stars and had found in their shapes images of what was on earth below. . . . She scarcely listened . . . only the aura of them, of timelessness, of vastness, of eternal things that had been before her and would be after her remained, and entered into her with a great hurt and longing.[13]

For John Berger, the stars are a metaphor for the way photographs are perceived by the viewer. He speaks particularly of how images become resonant when the viewer reacts to the framed subject with his or her experience, knowledge, and imagination. The viewer's position is not fixed and, in dialectical interaction with the image, both become open to a plurality of meanings and interpretations. The number of possible meanings available, both to the image and to the viewer's perception, removes the need for an explanatory text that would narrow the fluidity of interpretation and impose a repressive narrative. This interactive process between image and viewer connotes Berger's "invisible lines" between the stars.

In his argument, Berger states that the existence of the invisible lines "must be assumed." However, before this assumption can be made, it is important to be aware of the distance between the stars, that is, the space between image and viewer that signifies a material social context. Carol Schloss notes that "the space between who is framed and the one who frames is a place of political action."[14] Making the connection is therefore an ongoing political process which, like any other in capitalist society, is constrained and manipulated by issues of class, race, and gender.

Using the passage from *Yonnondio,* the inadequacy of Berger's theory is made clear. Maizie, the six-year-old daughter of Anna, is told how individual stars are part of constellations that help explain the meaning of her identity. However, her economic circumstances and lack of education mean that she is unable to make the connection for herself. She feels only "the aura" of the words, and a sense of "great hurt and longing" at her inability to articulate their meaning for herself.[15] In this sense, Maizie's inability to recognize and understand the literal meaning of the constellations not only undermines Berger's theory, it also subverts Walter Benjamin's suggestion that photography is an implicitly radical artistic medium which, in its endless reproductions of images, removes the exclusive "aura" of middle-class aestheticism through a process of mass consumption.[16] Her desire is not to achieve a sense of collectively formed revolutionary or proletarian consciousness, but to be able to comprehend cultural meaning for herself. Thus, the tragedy of Maizie's point of view in relation to the constellations is given political significance beyond Berger's and Benjamin's theories, in that—as an individual working-class girl—the possibility of self-signification on her own terms cannot even enter her consciousness.

Following on from the difference between John Berger's and Maizie's perspectives, my aim is to examine the work of three women photographers who worked for the United States government between 1935 and 1943—Dorothea Lange, Marion Post Wolcott, and Esther Bubley. My investigation begins with the view that theoretical discourses concerning self-signification are unhelpful unless prefaced with an understanding of the material circumstances necessary to free oneself from the impositions of representation. I will be looking generally at the work of each photographer, and specifically at images made of working-class subjects, especially working-class women. This will necessarily include an analysis of their living conditions, family situations, and work environments in relation to government photographs. Moreover, I will be concerned with the relationship of these images to government policy, New Deal rhetoric, and specific legislation that affected the lives of working-class women. These issues will be discussed within the context of the political imperatives that began this introduction—the need to establish a basis of representation against which working-class women can identify themselves and consequently be able to find the means for self-expression: creative, theoretical, and political. By comparing the photographs of Lange, Post Wolcott, and Bubley, I will attempt to show how a workable context for this point of view can be found.

In considering composition and ways of approaching a subject, I want to show how photographs by Lange, while politically sensitive and manifestly aware of the complex issues that caused and perpetuated migration and tenancy, could be so successfully used to generate positive publicity for the FSA during the 1930s, and subsequently were so easily appropriated into the artistic establishment and the realms of iconography. In short, what is it about Lange's photographs of migrant mothers and tenant farmers' families that does not allow a working-class woman's point of view to be articulated beyond framed subjecthood?

In contrast, Marion Post Wolcott chose subjects (often without official blessing) that raised questions about economic inequality and undermined the political rhetoric of the New Deal. Unlike Lange's photographs, which focused on the physical and emotional effects of institutional breakdown on individuals, Post Wolcott photographed the hierarchical dynamics of the economic and social system itself. However, while her photographs offer a radical analysis of capitalist economics, particularly in her images of women, she does not provide space for self-identification from the perspective of a working-class woman. Instead, her pictures reframe working-class subjectivity, as it was defined by liberal rhetoric, into the totalizing perspective of a vaguely Marxist ideology.

In conclusion, I will consider photographs by Esther Bubley that, in their unusual construction, lighting, and ways of approaching, allow her subjects to speak for themselves in a way that challenges the social and material context in which they are placed. Her images portray a disconnection and isolation from society that is disturbing to the viewer, and which does not allow for the possibility of an imposed narrative. Accepted points of interaction between subject and viewer are undermined and rearranged in a way that allows for the possibility of a working-class point of view. Subjecthood is not fixed within the frame since her photographs provoke a reaction that is uncomfortable, unsure, and necessarily incomplete. Her photographs do not fit easily with popular notions of working-class female experience in the 1930s and 1940s, nor are they included within the mythologized aestheticism that has come to denote the visual history of those decades. As a result, Bubley's images are able to release working-class identity from framed subjecthood, and also provide space within the image for self-signification.

As I consider the politically empowering context that emerges from a comparison of the work of these three women, I will also take note of their historical continuity. Lange worked for the RA and FSA between 1935 and 1940, Post Wolcott joined on Lange's departure, staying until 1942. Bubley worked under the jurisdiction of the Office of War Information from 1941 to 1943. My discussion will therefore consider the relevance of each photographer's work within her historical context, and will ask whether this is relevant to an interpretation of her images. If Lange's images represent the epitome of FSA photography in the 1930s, what relationship does Post Wolcott's work bear to this perspective? Her years spent in Europe, her progressive education, her association with Paul Strand, and her interest in the Group Theater suggest influences of the artistically Modern and the politically communist. Do her photographs, taken when the United States was becoming economically prosperous as it prepared for war, reflect these influences? Similarly, does the style of Esther Bubley's work emerge from her photographic education working for *Vogue*? Or from the context of the war years in which her images were made? Does the paradoxical nature of her images, which were used for overt propaganda purposes (unlike the FSA) and yet depict an uncertain and unfixable sense of identification, highlight an undermining of a universalizing modernist sensibility that was fragmented by the experience of a second world war?

In these respects the following examinations center on the ways in which critical investigation of photography has utilized postmodernism and poststructuralist theories. While these approaches have focused on the concept of self-signification in order to free the depicted subject and the viewer from ideological discourse, such inquiries provide little basis for overcoming material inequality. Consequently, these applications of poststructuralist theory, though vital for an understanding of how inequalities based on race, gender, and class identity are socially and politically inscribed, simultaneously limits this knowledge by ignoring the material circumstances of racism, patriarchy, and economic disadvantage. Thus, the self-signifying awareness that is poststructuralism's premise for political change, enshrines a middle-class point of view and circumscribes working-class selfhood within representation. As a result, it is necessary, and politically important, to examine photographs of working-class women in order to articulate the perspective of the economically deprived and socially marginalized subject, rather than the materially privileged viewer.

1

Dorothea Lange:
Representing Rural Poverty

History and Mythology

Myth traditionally provides the central drama of any social order. But history offers something vastly different in its ideal form, since it is concerned with change, more an ideology as distinguished from a utopian vision. But the two frequently work hand in hand. Myth provides the drama and history puts the show on the road.[1]

Warren Susman describes the 1930s as a time when America "was suspended between two quite distinguishable systems and ways of life."[2] First, an emotional reliance on traditional ethics of individual self sufficiency and moral steadfastness; second, an aspiration toward a "culture of abundance"[3] formed by new mass communication technology and emphasizing social democracy within consumer capitalist economics. The collapse of traditional family farming in the South and Midwest, and the subsequent migration of dispossessed sharecroppers and tenant farmers into California, became uniquely symbolic of this historical dichotomy.

Rural traditions were considered untenable in relation to a modern system of farm production. At the same time, the shortcomings of new modes of corporate, mechanized farming were felt acutely by those dispossessed from their land and subsequently failed by the mythological promises of consumer economics. Nevertheless, economic progression toward a culture of abundance was a central tenet of New Deal politics. The historical inevitability of a technocratic, managed economy was successfully communicated within a rhetorical discourse that simultaneously—and paradoxically—utilized the traditional symbolism of homestead farming, agrarian sentimentality, and moral stoicism in the face of hard times. The photographs taken for the Historical Section of the Resettlement Administration, and later the Farm Security Administration, were a visual manifestation of this incongruous context.

Roy Stryker, the head of the Historical Section, was himself a curious combination of western frontiersman—borne from his cattle-herding youth in Colorado—and Eastern Academic. Stryker was inspired to participate in New Deal politics by Rexford Tugwell, his economics professor at Columbia and the future administration of the RA.[4] Tugwell was a central advocate of economic planning at a national level in the New Deal government, and favored a large-scale restructuring of the agricultural economy in particular. Stryker served as Tugwell's loyal publicist in the Historical Section, fulfilling a mandate that provoked congressional and public sympathy for the alleviation of rural poverty, while furnishing evidence in support of increased mechanization of agriculture that would, in turn, lead to a systematic resettlement of the families consequently driven from their land. To this end, Stryker commanded his photographers with an authoritarian precision. Seemingly whimsical shooting scripts belied vigorous and draconian editorial practices: from cajoling correspondence directing photographers in the field, to the sometimes arbitrary destruction of negatives, to a complicated and purposefully mystifying bureaucracy, applied in order to maintain the ideological clarity of the file. Stryker confirmed his controlling position—somewhat disingenuously—in *In This Proud Land*: "I never took a picture, yet I felt a part of every picture taken. My ideas, my biases, my passions, my convictions."[5]

Maren Stange contends that an awareness of Stryker's editorial impositions under the auspices of New Deal ideology reveals "the terms on which such a government sponsored project might exist in a time of great and painful change."[6] The RA and FSA images depicted a dialectical convergence of cultural tradition and technological "progress," which celebrated the passing of rural life in a way that legitimated and perpetuated its destruction. The photographs captured the interwoven effects of mythology, history, folklore, and fact, while transforming poverty into a drama of representation, where the rural poor existed as heroes or victims displayed before an audience of photographer, government, and concerned public, whose emotional and political responses ultimately controlled the fate of the subject.

Deviation from the official vision often caused conflict between Stryker and the photographers in his employ. Walker Evans's attempts to make photographs that were "pure record, no propaganda,"[7] led to accusations of unreliability and underproduction that eventually led to his dismissal in 1936. Similarly, Dorothea Lange became engaged in a constant battle with Stryker over editorial control of her negatives. Her subsequent reputation for being demanding and difficult caused her to be dropped from the government payroll twice (in 1938 and 1939), when she was asked to provide negatives on a per diem basis. In early 1940 she was dismissed permanently. More telling than the practical reasons for her dismissal, however, was Lange's visual criticism of an FSA policy that consolidated the erosion of farming traditions and local cultures. As Maren Stange suggests, "[I]t was certainly the force of this perception that gave political animus to Lange's disputes with Stryker over matters that seem on the surface merely technical or bureaucratic."[8] Nevertheless, despite this assertion of the apparently subversive content of the images, Stange does not mention that Lange's photographs were the most frequently requested material of any FSA photographer, and that her work was widely reproduced in newspapers, pamphlets, congressional reports, and exhibitions. The new commercial photo-magazines, *Life* and *Look*, were especially interested in Lange's images. Consequently, it was through Lange's eye that contemporaneous impressions, and subsequently visual memories of the Depression—and of migrant labor in particular—were formulated. It is also significant that it was "Migrant Mother" that Roy Stryker lovingly framed as his most precious memory of the photographic project, noting in his memoirs that the image had made an indelible emotional impact on his consciousness: "When Dorothea took that picture it was the ultimate. She never surpassed it. To me, it was *the* image of Farm Security. The others were marvelous but that was special."[9]

Thus, Dorothea Lange's photographs represent a paradoxical context for the cultural and economic dichotomy in which they were made—undermining the fundamental principles of technological advancement, and simultaneously subverting Stryker's alternately sentimental and dogmatic vision. Yet, her photographs were also successfully and widely utilized as images that clearly justified a continuance of FSA policy. An understanding of Lange's photographs as sites where these apparently mutually exclusive economic situations and ideological purposes converge is therefore fundamental to any examination of her work. Moreover, a clear perception of this antagonistic context is a prerequisite for an analysis of Lange's photographs as representations of the rural working classes.

Photography by the Historical Section was intended to make the Depression—as it was lived by those most affected—accessible and familiar to those most distant from it. As a result, the emotional impact of the images clearly reflected the broad liberal rhetoric of the New Deal, perfectly illustrating Franklin Roosevelt's pledges to help the "forgotten man," while at the same time engendering a sense of social responsibility into the consciences of middle-class Americans.[10] Ostensibly, documentary representations of rural poverty were undertaken in order to gain public support for social welfare and work relief programs. More fundamentally, the images were intended to reestablish confidence in capitalism, and to rejuvenate the ideology of the American Dream.

Ironically, then, one-dimensional representations of rural poverty belied a fundamental political focus on the middle-class viewer rather than the working-class subject. Reflecting this ideological purpose, poverty, deprivation, and dislocation were depicted as ahistorical, personalized experiences that could easily be appropriated into a middle-class perspective.[11] The working-class subject's point of view was consequently repressed and marginalized in a dialectical opposition between government inscribed mythology and historical sensitivity towards the causes of rural poverty. An examination of this opposition is therefore important for a more complex understanding of the political, social, and economic circumstances depicted in Lange's photographs. More significantly, an evaluation of the specific political effects of this dichotomous context on her photographic methods also reveals how far her images were able to represent rural poverty from the perspective of the working-class subject rather than the middle-class viewer.

Politics and Ideology

In 1934, after Dorothea Lange had photographed the White Angel Breadline and San Francisco's general strike, and before she began her work with the Resettlement Administration, Willard Van Dyke published a critique of her work in the October issue of *Camera Craft*. In it, he appraised her visual understanding of the poverty and social unrest that were prevalent in the early years of the Depression:

In approaching the subject or situation immediately before her she makes no attempt at a personal interpretation of the individual or situation. Neither does she encompass her work within the bounds of a political or economic thesis. . . . She is not preoccupied with the philosophy behind the present conflict, she is making a record of it through the faces of the individuals most sensitive to it or most concerned in it.[12]

Van Dyke's assessment is typical of many responses to Lange that described her photographs as sympathetic, sensitive portrayals of individual hardship and suffering depicted in a way that reflected a basic human connection with her subject's plight. Van Dyke's article goes on to explain Lange's approach toward her subjects: "[L]ike an unexposed film she [eradicates] from her mind, before she starts, all ideas which she might hold regarding the situation."[13] In other words, Van Dyke suggests that Lange's response to scenes of poverty, dislocation, protest, or devastation, was primarily emotional and intuitive in ways that were somehow transcendent of any intellectual interpretation, and advantageously lacking any historical or political understanding of the situation portrayed.

Van Dyke goes on to describe Lange's technique as an extension of the camera's natural function that "must make its record out of context, taking the individuals or incidents photographed as climaxes rather than as continuity."[14] This assessment of Lange's unique success in utilizing the camera's inherent ahistoricism is illuminated by Edward Steichen's opinion of her contribution to his 1962 exhibition, "The Bitter Years." Steichen believed Lange to be a superlative photographer because she was a woman. Commenting on the gender specificity of her artistic skill he noted: "[W]omen have that curious thing which is intuition, stronger than men have. Intuition is simply keen perception and evaluation. They [women] know how to value their perception, which is something a man is very poor at as a rule."[15] Steichen's identification of Lange's distinctively female photographic instinct was also described by Roy Stryker as an important way of establishing a sense of reciprocity between the audience and the depicted subject. He explained to Nancy Wood how Lange "would go into a field and a man would look up and he must have had some feeling that there was a wonderful woman and she was going to be sympathetic."[16] The implications of Van Dyke's original assessment are made clear by Steichen's opinion and Stryker's apparently innocuous comment. They suggest that Lange produced emotionally gripping photographs because she utilized an innately female ability that allowed her to communicate with the rural poor simply and nonconceptually, in ways they could understand. Paternalistic wonderment at Lange's maternal instinct established a one-dimensional connection between femininity and working-class identity in her photographs. This perspective also critically removed her work from the meticulous economic and historical contexts she had intended to portray. Moreover, the suggestion of a fundamental sense of mutuality between Lange's emotional, biologically instinctive sense of empathy, and the fatalistic simplicity of her subjects, enabled her images to be perceived as representative of the ideological imperatives of the New Deal. This gender specific criticism meant that Lange's photographs were less likely to be understood as incisive depictions that provoked deeper understanding of rural poverty as a phenomenon too complex to be captured on an individual face within a single frame.

The one-dimensional conflation of femininity and working-class identity that was ascribed to Lange's photography also allowed her historically diverse images to be appropriated within the mythological facade that defined the government's policy towards rural poverty. Sentimental evocation of agrarian imagery was undermined by a legislative purpose that regarded the family farm as obsolete. Despite the rhetorical claims of those agencies created to combat rural poverty, their ultimate goal was to integrate traditional farming culture with the needs of the commercial market. In practical terms, policies of resettlement and rural rehabilitation were helpful to destitute tenant farmers and sharecroppers. The RA, and later the FSA, provided funds for new equipment, stock, medical care, and the alleviation of debts. They also formulated a tenant purchase program, and a policy that relocated farmers from submarginal land to more fertile fields. As well as this, the government helped improve tenancy agreements and encouraged more cooperation between tenant families, hoping to engender a sense of solidarity within the community founded on mutual need. Despite these pragmatic measures, however, the RA and the FSA were formulated by a political mythology that, even as it decontextualized rural poverty from its historical causes, simultaneously weakened the cultural traditions that gave its population an identity. RA and FSA policies were intended to "instill . . . new patterns of social and political behaviors" into rural life.[17] To this end, the circumstances of poverty were exploited, and the rural poor were marginalized further by economic and political planning that considered them to be an anachronistic liability.

Reflecting these purposes, rehabilitation and resettlement policies intentionally bypassed the needs of the very poorest farmers and tenants, helping only "those who needed help less because those who needed it more did not count politically."[18] For those chosen, the price of rehabilitation and resettlement was to relinquish traditional ways of life to government planners. The recipient of a loan had no control over how it was spent and had to adhere to a meticulously detailed spending plan that was enforced through a joint bank account with the county supervisor. Traditions such as "settlement time," when at the end of a crop year tenants and sharecroppers usually bought a special item of clothing or furniture in celebration, were considered frivolous by FSA officials, an example of the kind of ignorance and simplemindedness that had caused rural poverty.[19] Furthermore, resistance to government efforts was common among a rural population that was proudly individualistic, self-sufficient and suspicious of charity. Government officials were consistently amazed by such resentment, displaying a lack of insight that reflected their acceptance of mythologized representations of the causes of rural poverty.

Institutionalized narrow-mindedness was exemplified in the words of Rexford Tugwell. He saw the family farm as a place of degradation borne from a simplistic faith in a land infected to almost biblical proportions, and inhabited by people who were ignorant, stubbornly naive, and innocently victimized to the point of insanity:

A farm is an area of vicious, ill tempered soil, with a not very good house, inadequate barns, makeshift machinery, happenstance stock, tired over worked men and women—and all the pests and bucolic plagues that nature has evolved . . . a place where ugly brooding monotony, that haunts by day and night, unseats the mind.[20]

In Tugwell's comments, the causes of rural poverty are described as emotional and elemental rather than social and economic. In opposition to this rhetorical view, large-scale technological agricultural production was considered to be an inevitable historical progression to which the rural poor must adapt or else cease to make a living from the land. Representations of the rural poor gave social legitimacy to this ideological purpose. The rural poor brought the potency of agrarian symbolism to commercial farming even as the material basis of their history was being destroyed.

Framing a Context: An American Exodus

People don't see the big story . . . which is the story of our natural resource . . . they will photograph the conditions but they don't go behind and put them in the right place.[21]

In 1933 Dorothea Lange left her portrait studio permanently and began to take documentary photographs on a full time basis. Although driven by a sense that the upheavals and injustices around her should be recorded, she was unsure how her photographs might be used to affect change in the circumstances she had portrayed. At first, she put her faith in the emotional immediacy of the photographic process, as is clear in her description of the impetus behind her documentation of the May Day demonstrations of the unemployed at San Francisco's Civic Center in 1933: "I will set myself a big problem. I will go down there, I will photograph this thing, I will come back, and develop it. I will print it and I will mount it and I will do this to see if I can grab a hunk of lightening."[22]

Her belief in the power of the image was given another dimension in 1939 when she met Paul Schuster Taylor, a professor of sociology at Berkeley and her future husband. The meeting was pivotal for both Taylor and Lange. For Taylor, the camera added an extra visual dimension that was vital to his documentation of rural poverty in California. Commenting on the emotional and political power of images in relation to analytical reports and statistical evidence, he noted that "no other amount or quality of words could alone convey what the situation was that I was studying."[23] Similarly, for Lange the visual language of photography was enhanced by documenting and recording the words of the people she was portraying, and by placing each image within a wider social, economic, and historical context. By combining and integrating their individual skills, Lange and Taylor were able to construct what they considered to be a complete visual and literal narrative picture of the circumstances of rural poverty. Working with Taylor, Lange was able to extend the representational framework of her images to create a visual record of rural poverty, which could be articulated in the simple language of subjective experience and understood within a frame of sociological, historical, and economic interpretation.

Lange wanted to continue the approach she had developed alongside Taylor in her work with the Historical Section. She embraced her position as part of a liberal agency that was trying to improve the conditions of the rural poor. Since this purpose was backed by an ideological intent that had no political stake in preserving the traditions of subsistence farming, however, Lange's three-dimensional investigation of rural poverty was often constricted by the narrow perspectives of government-sponsored images. Nevertheless, Lange tried to integrate an increasingly complex scientific analysis of rural poverty into a photographic project that reflected the government's political fatalism towards traditional farming. As Alan Trachtenberg suggests, the single theory that governed the Historical Section was the desire "to preserve what was already lost."[24] To this end, the images in the file invited sentimental reverie that arose from a politically motivated intention to marginalize the rural poor from historical continuity into decontextualized, nostalgic mythology. In contrast, Lange's photography was driven by a sense of historical urgency. As she and Taylor traveled from the migrant camps in California where she had begun her photography, Lange began to formulate a wider view of the causal relationships between technological "progress" and economic displacement. Traveling through the southern states, she recognized the connection between government sponsorship of mechanization in cotton cultivation, and the subsequent displacement of tenants, sharecroppers, and farm laborers. On June 3, 1937, she wrote to Roy Stryker explaining her conclusions:

Have uncovered here . . . a very interesting situation on tenancy—people put off farms, tenants, often of years standing and established. With tractors which were purchased by the landowners with soil conservation money. Not just a few cases. It's the story of the county. The ex-tenants are homeless and landless . . . working tomorrow on as complete a study of these abandoned tenant homes (tractor right up to the porch) as I can do.

P.S. This may turn out to be an important part of our California story, in fact I know it is now.[25]

Lange's view was corroborated by Taylor who, in a letter to Thomas C. Blaisden Jr. at the Division of Research and Statistics, wrote that he and Lange had recorded a picture of rural poverty that challenged the mythologized belief that migrant workers had been "dusted out" of their native states:

There's drought and the well known criticism of the crop reduction program, but the driving force is economic and powerful mechanization. It's a force that can hardly be checked even if we could. . . . Any program for the relief of tenants and other low-income groups in cotton must reckon with machine methods of production. They are here and will spread fast.[26]

As well as formulating her own multilayered investigation of rural poverty in California, Lange also believed that it was vital to integrate her work with the impressions of the other FSA photographers. She believed that the images in the file were "interlocking pieces of a giant jigsaw"[27] that formed a complete and complex picture, "filed and cross filed . . . and buttressed by written material and by all manner of things which keep it unified and solid."[28] Her intention was undermined, however, partly because she was based in California and therefore quite distant from the political machinations in Washington, but largely because of Stryker's reluctance in keeping her informed of other photographers' work and the general progression of the file itself. As a result, the complexities of Lange's documentary record were somewhat marginalized from the official vision of the Historical Section. It was not until 1939, and the independent publication of *An American Exodus: A Record of Human Erosion in the Thirties*, that Lange and Taylor were able to complete a comprehensive photographic documentation of rural poverty that was fully integrated within its historical context.

According to Paul Taylor, 300,000 migrants arrived in California between the middle of 1935 and May 1939.[29] *An American Exodus* examines the historical causes of this migration using photographs captioned with the words of their subjects, factual information, and contemporary commentaries. The photographs are divided up into geographical sections—the South, Midcontinent, the Plains and the West—and are accompanied with a brief explanatory essay by Paul Taylor. Each region is shown as it developed in relation to technological "progress" in agricultural production, how that progression affected traditional farm culture, and finally how that process culminated in dislocation and migration. As such, the book is a discourse between layers of narrative: historical, economic, political, analytical, subjective description and objective analysis. The juxtaposition of Lange's photographs within this context transforms her images into visual sites where the various narratives converge and diffuse in a way that attempts to expose the mythological impositions of official representation.

Most dramatically, the book portrays rural poverty as a nationwide phenomenon, relating agricultural traditions of the plantations in the Deep South to the small holding culture of the Midwest and Great Plains. The displacement and poverty experienced by African-American sharecroppers and laborers in Mississippi and Georgia is visually connected to the plight of white subsistence farmers in Oklahoma and Arkansas. The related economic effects of over-cultivation and land and labor exploitation were consolidated by short-sighted mechanization, by paternalistic plantation owners in the South, and by absentee landlords in the Midwest—a process that inevitably led to increased tenancy, foreclosure, unemployment, and the development of a rootless migrant work force dependent on seasonal employment for their survival.

Lange's photographs perfectly illustrate the intra-continental, macro-economic nature of rural poverty. One picture of a woman standing at the entrance of an enormous pillared mansion relates the South's destructive reliance on the plantation system (fig. 1.1). The imposing building, which was once symbolic of the wealth of cotton production in the South, is dilapidated and corroding. The excesses of an economic system founded on exploitation of land and labor are becoming visible in the decaying paint work and rotting foundations of the mansion. The woman, dwarfed by the building, leans against a pillar, but the insubstantiality of its once opulent facade can no longer offer any support. The photograph highlights the intrinsic ironies of an economic system founded on exploitative and paternalistic dependency, and perpetuated by a shortsighted faith in its indestructibility. Standing at the top of some fragile-looking steps, the woman is isolated further. Her entrapment is compounded by the photograph's frame, which crops away what lies beyond the mansion's edge. She is symbolically stranded by the legacy of cotton culture, the destructive insularity of which made its economic collapse inevitable.

The erosion of small-scale subsistence farming in the Midwest is similarly depicted (fig. 1.2). A family of ten sit on the tiny porch of a broken down farm house. Adults and children are closely connected; their gazes are directed towards each other's faces rather than toward the camera. Their unity is visually underscored by the photograph's construction, foregrounding the platform on which they sit and reframing

Fig. 1.1. Dorothea Lange. "Ante-bellum plantation house Greene County, Georgia." July 1937. Reproduced from the Collections of the Library of Congress.

them between the wooden struts that hold up the porch roof. The sense of emotional connection is made emphatic—they are a family and this is their home. The image resonates with family love and pride. The house is ramshackle, but despite its worn out state the father—his legs crossed and holding a small child—appears relaxed in the security of his position as the successful provider of shelter, food, and material stability for his family. A woman, perhaps his wife, sits next to him on the bed, she is

Fig. 1.2. Dorothea Lange. "Midcontinent, returned from California." 1938. Copyright of the Dorothea Lange Collection, The Oakland Museum of California, The City of Oakland. Gift of Paul S. Taylor.

smiling radiantly outward and the children around her are happily self-contained. Beneath their own roof they can feel safe and protected.

Despite the tangible sense of security depicted in the photograph, however, the family's apparent assuredness within the frame of their porch is undermined by the caption above the image: "Whole families go to Los Angeles, Phoenix, Bakersfield. Half the people of this town and around here have gone out there."[30] In relation to these words, the family members appear to be huddled together for protection against the inevitability of their displacement. In the light of the caption, the fore-grounding of the family on the porch is suggestive of the erosion of sub-sistence farming. The family's security is precariously poised on a raised platform that is buckling under the weight of their dependence. The fragility that has become evident within the image undermines the optimistic appearance of the family group. The photograph, cropped around the front of the house, now seems claustrophobic. The land they have lived from is disappearing into the background and the ground around them is muddy and strewn with rubbish. There is not even enough space left for their furniture.

The close symbolic relationship between these two images reveals a visual language in Lange's photographs that interacts with the text of *An American Exodus* to create a unified theory of the causes of rural poverty. The discursive arrangement of text and photographs gives an historical continuity to this thesis. Migration is seen to be the culmination of an economic process that was not natural and inevitable, but manmade and therefore avoidable. Traditional farming culture could have adapted to new methods of production; instead, mechanization and technological farming simply extended an already wasteful single-crop, short-term profit system. Images of tractor furrows, right up to the doors of plantation cabins in the Mississippi Delta and to the porches of homestead farms in the Texas plains, attest to the results of such shortsightedness. Mass overcultivation led to soil erosion that precipitated the dust storms of the 1930s. At the same time, displaced small holders, tenant farmers, sharecroppers, and laborers, in the South, in the Midwest, and in the Great Plains, became important only as an inexhaustible supply of cheap and desperately willing labor. They were exploitable and expendable—given their vast numbers—and so ideally suited to the dynamics of industrialized farm production in the fields of California. By placing the causes of rural poverty in this historical context, Lange's images of migrant workers in California do not show the tragic but unavoidable result of a necessary modernization of agricultural production, rather they depict a future rendered inevitable by the politics of commercial economics. As such, *An American Exodus* undermined the government's interpretation of the causes of rural poverty, and consequently exposed the limitations of legislation designed to combat it.

The photographs in the penultimate chapter of *An American Exodus* echo images of the rural poor in previous pages. The despair of African-American laborers and the defiance of displaced tenant farmers in North Texas are repeated in the faces of migrant workers squatting on the edge of fields waiting for the opportunity to work. Their appearance is also echoed in the expressions of men idling in the streets of Californian towns, disempowered and degraded, standing in line for welfare checks. Similarly, laborers hoeing in the cotton fields of Mississippi have their visual counterparts in the pea fields of the Imperial Valley.

Continuing from this narrative of displacement and poverty, there is a visual progression in the California section of *An American Exodus,* from despair and subjugation, to unity and resistance that is shown to have significant political and economic ramifications. Two families are stuck on a muddy highway on the way to Nipomo, California; the caption reads: "Us people has got to stick together to get by these hard times."[31] A photograph of field workers is captioned with an observation that commercial farming has produced "a large, landless, and mobile proletariat."[32] A following image shows a sign displayed during a cotton strike in Kern County, California: "This is your country don't let the big men take it away from you."[33] The opposite photograph shows a migrant worker standing imposingly in front of a political poster. The caption is a quote by George Mason, a delegate from Kern County: "We ought to attend to the rights of every class of people . . . "[34] The progression of visual and textual language in the penultimate chapter of *An American Exodus* arrives at the conclusion that since the development of agricultural production brought sweatshop-like conditions to the field, then agricultural workers must organize, protest, and be represented along the class lines formulated by industrial capitalism. As such, Lange and Taylor have attempted to expand the historical continuity of rural poverty beyond the symbolic frame of official representation, to where the rural poor are potentially able to control their economic progress into the future.

In his sympathetic analysis of the FSA, Stanley Baldwin suggests that the government "approached the task of [combating rural poverty] as existentialists," believing that rehabilitation was a simple matter of supplying poverty-stricken farmers with modern equipment, a new building, or an extra mule.[35] Baldwin goes on to state that this apparently practical response was founded on a realization of the "ideological potentiality" of agrarian symbolism.[36] As a result, the government's understanding of rural poverty was limited to representation, as a way of dramatizing the New Deal's social conscience, as an opportunity for reorganizing the economic structure of agricultural production, and as a means of revitalizing the mythology of the American Dream. Dorothea Lange's photographs in *An American Exodus* add another dimension to agrarian symbolism, but the potential for solidarity and political organization she envisioned was equally as detached from the individuals she portrayed. The following analysis of Lange's most famous photograph will reveal how her efforts to create a complex context for each of her images was measured against her own aesthetic, political, and ideological agendas.

Florence Thompson and the Migrant Mother

In February and March 1936, Dorothea Lange was assigned to take photographs of migrant workers in the pea fields of California's Imperial Valley. It was during this trip that she made some of her most emotionally resonant photographs, including her famous portraits of a thirty-two-year-old, part Cherokee woman, the mother of seven children, struggling to survive on the sparse income offered by occasional work in the fields. The series included the image known as "Migrant Mother," a photograph that came to symbolize both the social intention and the aesthetic style of the Historical Section's photographic project.

"Migrant Mother" has been described and evaluated in many different ways: as an image that captured a specific historical moment, and as an image that transcended history and portrayed the eternal nature of the human condition. This is an opposition that highlights the political, ideological, and artistic contexts that informed a basic duality in Dorothea Lange's approach. Her fastidious recording of the subject's words, and her informed sensitivity toward historical context, were accompanied by a need to construct an emotional hook within the image that would appeal directly to the middle-class viewer. In her description of the way she made the "Migrant Mother" photographs, Lange emphasizes the intrinsic importance of sentiment, pathos, and decontextualized emotion in her photographic method:

I was following instinct, not reason, I drove into that soggy camp and parked my car like a homing pigeon. I saw and approached the hungry and desperate mother, as if drawn by a magnet. I do not remember how I explained my presence to her, or my camera, but I do remember she asked me no questions. I made five exposures, working closer and closer from the same direction. I did not ask her name or her history. She told me her age, that she was thirty-two. She said that they had been living on frozen vegetables from the surrounding field and birds that the children had killed. She had just sold the tires from her car to buy food. Here she sat in a lean-to tent with her children huddled around her, and seemed to know that my picture might help her, and so she helped me. There was a sort of equality about it.[37]

In all Lange spent only ten minutes in the camp yet she felt she had "recorded the essence" of her assignment.[38] Lange's description of her brief, almost perfunctory meeting with the woman who was to become "Migrant Mother" is remarkable in that it is so far removed from her usual photographic practice. Normally, before she made any photographs, she would spend several hours with the migrant workers, letting the children play with her equipment and getting to know the adults, asking them questions: their names, their histories, and their opinions. Then she recorded all the information, carefully captioned her images, and fitted the stories she had heard with the history and politics of each subject's circumstances. In this case, however, she describes having been driven by an impulse that belied the historical and sociological complexities of her usual photographic approach, and—somewhat ironically—echoed the paternalistic, one-dimensional assessments made of her work by Willard Van Dyke, Edward Steichen, and Roy Stryker. Reflecting this, Stryker summarily rejected any suggestion that the woman in Lange's photograph had been artificially posed, noting—in language significantly similar to Lange's description of the natural, almost mystical, connection between herself and her subject—"people would say to me, that migrant woman looks posed and I'd say she does not look posed. That picture is as uninvolved with the camera as any picture I've ever seen."[39]

In reality, as recent critics have noted, the "Migrant Mother" image was systematically arranged, edited, dissected, retouched, and artfully framed by Lange in order to fit the ideological imperatives of government policy. James Curtis describes how Lange manipulated her subject, beginning by withholding one photograph from the FSA file that apparently did not meet her own artistic standards, but that nevertheless revealed how she gradually arranged the migrant family in order to fit the political, ideological, and aesthetic criteria of the Historical Section.[40] In this first image, the migrant woman and her children are scattered around the edges of the photograph's frame, most of their faces are obscured or turned away from the camera, apart from one child who has turned her eyes toward Lange and begun to smile. As Curtis notes, this initial "trial picture" is "a rather chaotic image, lacking control and a central focus." In the next photograph Lange's subjects are arranged more formally.[41]

Here, all of the family face the camera and are framed within the edges of the tent except for the teenage daughter who is posed rather self-consciously on a rocking chair in the foreground of the photograph (fig. 1.3). Lange gradually progressed from this image and focused more and more closely on the mother in the next four exposures. In so doing, she decided to remove several of the children from the frame and excluded the family's lean-to tent house. She chose not to include their scant belongings; she completely ignored any mention of the family's father, and she asked the children left in the final image to turn their faces away from the camera. This systematic dissection of the migrant family was completed when the famous sixth image was exhibited at the Museum of Modern Art in 1941. Lange had been troubled by her sub-

Fig. 1.3. Dorothea Lange. "Destitute pea pickers in California, a 32-year-old mother of seven children." Feb. 1936. Reproduced from the Collections of the Library of Congress.

ject's thumb, which had moved into the edge of the frame as the mother grasped her baby. Disturbed by the aesthetic imbalance of the woman's body, Lange chose to retouch the negative and remove the "glaring defect." In so doing, Lange "removed the last traces of the one instinctual motion that Migrant Mother made."[42]

A close analysis of the "Migrant Mother" series shows how through instruction and manipulation, Lange was able to produce an image that perfectly symbolized the documentary style of the Historical Section. Moreover, Lange's approach to her subject was shaped by the political ideals and moral perspectives of the middle-class viewers towards whom the FSA images were directed. As such, the smile on the face of the child in the first image was considered unappealing. Middle-class sensibilities demanded wide-eyed, uncomprehending innocence from poverty-stricken toddlers. In the same way, Lange chose to include only three of the children in her final image. To photograph all seven would represent a challenge to middle-class conventions about how large a family might be before compromising the morality of its parents. Three children was the average in professional, liberal society—usually the audience for FSA images—any more might have suggested selfishness and social dependency. The teenage daughter was excluded from Lange's photographs after the second exposure for similar reasons. A middle-class viewer might have wondered why this older child could not take care of herself, or at least why she was not working to take care of the younger children. Furthermore, her age might have cast aspersions on the mother's moral culpability, suggesting that she had begun reproducing at a licentiously young age. For similar reasons, Lange focused away from the dirty interior of the family's tent because "the public might be less sympathetic to migrants who could not even pick up their personal belongings"[43] (fig. 1.4). Thus, the self-identity of the migrant woman, her personal history, her family situation, her economic position, and even her facial expression were suppressed, and effectively removed from the image Lange produced.

The systematic exclusion of the subject's perspective from the "Migrant Mother" photograph was extended further in the way the woman was posed by Lange so as to invoke the visual language of Madonna and child paintings. The arrangement of the angelic, blonde-haired children around the mother as she holds her baby evokes classic paintings of the Virgin Mary surrounded by attendant angels as she nurses the infant Christ (fig. 1.5). Similarly, in the final photograph, Lange emphasizes the mother's pale skin and dark hair as the light falls onto her head like a halo reflected in the fair hair of her child.[44] The use of such religious imagery was consistent with the rhetorical tenets of

Fig. 1.4. Dorothea Lange. "Destitute pea pickers in California, a 32-year-old mother of seven children." Feb. 1936. Reproduced from the Collections of the Library of Congress.

Fig. 1.5. Dorothea Lange. "Destitute pea pickers in California, a 32-year-old mother of seven children." Feb. 1936. Reproduced from the Collections of the Library of Congress.

FSA representation and New Deal ideology. The causes and effects of the Depression were continually defined in terms of natural disaster and divinely inspired fate. Consequently, images that inscribed the possibility of redemption reassured middle-class audiences that they could offer charity and be repaid with a cathartic measure of magnanimous gratitude. Moreover, by giving her subject the appearance of a Madonna, Lange constructed a palpable quality of forgiveness within the image, projecting from the "Migrant Mother" in the photograph toward the middle-class viewers. In this way, Lange introduced a superficial sense of mutuality—almost a symbolically rendered conversation—in her photograph, which effectively articulated the perspective of the middle-class audience. The material circumstances, individual experiences, and self-expression of the working-class subject were simultaneously disguised with a facade of classical religious imagery.

Lange's symbolic utilization of the Virgin and Child in the "Migrant Mother" image, led the photograph to be alternately entitled "Migrant Madonna" (fig. 1.6). Taken together, these two titles amplify the metaphorical importance of femininity—specifically motherhood—alongside the spiritual rejuvenation and redemptive possibilities contained within the "Migrant Mother" photograph. Representations of mothers provided a complimentary set of reassuring symbols in FSA photography. Images of women who remained strongly protective of their children, and who looked like they would ensure the survival of their families despite economic hardship and homelessness, offered hope to middle-class Americans that traditional family life would endure and outlast the ravages of the Depression. Reflecting this, Lange cropped the "Migrant Mother" photograph closely around the woman, placing her at the center of the image so that she appears to dominate the frame. The two children beside her turn away from the camera, leaning on their mother's shoulders and burying their faces in her neck. Conversely, the woman does not lean back towards her children, instead she has been directed by Lange to look outward beyond the camera, and to put her hand on her chin in an attitude of uncertainty and worry. The powerful impact of the mother's face is emphasized by the children's anonymity. This construction ensures that the woman is not seen as the individual mother of a particular family in a state of destitution that affects her own personal circumstances. Rather, she becomes a representative "Migrant Mother," symbolizing constancy, self-sacrifice, and the possibility of renewal.

Andrea Fisher notes that the symbolic centrality of motherhood in the "Migrant Mother" image reflected contemporary assessments of Lange's photographic approach which, as was made clear in the com-

Fig. 1.6. Dorothea Lange. "Destitute pea pickers in California, a 32-year-old mother of seven children. [Migrant Mother]" Feb. 1936. Reproduced from the Collections of the Library of Congress.

ments made by Van Dyke, Steichen and Stryker, assigned to her a distinctly female sense of intuitive connection with her subjects. Lange's public persona echoed the metaphoric resonance of the working-class women in her photographs:

She was repeatedly represented in popular journals as the "mother" of documentary: the little woman who would cut through ideas by evoking personal feeling. Through her pathos for destitute rural migrants, the New Deal's programs might be legitimized, not as power, but as an exercise of care. . . . Where [Walker] Evans was thought of as the guarantor of honest observation, with his flat-lit frontal shots, Lange was lauded as the keeper of documentary's compassion.[45]

Fisher asserts that such descriptions of Lange revealed a subversively feminist element in her work—especially in her portraits of rural working-class women—that overturned paternalistic suggestions that she was merely an emotionally driven, highly intuitive photographer. According to this assessment, Lange intentionally placed women's lives and female experiences at the center of her documentary photography in such a way that poverty, destitution, hunger, and homelessness were expressed through a common bond between the female photographer and the female subjects of her work. According to this analysis, the sense of mutuality between the perspective of the woman in the "Migrant Mother" image and the photograph's enthralled viewers might be understood as an expression of Lange's apparently wholly equalizing feminist position. This analysis is complicated, however, when the undoubtedly unprecedented visibility of middle-class women photographers and working-class women subjects in the 1930s is placed within the context of the feminist attitudes of women employed by the New Deal government.

The Roosevelt Administration had increased the number of women working in the government by more than 90,000 by 1939. According to Susan Ware, their duties included everything from "[marking] airstrips for the Aeronautics Board up to the Secretary of Labor."[46] Significantly, however, female participation in politics was institutionally and popularly regarded as an extension of what were considered peculiarly female concerns. Consequently, women's jobs were concentrated in the areas of health, education, employment regulations, and social welfare legislation. Women saw their role in government as being equivalent to their domestic duties, a natural progression borne from the female propensity for nurturing, empathy, and instinctive emotion. The engendered division between male and female political talent was made clear by Eleanor Roosevelt when she noted that the Depression could be defeated by utilizing "the ability and brains of our men and the understanding heart of the women."[47]

The notion of social welfare legislation being a specifically female political mission was an extension of the philosophies of several middle-class ladies' organizations to which the majority of female politicians had belonged. Groups such as the National American Women's Suffrage Association, the League of Women Voters, the National Consumer League, and the Women's International League for Peace and Freedom, had campaigned vociferously for social reform. Significantly, as an investigator for the juvenile court system in New York City, Lange's mother, Joan, was an archetypical participant in these agencies of female social work.[48]

Women reformers fully embraced their socially legitimated female sphere in government, and focused their political energies on promoting an inspirational image of the American family. Specifically, they were concerned with abolishing child labor and improving conditions for working women. To this end, in 1933 they fought within the National Recovery Administration to include shorter hours and minimum wage rulings for female employees. Similarly, as part of the Fair Labor Standards Act of 1938, women politicians were at the forefront of efforts to reduce the number of children working. Despite the active feminization of such campaigns, however, the circumstances of economically underprivileged women were often misunderstood by female legislators. Indeed, their political activities often increased the social degradation and marginalization of working-class women in America. The reduction of child labor in 1938, while morally appealing to middle-class reformers, took no account of the necessity of children's wages for the survival of working-class families where a household's most valuable resource was the wage-earning power of its members.[49] Consequently, the removal of a child's income ironically added to the emotional and physical strains of already overburdened working-class mothers. Furthermore, middle-class definitions of responsible motherhood persistently attacked the self-identities of poor women. Economic destitution and lack of education meant that working-class women were deprived of the right to control their own fertility. Abortion was a privilege closely guarded by judgmental relief agencies. The usual response to unwanted or financially impossible pregnancies among working-class women was enforced sterilization or alternatively, back street or self-inflicted abortion.[50]

The disparity between legislation inspired by women reformers in the New Deal government and the experiences of working-class mothers in actuality was manifested in the "Migrant Mother" photographs. Contrary to the insistence of Lange's male critics in the 1930s, and despite more contemporary feminist analyses, the biological affinity between Lange and the woman who became the "Migrant Mother" could not transcend the social and economic differentials between the working-class subject and the middle-class viewer. As a result, the woman in the photograph was presented as a symbolic construction of expectations that defined femininity and motherhood from an exclusively middle-class point of view. This was a portrayal that produced a socially and politically resonant image of a "Migrant Mother" that might have served the cause of social reform, but which simultaneously removed the identity of the woman from the frame of the photograph.

By placing the "Migrant Mother" images within the social and aesthetic contexts of New Deal politics and woman-centered social reform legislation, it becomes clear that Dorothea Lange's encounter with the woman who was to become the symbolic center of the Historical Section's documentary project was far more problematic than her enthused description suggests. Nevertheless, despite her various manipulations of the scene, Lange continued to believe that her role as a documentary photographer enabled her to transfer the unembellished, rational truth of what she saw to whoever might be looking at the image. She claimed that her photographs portrayed poverty, hunger, and dislocation, as a "simple drama" that depended on an unadulterated sense of mutual understanding between the subject and the viewer of the photograph.[51] Thus, she explained that her images showed a middle-class audience "that this is where any of us would find ourselves if we packed up and hit the road."[52] In the same way, she believed her work gave her subjects an opportunity to "tell what they were up against to their government, and to their countrymen at large."[53] Thus, documentary representation seemed to provide the rural poor with a unique chance to converse and be heard on equal terms with those powerful enough to affect their circumstances.

Lange contended that the primary task of a documentary photographer was to keep the visual channel between subject and viewer as uncluttered as possible. To this end, she shrouded herself in what she called a "cloak of invisibility," which psychologically enabled her to become a conductor of pure information, free of her own biases and opinions.[54] At the same time, however, Lange's self-defensive pose also endowed her with the power to observe and investigate her subject while protecting herself from any reciprocal inspection. The power of Lange's position in relation to her subject is made clear by suggestions that while Lange was able to maintain what she called "that self-protective thing," she induced her subject to drop her defensive expression. For example, in the third photograph of the "Migrant Mother" series, the woman "looked downward, as if wishing to shield herself from the scrutiny of the camera." Significantly, she made the "kind of face [that] spoiled Lange's image."[55] That is to say, the woman in the photograph appeared self-enclosed, uncooperative, and unwilling to present herself in the way that Lange—and her middle-class viewers—demanded. As a result, Lange had to work carefully in order to be sure of creating an image of the woman that she could present as a symbolic "Migrant Mother." In order to do so, she had to control and disguise the woman's countenance, disallowing any individualized expression and effectively silencing, rather than articulating, her subject's point of view.

In such a way, the woman who was the subject of the photograph was systematically separated from her famous image. This was a process of fragmentation that was socially legitimated in the 1930s and gradually compounded as the photograph became a cultural icon. The "Migrant Mother" image was first published in *Survey Graphic* in September 1936 and then again to illustrate an article for *Life* magazine in 1937. The title of the *Life* piece, "Erosion of Soil Has Its Counterpart in Erosion of Our Society" typically addressed an audience of concerned and politically liberal readers toward whom the rhetorical devices of documentary photography were directed. At the same time, however, "Migrant Mother" became a recognizable work of art. After seeing the image in *Survey Graphic*, the editors of *U.S. Camera* asked Lange to submit it for an exhibition as "one of the outstanding pictures of the year."[56] As time progressed, this combination of aesthetic brilliance and emotive appeal meant that "Migrant Mother" often transcended its original historical context. In an article for *Popular Photography*, Marjory Mann revealed the extent to which Lange's photograph had been absorbed into American culture:

Not long ago I passed the display window of an artist who would paint your portrait from your photograph, and amidst his samples, the glorified girls and the thirty year old, sly smiling Bette Davis and the muscle men, sat, "Migrant Mother," big as life, in blue and yellow and lilac.[57]

Milton Meltzer also recognized the photograph emblazoned on the cover of a Black Panther newspaper in 1973. In this version "Migrant Mother" had been given "black features and hair [and] the caption 'Poverty is a crime, and our people are the victims.'"[58]

Eventually, Lange herself became concerned that the cultural significance of the photograph might overtake her own reputation as a versatile and complicated artist. Her frustration is clear in one interview where she commented, "I am not a 'one picture' photographer. I don't understand it, . . . I don't know why. It seems to me that I see things as good as that all the time."[59] Ironically, Lange's statement seems to suggest that the cultural prominence of the "Migrant Mother" image had finally led to a circumstance where the photographer and the woman in the photograph became equally anonymous. The postmodern appeal of this scenario is complicated, however, when analyses of "Migrant Mother" lead inevitably toward an investigation of the photographer who created the image, or the historical and political contexts that inspired its conception, rather than of the woman who became its subject.

In 1978, living in a trailer in Modesto, California, on a social security income of $331 per month, seventy-five-year-old Florence Thompson confessed that she was proud to be the subject of the world's most reproduced photograph. She kept a copy of the picture in a frame, together with an edition of *In this Proud Land* also bound with the image of herself. Contrary to this appearance of pride, she spoke of her disappointment and resentment that her picture was "hanging all over the world, and I can't get a penny out of it" asking finally, "What good is it doing me?"[60] In 1983, Florence Thompson appeared in the news again alongside the famous photograph. She had suffered a stroke that prevented her from speaking, and she had cancer. Her children had reprinted the "Migrant Mother" image in order to elicit sympathy that might help raise funds for their mother who had no medical insurance. The publicity was successful and raised almost $30,000, but it was too late for Florence Thompson who died a few months later.[61]

Perhaps, as some have suggested, the fundraising effort made on behalf of Florence Thompson reveals the continuous power of Lange's image, which was at last being utilized for the benefit of its subject. Such assessments are correct in that "Migrant Mother" eventually did Florence Thompson some financial good. Equally, the image provided the impetus to improve general conditions for the rural poor in the 1930s. Nevertheless, despite these long overdue and easily displaced practical measures, "Migrant Mother" was successful and lasting precisely because of the distance between the symbolic resonance of its construction and the individual life of its subject. "Migrant Mother" was never intended to be a portrait of Florence Thompson, rather it was conceived as a depiction of middle-class preconceptions about how the experience of poverty should appear. Consequently, when Florence Thompson did not cooperate with Lange's ideological mandate, the photograph was considered aesthetically inferior—and even less historically accurate—in comparison with the final image.

Inevitably, then, instead of receiving the personal assistance that Florence Thompson thought might be forthcoming if she "helped" Lange, she had to be satisfied with the generalized—for her, inconsequential—improvements that were inspired by "Migrant Mother." Thus, Florence Thompson's position as a working-class woman remained unchanged and consistently marginalized from the social, political, historical, and artistic discourse surrounding her image. Curiosity about Florence Thompson existed only because she was "an incongruity, a photograph that has aged. . . . of interest solely because she is a postscript to an acknowledged work of art."[62] Moreover, the economic differential between working-class subject and middle-class viewers was reemphasized by this reinvestigation. Readers of the *New York Times Magazine*[63] or the *L.A. Times* could see that although the "Migrant Mother" lives in a trailer rather than a tent, and that she receives meager social security payments rather than starving or begging, "the relative distance [between viewer and subject] has not been abridged; we [the middle-class viewers] are still doing much better than they [the working-class subjects]."[64] As such, the insignificance of Florence Thompson's contribution to Lange's photograph is made historically concrete. As well as voyeuristic satiation, middle-class interest in the "Migrant Mother" has been maintained by the constancy of economic inequality since the 1930s, and with nostalgic representations of how it might be resolved. At the same time, with tragic irony, Florence Thompson's invisibility was maintained by almost fifty years of material deprivation, an unchanging situation which—despite the desperate reappropriation of the image by her children—led to her silent death.

2

Marion Post Wolcott:
The Economics of Deception

The Political Landscape

The drive over here was beautiful. I was sorry I hurried so after I arrived and found that no arrangements had been made for the pix here. It wouldn't have mattered if I had taken my time and gotten some photographs of the spring & planting, etc., on my way. Perhaps it was better so—the lab might have gotten too many apple blossoms and budding trees and spring clouds to print. More FSA cheesecake. Or if I had stopped I might have begun to dig in the red brown earth in some farmer's garden & just stayed there.[1]

Until recently Marion Post Wolcott was considered a minor contributor to the FSA documentary project. Her most widely published images, of sumptuous landscapes, sleepy New England towns and romantic farm scenes, were thought aesthetically pleasing but politically shallow, especially in relation to Dorothea Lange's migrant families, Walker Evans's southern sharecroppers, and Arthur Rothstein's images of droughts and dust-storms. Against such an impressive gallery of social iconographers, Post Wolcott's work appeared undramatic and unportentous. Accordingly, Roy Stryker was not inclined to include her work in *In This Proud Land*, and remembered her simply as a "girl who had never had the real guts for the job."[2] Reflecting this evaluation, in *Portrait of a Decade*, F. Jack Hurley paid cursory attention to Post Wolcott's work, characterizing her as energetic and enthusiastic, with an eye for impressive scenery and possessing a girlish sense of humor, but as intellectually empty headed, with limited photographic skill and even less social acumen: archetypically "FSA cheesecake."

Since these first assessments, however, Post Wolcott's work has undergone a critical reevaluation.[3] The subject range of her published images has been extended to show insightful and protracted analyses of economic and social deprivation as well as landscapes and country idylls. Moreover, her photographic approach has been reexamined to

55

reveal a distinctively feminist perspective. This stance was provocatively depicted in her images of mothers and children, in her visual critique of gender roles and racial interaction, and in her concentration on sexual identity. Subsequently, in 1989, F. Jack Hurley revised his opinion of Post Wolcott, praising her for her skillful utilization of photography as an instrument of social research.[4]

Individually and collectively, these reappraisals have directly challenged, and occasionally undermined previously stereotypical interpretations of Post Wolcott's work, and for the first time have revealed the complicated extent of her professional abilities and personal convictions. Now she is presented as a photographer whose "distinctive interests constitute an unsentimental, provocative departure from the dominant themes of FSA photography."[5] With this view in mind, Post Wolcott's images are selected, deconstructed, and analyzed as evidence of her radical perspective. Significantly, however, these analyses often do not include Post Wolcott's scenic images. Instead, her "pastoral views"[6] are mentioned only as the photographs Post Wolcott was required to take when she really wanted to picture the human effects of economic and social stratification. These later assessments of Post Wolcott create a diametric opposition; between a monolithic FSA orthodoxy that transformed Post Wolcott into a lightweight pictorial photographer, and an authenticating critical deconstruction. Debunking the "cheesecake" image, the real Marion Post Wolcott is apparently revealed, uncensored, and expressing a complicated and sophisticated social analysis in her photographs. The image of an FSA airhead is thus effectively replaced by a representative FSA rebel.

My aim here is to examine the opposition between sexist stereotyping and the one-dimensionality of some revisions. The letter that Post Wolcott wrote to Stryker highlights the historical and political contexts that inform a more complex definition of her photographic approach. Read superficially, the letter reveals nothing new. Post Wolcott is apparently dismissive of the prospect of photographing more "apple blossoms and budding trees," typically expressing her frustration at the limitations of her FSA mandate. Nevertheless, her cursory attitude is balanced by an obvious emotional attachment to the land she was required to photograph. Simple appreciation of scenic beauty at the beginning of her letter is later expressed as a psychic need to "dig in the red brown earth in some farmer's garden and just stay there." The letter continues: "Parts of the country driving reminded me of France which I drove through one Spring. War news, international & national happenings, always seem to be even worse & more terrifying when I'm away & I don't have anyone I know to talk about it."[7]

The letter, dated May 15, 1940, was written at a time when most of Europe had fallen to Hitler. Germany was poised to enact its plans for an invasion of Britain at the end of the year, and Allied defeat seemed inevitable. In the United States, President Roosevelt was gathering congressional support for American entry into the war. In order to promote the government's interventionist policy, the ideological direction of the FSA project shifted from images of a country ravaged by drought, dust, and poverty, to photographic visions of a beautiful and fertile landscape. Post Wolcott's shooting scripts were intended to recapture the notion of America as a land that was worth defending. This pictorial approach also emphasized small towns and family farms inhabited by "simple Americans," rather than by symbolic heroes or pathetic victims. The threat of war was conceptualized and depicted in pastoral—rather than iconic—terms. Reflecting this, in 1939, one observer commented: "Everyone—little people like taxi drivers, drugstore clerks and farmers in the Shenandoah and the like, are saying we'll sure get into it."[8] Accordingly, the Historical Section wanted to produce images that would inspire patriotism in these "ordinary citizens," by portraying the country in a way that reflected individualized conceptions of personal history, family tradition, and national identity. To this end, the FSA tried to make images of a popularly perceived conception of home.

Post Wolcott's letter reflects the idealized emotional foundations of the government's propaganda tactics. Her personal insecurity and fear at the imminence of war is counteracted by her desire for stability and constancy as she perceived it in the landscapes she photographed. Moreover, her letter also implies the engendered terms on which the government's ideological campaign depended. As war approached, symbolic reverence of the land gained a distinctly female identity. This is made clear in Samuel Chamberlain's illustrated book, *Fair Is Our Land*, published in 1942 and including several of Post Wolcott's photographs. The accompanying text, written by Donald Moffatt, describes the landscape as "a picture of peaceful America, the land that awaits the returning soldier, serene and comforting,"[9] and reminded the reader: "All lands are fair. But the matchless beauty of our land we now see in a new and clearer light. Now, when we are learning to forget ourselves and fight to keep this beauty undefiled."[10]

Images of countryside and small towns became metaphoric depictions of loyal wives, proud mothers, and faithful sweethearts waiting for the return of their heroic menfolk. These allusions were extended to evoke images of female sexuality. To this end, Moffatt's narrative not only suggests that women should remain chaste while their men were away, but that in defending the beauty of the American landscape, soldiers were also implicitly protecting the collective sexual honor of American womanhood. In the same way, sexual loyalty was perceived as a woman's patriotic duty, reflecting a landscape that was depicted in terms of potential defilement and destruction.

In the light of this representational ideology, Post Wolcott's use of the word "cheesecake" to describe the landscape she was portraying implies a more sexualized subtext, which refers to a symbolically depicted female body utilized to appeal to a metaphorically male audience. This gender differential—between a feminized landscape and a controlling masculine point of view—was compounded by the way Post Wolcott was consistently perceived. According to comments made by Stryker, by the popular media, and in later assessments of her work, Post Wolcott was defined in the same sexualized terms as the landscape she photographed.[11] She was presented as the embodiment of a certain female sexual vibrancy that was ideologically employed to inspire men to become soldiers by offering the promise of a sexual reward on their return from war. Moreover, Post Wolcott's travels alone through the country carrying only a hatchet for protection suggested an appealing desire for adventures that might—at the very least—compromise her personal security. At the same time, however, Post Wolcott's apparently fearless predilection for physical challenge was counterbalanced, since she also remained "white-gloved" and appropriately virginal despite her apparent vivaciousness.[12] Consequently, she was frequently portrayed as "a pretty girl photographer . . . too young looking to be taken seriously."[13] Stryker noted that Post Wolcott "suffered from being an attractive young girl, and I always wondered how she could get along."[14] His paternalistic concern was tempered, however, by his recollection of Post Wolcott's response: "I asked Marion one time, I said, 'Marion, don't you have some trouble around sometimes.' She said, 'Yes, very often a local policeman picks me up. We have a Coke, and he asks me something about my sex life, and I ask him about his, and by this time I look at my watch and say "If I don't get back to work I'm going to get fired!" ' "[15]

Stryker's dualistic expression of concern and delight toward Post Wolcott's sexuality was reflected in the work she was asked to do for the Historical Section. Stryker utilized her physical attractiveness to charm recalcitrant local officials. As a result she was assigned to a disproportionate number of standardized projects for government agencies, rather than being allowed to pursue her own independent perspectives.[16] Stryker wanted Post Wolcott to function "not as a photographer but also as a public relations person for the central office in Washington."[17] Stryker's reluctance to allow Post Wolcott the freedom given to other

FSA photographers might also have stemmed from his distrust of the politically challenging photographs that she made when left to her own devices.[18] Whatever the reasons for his circumscription of Post Wolcott's work, Stryker's opinions were couched in familiarly gender specific terms. His memos suggest that he felt he was protecting her from the sexual threat he imagined as being integral to rural working-class life. This was a view he expressed clearly in a letter written on July 14, 1938, while offering a strict opinion on her style of dress:

I'm glad that you have learned you can't depend on the wiles of femininity when you are in the wilds of the South. Colorful bandannas and brightly colored dresses, etc. aren't part of our photographers' equipment. The closer you get to what the great back-country recognizes as the normal dress for women, the better you are going to succeed as a photographer. I know this will probably make you mad, but I can tell you another thing—that slacks aren't part of your attire when you are in the back-country. You are a woman, and "a woman can't never be a man."[19]

Post Wolcott's position as female photographer employed by the government was delineated by the gender oppositions implicit in such comments, and which also informed the ideological discourse of FSA photography as America prepared for war. An independent woman like Post Wolcott might believe she was able to cope on her own but, in the same way that the American landscape was presented to offset the imminent threat of conflict, the female body was essentially depicted as a desired space that had to be defended against aggressive foreign advances by a protective male presence. As such, Post Wolcott's publicly perceived innocence reflected the symbolic resonance of her scenic images. Her femininity was inextricably bound to the patriotic sexual morality evoked by the American landscape.

Some critics have suggested that although the landscape was presented as essentially feminine in a way that simultaneously nurtured and satisfied the expectations of a male viewer, it was also possible to depict the landscape as a woman-centered vista that might reflect and express a feminist perspective.[20] Annette Kolodny highlights this difference in perception when she suggests that defining the land as feminine from a feminist point of view rather than an aggressively male one would "at once do away with the notion of the land as something to be either exclusively possessed or preyed upon—like a sexual object—and suggest instead an intimacy based on reciprocity and communality."[21] The emotional need expressed by Post Wolcott in her letter to Stryker perfectly reflects Kolodny's assertion. Post Wolcott wrote of her desire to halt her continuous journey around the country gathering evidence, documenting facts, reporting and measuring economic and social circumstances, and instead stop in a fertile field where she could take root in the earth and become part of the landscape.[22] Her longing to conjoin with the countryside as a reaction to her solitude also fits Kolodny's perspective. Other FSA photographers—Jack Delano, Ben Shahn, and Dorothea Lange—took their spouses out into the field. In contrast, Post Wolcott invariably traveled alone. In relation to this isolation, her connection with the environment seems to connote a longing for company—not simply for a husband— but for a community that might offer her the same sense of stability and security that she describes as being inherent to the landscape. Post Wolcott reiterated these feelings in another letter:

One has the feeling of not belonging anywhere, of having no roots or base. It is a kind of numbness. One never really participates in anything. At times nothing seems real to you, or part of your life. Nothing affects your own life. One has the feeling of being suspended, of never being relaxed, or at home, or accepted for who or what one really is, or has been, and what one believes. One never has the same feeling of belonging as one does when with former acquaintances and friends. It is a need to be with familiar people, to walk known streets and recognize familiar places. It is not good to feel always that one must go on, leaving everything unfinished and incomplete—both work and human relationships.[23]

Clearly, then, Post Wolcott's landscape work was not merely routine and irrelevant, but was an expression of the often antagonistic ideological contexts in which she was working. Thus, her photographs of the American landscape can be interpreted as representations made from an essentially feminist perspective that valued community, stability, emotional love, and psychological attachment over aggression, conquest, individuality, and selfish desire which, in opposition, are inevitably defined as male. At the same time, this analysis undermines the suggestion that her landscape images were simple depictions of official propaganda, and thus reflections of the contradictory sexist impulses that defined her identity as a government photographer. In either case, Post Wolcott's responses to the American landscape fundamentally informed more obviously complex depictions of economic and social inequities in her photography, while providing an important basis from which to examine the political convictions, radical perspectives, and aesthetic styles that inspired her work for the FSA.

American Radicalism

Marion Post Wolcott was born on June 7, 1910, in Bloomfield, New Jersey. Her father, Walter Post, was a doctor, described by Post Wolcott as "distant, conservative, authoritarian, judgmental, and emotionally boundup."[24] In contrast, her mother, Nan, was considered an unconventional woman in genteel, conservative Bloomfield. She was a trained nurse and a scandalously strong advocate of contraception. She was also politically radical, supporting the Russian Revolution and defending union rights and racial equality in the United States.

Nan was divorced from Walter in 1924, after an affair that shocked neighbors and relatives who had been unmoved by Walter's many similar liaisons. After the separation, Post Wolcott was raised entirely by her mother. Nan worked full time with Margaret Sanger in order to support her family, and encouraged her daughter to revel in the physical and sexual freedoms that family planning afforded women. Accordingly, Marion wore bloomers and emulated her mother's apparently outrageous style of dress.[25] Typical of these recollections was Marion's first dance, when her mother persuaded her to wear an evening dress despite the risqué nature of such attire:

I remember when I was in junior high getting invited to a prom. My father said, "She cannot wear an evening dress, it's out of the question." Mother said, "She will have an evening dress. Maybe it won't be cut quite as low as I personally would like, but she will have an evening dress."[26]

Nan Post's belief in the liberating power of physical expression for women extended into her appreciation of art and theater. Contrary to her husband's wishes, she took Marion to see Isadora Duncan perform in New York City. The experience had a lasting effect on Post Wolcott, who immediately decided to pursue a career in modern dance. She attended the Denishawn School in New York where she studied with Ruth St. Denis, and later went to classes taught by Doris Humphrey at New York University. The emphasis these dancers placed on physical self-expression as a means of achieving psychological and emotional release played an important part in the development of Post Wolcott's photographic skills.[27] Thus, it was no coincidence that when Post Wolcott left the United States for Germany to study dance with Mary Wigman, she also began to take photographs.

Post Wolcott arrived in Europe in 1933 and settled in Austria along with her sister, Helen, who had been studying with portrait photographer and self-styled bohemian Trude Fleischmann.[28] Post Wolcott became an enthusiastic student of Fleischmann's and, as she became more accomplished as a photographer, she also became increasingly influenced by the political developments in Austria. She remembered that witnessing Hitler's rise to power first hand "made me very antifascist, as well as against all forms of racial intolerance for the rest of my life."[29] Her personal response to such manifestations of fascist violence as "swastikas burning in the front yards of peasants" and "lying awake and listening to the bombing out in the Floridsdorf district of the city"[30] matched those of the artistic circle around her. Vienna's left-wing radicals were self-consciously disturbed by events affecting those racially or politically attacked by fascists. Post Wolcott recalled the existential ennui that infused and paralyzed the Bohemian community:

Oh, you'd sit around in wicker chairs at cafes—everybody did this—and read the papers forever. . . . If you weren't attending classes, you were at Trude's, or maybe going to some semi-radical student meeting. . . .

   I think it was perfectly legitimate idealism. I suppose it was my urge, the urge of any of us, to try and discover alternative political systems.[31]

Post Wolcott's involvement in radical politics was, according to some interpretations, "innocent,"[32] rather in the same way that her approach to FSA photography was considered superficially naive by Roy Stryker. Nevertheless, her attitude toward the developments in Europe reflected her belief that psychological freedom and personal self-expression allowed individuals to transcend their material circumstances, while providing an elemental sense of identification between people divided by social, political, and economic inequities. This point of view—which extended from the liberating physicality she experienced as a dancer—was developed when she returned to America in the summer of 1934.

Post Wolcott's experiences in Europe were balanced by the time she spent teaching at an elementary school in Whitinsville, Massachusetts. Her students were the children of managers at a nearby mill in the town, and while she was employed at the school, Post Wolcott boarded with the mill workers. The economic differential between the lives of Post Wolcott's relatively well-off pupils and the experiences of the mill workers' families at the boarding house first introduced her to "social and class oppression in the United States."[33] Paul Hendrickson concurs that Post Wolcott's brief stay in the Whitinsville boarding house was "an eye-opener to the poison of class bigotries in America."[34] F. Jack Hurley similarly asserts that the Whitinsville experience was central to her later investigations of economic oppression in FSA photography. He notes that Post Wolcott's position as an intermediary between "the working-class men in her boarding house" and the "clean bright children" in her classroom allowed her to observe social and economic stratification as a process of physical and psychological separation that began at the earliest stages of education.[35]

According to these assessments, Post Wolcott's insights into social hierarchy resulted from a radical upbringing that had allowed her to express her self-identity through an awareness of her physical, sexual, and psychological being. These early experiences nurtured her self-confidence and provided her with a sense of bravado, both necessary qualities if a young middle-class woman was to board with a group of working-class men. Despite this self-conscious ability to transcend class boundaries, Post Wolcott's experience at Whitinsville also revealed the limitations of her political outlook. Post Wolcott perceived the material inequities of class circumstance as being psychologically equivalent. From her privileged point of view, mutual understanding between physically divided workers and students was prevented only by the superficial confinements of a particular economic situation that unfortunately "prohibited against direct contact between classes."[36] Thus, Post Wolcott did not believe her presence in a working-class community to be incongruous. Similarly, she did not consider that her apparent insights into their mental processes might have been somewhat presumptuous. Rather, she believed that both experiences were evidence that social mobility was possible if individuals could free their minds from the confinements of their respective material situations. Therefore, according to Post Wolcott, middle-class ignorance of economic oppression and working-class unfamiliarity with liberal education were equally tragic. Significantly, then, the perception that most disturbed Post Wolcott at Whitinsville was that "the working-class men in her boarding house knew nothing of Progressive education, and . . . the children whose minds [she] spent her days stimulating, knew nothing, indeed might never know anything, about the necessity of working in order to eat."[37]

In reality, however, material circumstances were psychologically defining. Economic and educational privileges might have given Post Wolcott access to a working-class environment, but working-class exclusion from the same advantages made the reverse impossible. In this hierarchical social context, the physical strains and the psychological and emotional debilitations caused by economic oppression left no space for working-class self-expression. As a result, in Whitinsville, the mill workers' opinions were easily appropriated into Post Wolcott's personal sense of mutual exchange, where middle-class interpretations of oppression and equality were reassuringly undisturbed by diverse economic perspectives that were always represented, but never self-defined. The Whitinsville experience was undoubtedly important in the development of Post Wolcott's photographic approach. Working for the FSA, she consistently depicted a community of Americans economically and racially fractured, but displaying identical psychological needs and emotional characteristics—communication, love, relaxation, sexuality—even in the most disparate physical circumstances. The spirit of psychic wholeness and communality was symbolically resonant in her photographs of a rich and fertile land framed by the context of approaching war.

Post Wolcott's experiences at Whitinsville were given further support by a community of left-wing and radical organizations that, by the mid-1930s, had re-defined revolution as an all inclusive, all-American, activity rather than an antagonistic political movement.[38] In particular, the Photo League that Post Wolcott joined in 1935 had disassociated itself from its original proletarian prefix and its accompanying mandate that membership should be "mainly working-class, with a sprinkling of middle-class intellectuals and technicians sympathetic to our progressive goals."[39] By 1935, the League, which had previously criticized the New Deal Government for betraying working-class interests, now included almost all of the FSA photographers in its ranks. The League also welcomed Roy Stryker to deliver guest lectures at its meetings and, in its weekly newsletter, *Photo Notes*, actively praised government photography for presenting an objective "spirit of realism [with]. . . . scientific, uncompromising honesty."[40] Significant, in relation to Post Wolcott's membership, was the League's rejection of a former dictate that pejoratively judged all portraits, nudes, landscapes, and still lifes to be "bourgeois."[41] Post Wolcott's approach to documenting poverty and inequality was far more suited to an artistic and political rubric that claimed to depict working-class identity as a symbolic facet of a fundamentally democratic society, temporarily divided by the Depression.

As the Photo League focused away from overt representations of archetypical proletarian themes (strikes, demonstrations against rent levels, etc.), its political direction became intertwined with other modes of radical artistic expression. Specifically, Post Wolcott's connections at the League combined with her new interest in the Group Theater. Photographers like Ralph Steiner and Paul Strand, whom Post Wolcott regarded as her mentors, often associated themselves with productions at the Group Theater.[42] Moreover, the method acting techniques used by Group members to express their political radicalism reflected representations of working-class subjects at the Photo League. The political commitment of both the League and the Group Theater stemmed from an eagerness to observe and portray working-class life without reference to the capitalist hierarchy that allowed them to do so. Ironically, Stanislavskian acting techniques and photographic concern with representations that emphasized mutuality between working-class subjects and middle-class viewers legitimized ignorance of economic oppression. Trust in the liberating possibilities of psychologically real performances or of absolutely objective photography sanctified the skill of the artist and the (middle-class) audience's understanding of the scene portrayed. At the same time, however, artistic emphasis on transcendent emotional truth marginalized the material realities of working-class experience, and so rendered the need for a self-identified working-class point of view unnecessary. Without a fundamental focus on working-class identity, political radicalism, at the Group Theater performances and in photographs at the League, was little more than a rhetorical or a visual facade. As a result, "left-wing activist" was an ideological position easily taken on in the artistic community to which Post Wolcott belonged. Bobby Lewis, an original member of the Group Theater, remarked: "Oh Hell, everybody was a Communist in one sense or another back then."[43] Similarly, Harold Clurman, the Group's founder, while noting the fervent socialism of his actors, commented that "even our kitchen staff was being propagandized."[44] The irony of this statement was lost on Clurman, and possibly most of his actors. Evidently, there was no time for food preparation in the midst of rehearsing *Waiting for Lefty*.

Post Wolcott's familiarity with the radical styles of the Group Theater and the Photo League is clear in her FSA work, particularly in her focus on the American landscape. As such, her work was commensurate with the aesthetic style and political contentions of Paul Strand, the photographer who recommended Post Wolcott to Stryker.[45] In his own work, Strand sought to portray a resonant contradiction between nature and society in a way that symbolically reflected the dynamic possibilities of socialist ideology. In so doing, he focused on archetypical American scenes—like the rugged mountains, spectacular foliage, and wooden buildings in New England—in order to suggest a renewable sense of revolution that he perceived as being implicit in the American landscape.[46] Much of this philosophy appears in Post Wolcott's images of idyllic country scenes. Her many images of snowbound New England towns recall the peculiarly American belief in a transcendent form of radicalism, centered on individual freedom, an elemental sense of resistance, and a sustainable revolutionary spirit that was symbolically represented in winter landscapes.[47] Despite this similarity with Strand, Post Wolcott developed her own analysis of the American countryside.

Viewed superficially, Post Wolcott's images represent a visual celebration of the land as a symbol of equality and community. She concentrated on small towns and working farms in order to highlight the liberating capacity inherent in every American's unique connection with the environment. This perspective is evident in one image: "Farm, Bucks County, Pennsylvania," June 1939 (fig. 2.1). The photograph shows a number of small farm buildings enclosed by trees. The surrounding fence makes a path that directs the eye into the central horizon and upwards into the summer sky. The buildings and the trees are portrayed in harmonious relation with each other, a connection that is metaphorically depicted as spiritually uplifting. Unlike earlier FSA photographs that vividly displayed the human cost of land exploitation, this image reveals the positive effects of an equalized relationship with nature, a connection that might create a context for developing a more democratic and egalitarian American community.

This simple visual affirmation of the traditional values that were portrayed as inherent to the landscape is complicated, however, by Post Wolcott's depiction of the ways society had been systematically divided by the inequities of industrial capitalism. For example, her photograph, "Coal mining community, near Welch, West Virginia," Sept. 1938, has a construction similar to her photographs of small farms (fig. 2.2). The mining town is nestled in a valley, the row of houses and the railway tracks lead the eye across and beyond the frame in symbolic lines of reverie. In contrast to the sleepy tranquillity of the Pennsylvanian farm, the landscape that encloses the mining town is a steep and oppressive hill, and only one tree, with stark foliage, is visible. The houses are built right up against the hillside and the image is cropped to emphasize the aggressive angle of the slope: a landslide appears to be immanent. The buildings are facing what looks like a muddy pit; its depth is not clear, but it seems equally as threatening as the hill. Also unlike Post Wolcott's romantic farm images, the railway tracks do not lead upwards to a transcendental horizon, but downwards into a dark tunnel underneath the hillside. The landscape is visibly scarred by human exploitation and the working-class community is consequently enclosed, threatened, and oppressed by its surroundings. The possibility of articulating an individual point of view beyond the frame of the photograph is consequently removed.

Similarly, another photograph, "Picking cotton, Nugent Plantation, Benoit, Mississippi Delta," Oct. 1939, shows African-American laborers harvesting a cotton crop (fig. 2.3). The field is enormous, stretching far off into the horizon, a vast distance made more extensive by Post Wolcott's oppressively close foregrounding of more cotton plants ranging beyond the edge of the image. The photograph is focused on a picker surrounded by cotton plants. Nearby, another two pickers are recognizable only by their white hats. Closer inspection of the photograph reveals

Fig. 2.1. Marion Post Wolcott. "Farm, in Bucks County, Pennsylvania." June 1939. Reproduced from the Collections of the Library of Congress.

Fig. 2.2. Marion Post Wolcott. "Coal mining community, near Welch, West Virginia." Sept. 1938. Reproduced from the Collections of the Library of Congress.

Fig. 2.3. Marion Post Wolcott. "Picking cotton, Nugent Plantation, Benoit, Misissippi Delta." Oct. 1939. Reproduced from the Collections of the Library of Congress.

dozens of white specks between the cotton plants, again reaching off into the horizon. The extent to which the structure of the southern economy, and its accompanying racism, engulfed the lives of African Americans is made clear in this image. The workers' bodies are overwhelmed by the cotton crop. In the distance, roofs of buildings—presumably the workers' houses—are also enclosed by the field. The sky is thick with clouds and a storm is threatening. Apart from a few trees, the landscape is completely covered by the cotton field. As a result, the possibility of a liberating connection with the natural environment has been removed. By portraying the landscape in such a way, Post Wolcott has symbolically depicted the enforced peonage of African Americans in the South, revealing their condition to be a perversion of nature, and a systematic negation of the values and ideals that Post Wolcott perceived as being fundamental to the American landscape.

Post Wolcott's portrayal of the landscape as a manifestly politicized space reflected the rhetorical devices of the artistic radicalism that informed her photographic approach before she was employed by the FSA. That her landscape images also happily fitted the one-dimensional requirements of Roy Stryker's dogmatically sentimental shooting scripts attests to the flexibility of the rhetorical facade that represented the New Deal to a predetermined middle-class audience. Post Wolcott's insight into social divisions as they were represented in relation to the land was consequently firmly delineated by her officially directed concentration on traditionally American landscapes: New England farms, southern plantations, and midwestern hillsides. By focusing on these reassuring scenes, and simultaneously away from depictions of poverty, land desecration, and economic disaster, the FSA wanted to exclude subjects that would disturb the nationalistic fervor of the middle-class viewer. As a result, landscapes that might contain an economically deprived or racially marginalized population were considered less suitable for representation. In order to oppose this official mandate, Post Wolcott had to artfully manipulate her landscape photography in order to include working-class or nonwhite subjects. Her apparently inclusive approach was compromised, however, in relation to the alternative perspective from which Post Wolcott began her investigation of the economic and social inequities that predominated in America during the 1930s. As has been seen, left-wing activity appealed directly to middle-class intellectualism and modes of cultural expression that subsequently removed working-class subjectivity from the dialectics of radical politics. In the same way, Post Wolcott photographed an American community physically divided, but spiritually equivalent in their connection with the land. From this point of view, the progression of radical social change in Marion Post

Wolcott's photographs of the landscape leads to an ahistorical point of transcendence, euphemistically defined as universal and naturally American. Her visual criticisms of American capitalism extended from this ultimately conservative political perspective.

Landscape and Sexuality

Post Wolcott's position in the FSA was an extension of official concentration on the landscape as a feminized space presented as simultaneously available and endangered. Her own personal sense of political and artistic principle, and subsequently her professional participation in the agency's project, were inevitably compromised as a result. In the same way, the FSA's mandate for photographing the landscape to reflect traditionally democratic and idealistic American values often excluded economically and socially marginalized subjects from official representation. Post Wolcott tried to undermine this repressive combination in her photographs by portraying the physicality—and in particular the sexuality—of her subjects as fundamentally rejuvenating and thus a politically radical part of the American landscape. From this perspective, while Post Wolcott photographed the West Virginian countryside ravaged by the inequities of industrial capitalism, her images of the individuals living there also revealed a tangible sense of sexual energy that appeared to challenge the debilitating inhumanity of the environment. Reflecting this, Post Wolcott described her impression of the woman pictured in "Unemployed miner's wife on porch of company owned house, Marine, West Virginia," 1938 (fig. 2.4):

This woman had TB. I think she was living in an abandoned store. It was in West Virginia, down near Welch, on that first trip I made for Roy. I can see the road in, I can see her leaning over that railing talking to me. There may have been four or five families living in that store. They were all piled together. She's pretty erotic, isn't she? I probably admired that. I knew immediately I wanted to shoot her. She was so beaten down by life and yet there was all this sexuality in her, not just sexuality but sensuality. I talked to her for a while and then I went on. But I knew I had it.[48]

The innate eroticism that Post Wolcott ascribes to the woman in her photograph is evident in the way she is posed, leaning over the dirty and broken-down rail at the front of the building, with her naked arms and chest exposed beneath a flimsy dress. The woman's physical openness is compounded by her expression, which is lit from the top so as to emphasize the smoothness of her skin and the welcoming demeanor of her posture. Post Wolcott notes that the woman's apparently natural sensuality

Fig. 2.4. Marion Post Wolcott. "Unemployed miner's wife on porch of company owned house, Marine, West Virginia." 1938. Reproduced from the Collections of the Library of Congress.

was made all the more attractive in relation to the squalor of her material circumstances. Her description suggests that the woman was able to survive and resist the oppressions of her economic situation because of the self-defining power of her sexuality. In this way, the photograph was also a manifestation of Post Wolcott's feminist impulses. The woman is positioned at the center of the image where her body symbolically dominates the front of the house which, as the title states, is owned by the mining company. This emphasis is compounded by the way the wooden rail reframes the woman's body around her exposed breasts and her hips. From this construction, her figure seems to counteract the economic situation that has defined her material circumstances. According to this perspective, Post Wolcott has portrayed the radical power of female sexuality in dialectic opposition to the oppressive force of industrialized capitalism which, in contrast, is logically defined as male. Nevertheless, the explicit politicization of the woman's body in this image allowed Post Wolcott to circumvent the economic realities that defined her subject's working-class identity. The one-dimensionality of Post Wolcott's point of view is clearly evident in the photograph. Despite the woman's physical exposure, her bones—attesting to malnutrition and disease—are more prominent than her décolletage. In this respect, rather than seeming to be a celebration of this woman's sexuality, Post Wolcott's perspective, looking up from below and focusing on her jutting skeleton, becomes at the least insensitive, if not explicitly cruel, presenting the woman as a sickening parody of the vampish poses popular among models and movie actresses at that time.

Post Wolcott's disavowal of the physical evidence of the woman's poverty extended from the superficiality of her radical perspective. Concentration on the sexuality of her subject suggested that, despite the deprivations of the woman's material circumstances or even, ironically, because of her poverty, she was fundamentally more attuned to the natural processes of the land than middle-class viewers of the image and so was less corrupted by the rational force of industrial capitalism. The visual affirmation of physical energy that was innately fertile, fundamentally organic, and naturally separated from economic or political development, integrated working-class identity within the conservative rhetoric of government representation. At the same time, in order to assign a sense of physical and sexual power to her working-class subjects, Post Wolcott had to create a sense of emotional equivalency in her photographs. To do this she often portrayed economically deprived subjects in a way that would encourage middle-class viewers to be aware of how their own physical identities were repressed by the vestiges of material wealth. The success of this manipulative approach is particularly obvious in another of Post Wolcott's portraits of the mining community in West Virginia (fig. 2.5).

The miner portrayed is, the title states, known as a "smart guy" and a "ladies' man." He is described as "supine [and] lecherous."[49] Indeed, the miner seems to be leering confidently at the photographer and at the viewer. Like the woman in the previous image, he is physically attractive, with dark hair and eyebrows and young-looking skin. His grin is somewhat lascivious, and his posture displays an openness that appears positively uninhibited. There is also a symbolically sexual dimension to the photograph as the man bites the end of his cigarette, looking directly at the viewer while placing his other hand next to his groin. The phallic suggestion is implicit in the image, but is nevertheless compounded by

Fig. 2.5. Marion Post Wolcott. "Smart guy, ladies' man, Marine, West Virginia." 1938. Reproduced from the Collections of the Library of Congress.

the man's physical confidence, by his seductive expression, and by the information given by Post Wolcott in the photograph's title. Again like the first image of the miner's wife, Post Wolcott's concentration on the man's sexuality detracts from his underfed body that is almost overwhelmed by his overalls, and also diverts attention from the physically debilitating circumstances of his labor. Hendrickson notes that the curve of the miner's posture emphasizes the expression of desire on his face. At the same time, his contorted body, which suggests "not a human form but the letter S,"[50] also reflects the cramped conditions down in the mine where he has to work long, arduous shifts, which actively restrict— rather than express—his physical being. Moreover, Post Wolcott is able to decontextualize the miner's body from the site of his labor by using her own sexualized persona as a means of communicating what she perceives as a fundamentally powerful, and politically radical, aspect of working-class identity. In this way, the miner is represented in opposition to Post Wolcott's identity as a young, single, attractive woman. At the same time, in relation to her perceived innocence, he appears to be somewhat threatening and to be exuding the kind of uncontrollable sexual urge from which Stryker felt Post Wolcott needed to be protected. Consequently, the representation of working-class identity as an energetic physical force that was symbolic of an incorruptible American landscape is simultaneously transformed into a potentially aggressive and dangerous presence that must be carefully controlled in order to ensure the moral sophistication of middle-class culture.

The dualistic representation of working-class identity as being inspirationally natural, and simultaneously threatening to a middle-class point of view, was compounded and extended into a concrete political context in Post Wolcott's representations of nonwhite working-class subjects. Typical is one image of an artisan of mixed race whom Post Wolcott photographed at the John Henry Plantation in Louisiana. Apparently, this portrait "haunted" Post Wolcott years after it was taken. Her impressions of the man she portrayed are described by Paul Hendrickson:

She doesn't get his name. The man is very skilled in woodwork and weaving. He has a broad flat nose and deep-set eyes and a two-day stubble, but most of all he has an enigmatic expression—not quite a grin, certainly not an apology. What is in this look, she wonders. Self-confidence? Yes. But tenderness. And dignity. And spirituality. And eroticism. The man doesn't seem nearly as repressed or silent as so many Louisiana black people do. . . . She wonders if he has Indian blood in him. . . . Years later, studying over and over her half dozen images of this man, rubbing her fingers at the border of the prints, a photographer will ask herself, "Was he telling you that day, Marion, 'You're stealing a layer of my soul, lady, a filament of my memory with your infernal magic box. Perhaps I should lie down with you and take something for myself.' "[51]

Post Wolcott's reaction to her subject transforms his self-defensive independence into a stance that reflects racist assumptions about his identity, and also negates the power of Post Wolcott's own position as a middle-class white woman working to support government policies that invariably failed to serve the interests of racial minorities. Post Wolcott's self-referential response to the man she photographed reflected Stryker's opinion that she was doubly compromised as a physically attractive white woman taking photographs of black people. In a memo dated July 1938 he warned:

There is another thing I raised with you the other day, that is the idea of your travelling in certain areas alone. I know that you have a great deal of experience in the field, and that you are quite competent to take care of yourself, but I do have grave doubts of the advisability of sending you, for instance, into certain sections of the South. It would not involve you personally in the least, but, for example, negro people are put in a very difficult spot when white women attempt to interview or photograph them. But I do not think this needs to be a serious consideration at this moment. There are plenty of things to be done in the various problem areas of the country.[52]

Stryker's letter implies that both Post Wolcott and the subjects of her photographs needed to be protected from the sexualized tenets of racist ideology. This suggestion that victimization was experienced equally by white women and black people is taken up by some feminist critics who have concentrated particularly on Post Wolcott's photograph "On Main Street of Wendell, North Carolina," 1939, as an example (fig. 2.6).

The photograph shows three African-American men, a white man, and a white woman, crossing each other's paths in front of a sign on the side of a drug store. The white man faces the camera head-on in a stance that Andrea Fisher has described as "staunch, blunt, even challenging."[53] A white woman is walking on the street behind him clutching something, perhaps a baby. Two African-American men are clearly visible walking around the woman while avoiding the white man, "cutting the widest possible arc so as to avoid close contact with either the woman or the stationary man."[54] Paul Hendrickson somewhat obtusely suggests that the African-American men are avoiding the woman "because they know their manners," or perhaps because "the woman with the baby has just spoken sharply to them."[55] Nevertheless, despite the apparent innocuousness of the incident, racial tension is presented quite clearly to the viewer.

Fig. 2.6. Marion Post Wolcott. "On Main Street of Wendell, North Carolina." 1939. Reproduced from the Collections of the Library of Congress.

Racism was a cultural orthodoxy in the South. Its most systematic and violent manifestations—segregation and lynching—visibly enshrined white power. At the same time, brutalization and political barbarism were transformed into moral dogma through complex systems of manners, religion, innuendo, and social rituals. Stein and Fisher contend that Post Wolcott's image successfully deconstructs this facade of politeness and tradition so as to reveal the paradoxes that defined southern society. Both analyses show how the photograph uses a seemingly everyday interaction to highlight a system of fear and intimidation that supported white male identity in the South. Thus, as the African-American men avoid the white woman, they are also deferring to the symbolic power of the white man's steadfast glare. Most clearly, for Stein and Fisher, this dialectical opposition is centered on the white woman's insecurity. She hurries by, avoiding eye contact with the African-American men, her vulnerability not assuaged by the presence of the white man.

Concentrating on the centrality of the white woman in the photograph's construction, Sally Stein places the image within the context of white women's organization against lynching in the 1930s. The Association of Southern White Women for the Prevention of Lynching had a membership of over 40,000 by 1939. Its moral platform declared "a strong critical stand against the way they [white women] traditionally served as pawns for violent crimes by white men against black men."[56] Andrea Fisher concurs with Stein's assessment that while white women remained politically disempowered, their sexuality could be easily manipulated for the benefit of white men. Thus, Fisher suggests, in Post Wolcott's photograph "the men's postures lucidly diagram a crude differential in power in which the woman is caught as a conduit."[57] Stein's reference to the ASWPL provides a context for possible change in power relations in Post Wolcott's image. Despite this radical assertion, however, the photograph's visual dynamic, and the accompanying concentration on the necessity for white women's self-empowerment, simultaneously marginalizes African-American self-identity. The political limitations of these analyses become clear in an examination of the ASWPL's "strenuous objections" against lynching.[58]

On January 11, 1935, a meeting of the ASWPL was held at Atlanta University. The meeting was attended by several prominent African-American women, including Mary McLeod Bethune, who expressed her gratitude at the ASWPL's activities. Another African-American woman, Nannie Burroughs, offered a more critical opinion of the organization's failure to endorse the Costigan-Wagner Bill against lynching:

When we are not part of an organization I don't know how much influence we can have after a position has been taken. We can express ourselves—disappointment or satisfaction—but here is a group of people in an organization proceeding as they think they can proceed. Now that is a privilege of an organization. You see we have to accept things as they are and not as we would have them.[59]

Ms. Burroughs concluded, expressing an understated frustration against a deep feeling of political marginalization from a campaign concentrated on the moral edification of white women: "I did not think this organization was going to endorse the Costigan-Wagner Bill, there isn't any use in my telling you in tears that I am so disappointed, because I did not expect you to do it."[60]

The frustration expressed by the African-American women toward the middle-class white women members of the ASWPL might have also been directed at Fisher and Stein, both of whom failed to register the significance of the third black man present in Post Wolcott's photograph. This man walks in the opposite direction to the other two African Americans. He is also much shorter than them, and the fact that he appears to be walking with the white woman—although a couple of paces behind her, suggests that he might be a young man in her employ. His presence—mentioned, then ignored by Stein, and completely obliterated by Fisher—complicates the assertion that this is an image centered around a racist ideology that oppresses white women and black people equally.[61] Rather, the white woman now seems to have been assigned a significant amount of economic and social power over the black men in the photograph. Moreover, the intractable presence of the white man is lessened, first because he does not seem to notice what is going on behind him and, more significantly, because the black men might be swerving simply to avoid colliding with the black man coming the other way, rather than from a sense of fear and deference toward the white man. In either case, the white woman's position can now be construed as far less significant than Stein and Fisher have suggested. Instead, Post Wolcott's image seems to be referring less to the sexual codes that underscored racism in the South than the economic hierarchy used to legitimize its continuance.

Although this assessment of the "Wendell, North Carolina" image complicates Stein's and Fisher's analysis of white female identity in the racial codes of southern society, Post Wolcott continued to represent African Americans in the same way as her working-class subjects, emphasizing what she perceived as their liberating physicality and their sexual dynamism. Consequently, unlike the white woman in the previous image, African-American subjects were decontextualized from the economic, social, and political conditions that defined their lives. For example, Post Wolcott describes taking a photograph titled "Young cotton pickers waiting to be paid in Marcella plantation store, Mileston, Mississippi," 1939 (fig. 2.7):

These Negro boys. Their bodies are so beautiful, the way they're draped along this wooden bench. Look at how natural their clothing is. It just seems to flow off their bodies. This one here is like a dancer. I suppose that's what I saw, what I wanted to shoot. It was how elegant they were without really knowing it.[62]

Here, Post Wolcott has constructed the photograph to emphasize the aesthetic lines of the cotton pickers' bodies. The curve of each posture is perfectly balanced by the straight backed pose of the adjacent person. This sense of symmetry is compounded by the contrast between the alternately white and dark clothes each worker is wearing. Moreover, as in the photographs of the miners in West Virginia, Post Wolcott has focused on the smooth-faced beauty of her subjects. Every one of them appears to be unscarred by the physical demands of their work. So far their bodies have resisted the destructive nature of their economic position. Reflecting this, they appear to be at the back of the line waiting to be paid. Post Wolcott has presented them as aesthetically pure in relation to the corrupting processes of capitalist production. In this respect, from Post Wolcott's perspective, their physical inhibitions, and their apparently unconscious beauty and poise, are an indication of their economic and political innocence.

Post Wolcott's response to her photograph belies the tired resignation that is also clear in the cotton pickers' eyes. In particular, the man sitting on the bench seems to be regarding the viewer with a look of weary suspicion. Also, notwithstanding Post Wolcott's own assessment of their poses, the way each young person leans on the bench might also indicate physical pain after a long day's work bending over in the field. Nevertheless, Post Wolcott's focus on the physicality of her subjects reflects her assertion of the political power that she considered to be radically inherent to individual physical expression. At the same time, her approach reflected the context of radical cultural expression that fundamentally informed her work for the FSA, enabling her to identify a common bond with economically and socially disempowered subjects that might be transferred to the middle-class viewer. Furthermore, this physically defining, sexually essentializing critique of institutionalized racism and economic oppression also allowed the viewer to respond self-reflexively to the image, to become aware of material corruptions of

Fig. 2.7. Marion Post Wolcott. "Young cotton pickers waiting to be paid in Marcella plantation store, Mileston, Mississippi." 1939. Reproduced from the Collections of the Library of Congress.

middle-class culture and thus to admire and aspire to the primitive naiveté presented as central to working-class identity.

The Economics of Deception

In a letter written to Stryker from Kentucky in 1940, Post Wolcott expands on the artistic and political philosophy that underscored her work for the FSA:

[T]hese more prosperous farmers, & middle "clawses"—they will have none of it [being photographed], unless they look right, well dressed, powdered, &

unless they know who you are and what it's for. They're all against the government, the agricultural program and much of the FSA. It's hard to get away with
just "taking pictures" any more. Every one is so hysterically war & fifth column
minded. Suspicious!

In fact, I've decided in general that it's a helluva lot easier to stick to photographing migrants, sharecroppers, tenants, "niggers," clients—& the rest of
those extremely poverty stricken people, who are depressed, despondent,
beaten, given up. Most of them don't object too strenuously or too long to a
photographer or picture. They believe it may help them, or they may get something out of it—a little money, or better houses, or a gov. loan.[63]

Post Wolcott's description echoes Dorothea Lange's account of making
"Migrant Mother." Both photographers perceived themselves as interpre-
tative conduits through which socially deprived subjects could communicate with an audience that was sufficiently powerful to help ease their
circumstances. Post Wolcott extended Lange's account, however, by
comparing the apparent willingness of working-class people to be photographed with middle-class suspicion of becoming a depicted subject.
According to Post Wolcott's perception, working-class subjects were
more open and amenable to photographic manipulation because they
were economically needy and politically marginalized. As a result—in
Post Wolcott's opinion—working-class subjects could be easily confined
within the frame of representation, and the liberal middle-class viewer
could thus assume a sense of sympathetic mutuality and a simultaneous
reassurance of their superior economic and moral status. At the same
time, middle-class viewers could feel humbled by a working-class experience presented as more genuinely humane than their own.[64] Unfortunately for working-class subjects, the political expression of such a
response was not a systematic redistribution of wealth and power, but
merely a reversal of power dynamics within the visual discourse of documentary representation.

Post Wolcott's difficulty in approaching middle-class subjects
attests to the economic foundation of the subject/viewer opposition in
documentary photography. For the working-class population, economic
deprivation and political marginality demanded a surrendering of selfhood to social representation and middle-class evaluation. Alternatively,
middle-class participation in documentary photography was based on
visual confirmation of their economic position and the presentation of a
redeeming opportunity for personal self-reflection. There was therefore
no need to depict a middle-class subject in a political and social context
that supported and promoted their status as the viewer of the image.
Without the defining imperative of economic necessity, the middle-class

viewer was able to choose whether or not to be a depicted subject. Moreover, because self-awareness was maintained by material security and social stability, the middle-class subject could decide how he or she wanted to be represented and for what purpose. Consequently, the vestiges of material and educational acquisition—which were often suggestively condemned as representing the artifice of middle-class complacency in Post Wolcott's photographs—simultaneously become the beneficial accouterments of disguise. Post Wolcott believed that the protective facade of economic advantage problematically guarded the middle-class subject from misrepresentation, manipulation, and politically concrete moral judgment. Despite the humorous tone of her letter, however, she continued to seriously investigate the social ramifications of economic disguise in her photography. Most significant was her 1939 documentation of the luxuriously wealthy population living in Miami Beach, Florida, which she juxtaposed with photographs of poverty-stricken migrant families working in nearby Belle Glade. The result of this counterpoint revealed Post Wolcott's critical insight into the economic and political advantages manifest in the power to deceive.

Post Wolcott had gone to Florida in January 1939 to photograph migrant workers, a typical FSA project that was delayed by a frost that destroyed the crops. While she was waiting, she recognized an opportunity to portray the enforced idleness that was such an integral part of migrant life. She documented how even the workers' spare time was transformed into an oppressive circumstance defined by their poverty. A letter to Stryker, dated January 19, 1939, described the insidiously destructive effect of this "hanging around":

A woman the other day told how she'd been waiting around the packing house all day long. They were told there'd be some work, finally something came in and she got nine minutes work. They never know, so they not only don't get paid, but they can't stay home to take care of the "house" and kids either. Then at the peak of the season they have to work 12, 16, 18 hrs. straight with 15 minutes rest every 3 hours.[65]

The delay in Belle Glade also allowed Post Wolcott to photograph another kind of idleness twenty-five miles away in Miami Beach. Stryker wrote encouraging Post Wolcott to continue her stay in Florida, and asking her to focus on how "the lazy rich waste their time. Keep your eye on the middle-classes too."[66] Post Wolcott was fascinated by the contrast. For migrant workers in Belle Glade, "leisure time" activities were expressions of frustration judged as characteristic of socially dysfunctional working-classes. Reflecting this, Post Wolcott wanted to capture "the life of the packing houses—the hanging around, the 'messing around,' the gambling, the fighting, the 'sanitary' conditions, the effects of the very long work stretch, the rest period, their 'lunch' —etc."[67] Conversely, similar pursuits in Miami Beach—cocktail drinking, fashionable parties, and race-track gambling—were considered the epitome of sophisticated taste.

The opposition of this temporal experience was reflected in the ways Post Wolcott approached her working-class and wealthy subjects. In Belle Glade, she took advantage of the delay in production to find families that would be suitable for her photographic requirements. She worked to gain access to their homes, trying to persuade workers that her photographs would benefit their situations. Sometimes, when her persistence failed, she overcame objections by returning to the migrant home when a suspicious family member was not there. In contrast, at Miami Beach, Post Wolcott kept her distance. Consequently, most of Post Wolcott's images of wealthy subjects "were made at a distance of ten or twelve feet, contain very little eye contact, and display little camera consciousness."[68] Brannan surmises that "evidently Post Wolcott did not feel the need for intimate pictures badly enough to interact more directly with her subjects, or tackle the problem of gaining access to private homes and family life."[69] Instead, Post Wolcott was most concerned with the artifice of wealth at Miami Beach. She photographed elaborately designed gardens, enormous decorated buildings, fashionable clothes, beautiful food, spectator events, mannered interaction—all the concrete and symbolic signs that constituted the protective shell that physically and psychologically separated the rich from the working-class people living in poverty in nearby Belle Glade, and even distanced them from those who lived in close proximity: working as servants, waiters, and hotel attendants. Furthermore, Post Wolcott presented the facade of consumerism and politeness as being spiritually destructive and morally deficient; a capitalist monolith that totally engulfed the humanity of the Miami Beach residents. One photograph of a hotel entrance is typical in this respect.

The image focuses on a huge arched doorway, intricately carved, with Corinthian style pillars on either side (fig. 2.8). The archway is framed by the front of a shiny black car on the right of the photograph, and the trunk of a palm tree on the left. The tree seems bare compared to the gaudy stonework. The construction gently suggests how subtle natural beauty has been overpowered by opulent superficiality in Miami Beach. This suggestion is compounded by the frame that is cropped to lead the eye toward the interior of the hotel. The contrast of bright sunlight and shadow gives a sense of one dimensionality to the image. Post

Fig. 2.8. Marion Post Wolcott. Reproduced from the Collections of the Library of Congress.

Wolcott has added to the feeling of flatness by leaving only a very narrow foreground. This lack of perspective creates an appearance of artificiality: the vast stone entrance appears to be as insubstantial as a movie set. Yet, from Post Wolcott's perspective, this fairy tale appearance concretely defined the lifestyle of the wealthy population. The man standing at the hotel entrance clearly symbolizes her opinion. Poised at the hotel's threshold, his white suit and hat reflecting the starkly lit archway and his face invisible, he seems to be included in the superficiality of the building.

The artificiality of wealth is repeatedly depicted in Post Wolcott's Miami Beach images, but only rarely deconstructed. In one photograph of a woman and two men at a swimming pool, however, Post Wolcott provided a singular instance of the disguise being dropped (fig. 2.9). The people are photographed standing in a tight group. The two men—one leaning against the woman's shoulder—turn towards the camera. The woman stands with her back to the viewer. She is dressed in the same fashionable style—bathing suit, earrings, head scarf, and high heels— that Post Wolcott had portrayed in many other images. But, rather than the serene pose more typical of similarly stylish women, Post Wolcott has captured the moment as the woman adjusts the back of her bathing suit.[70] Her awkwardness leads the viewer to inspect the woman more closely. The bathing suit is perhaps a little too small for her body, and she seems to be precariously balanced on her high shoes. Her discomfort is both humorous and telling. She is caught between poses, before she has had a chance to adjust her appearance and present herself to the camera as she would have liked to be seen. Consequently, for a brief moment, her humanity is exposed beneath the vain deception of her wealth.

In contrast, Post Wolcott could approach the migrant workers in Belle Glade without the hindrance of material deception. She was then able to photograph what she considered to be a fundamental quality of innocence that she had portrayed as having been so corrupted in Miami Beach. The preconceived difference in her views of wealth and poverty is clear in the number of photographs she made of migrant children, as opposed to the exclusively adult environment in Miami Beach. Several Belle Glade images focus on blonde, wide-eyed children, who seem angelic despite their shabby clothes, dirty hair, and bare feet. In the captions to her photographs, Post Wolcott documented how the children's eyes had been infected by caustic oil, how they were left by their parents to cook and to take care of younger babies. Despite these circumstances, Post Wolcott's photographs reveal a fundamental spirit of play: the children climb on cars and bathe and dress their dolls. This pathetic expression of childishness despite disadvantaged circumstance was symbolic of the potential for spiritual and moral rejuvenation that—Post Wolcott believed—was inherent to the migrant character and was perfectly reflected in the working-class children, but which remained hidden beneath a wealth of deception in Miami Beach.

Fig. 2.9. Marion Post Wolcott. Reproduced from the Collections of the Library of Congress.

Post Wolcott's insight into the dialectic of economic disguise extended beyond Miami Beach/Belle Glade contrast. The photograph "Colored maids with white child in stroller visiting together on street corner, Port Gibson, Mississippi," 1940 (fig. 2.10), represents an attempt to widen the visual discourse of documentary photography in a construc-

Fig. 2.10. Marion Post Wolcott. "Colored maids with white child in stroller visiting together on street corner, Port Gibson, Mississippi." 1940. Reproduced from the Collections of the Library of Congress.

tion that echoes Dorothea Lange's "Migrant Mother." Two African-American women, dressed in differently styled maids' uniforms, are portrayed standing either side of a white child. The woman on the left stands back, pushing the child to the center of the frame, while the woman on the right is positioned to the side of the child, leaning over to remove a white cloth that is hiding his face from the camera's view. The relevance of the black women's position in relation to the white child is assessed by Sally Stein as an expression of a socially inscribed assumption that "their own presentation to the camera is of less importance than the presentation of the child."[71]

The construction of the photograph reverses the opposition between the disguise of wealth in Miami Beach and the exposure of poverty in

Belle Glade. The blonde white child at the center of this image represents the epitome of middle-class wealth rather than the morally fortifying experience of poverty. The absence of parents therefore does not attest to the demands of labor but is a sign of possessing a disposable income and an increased amount of leisure time purchased at the physical and psychological expense of the two African-American women. The two women are hidden by their maid uniforms. Their self-effacing position in relation to the white child further removes any suggestion of individual self-identity. Unlike the decorations of wealth in Miami Beach, however, their clothes do not offer material protection but instead are signs of their deprived economic and racial status. Their poverty forces them to wear a dehumanizing disguise that ironically transforms them into yet another artifact of middle-class consumption.

Despite the critical insight of this image, Post Wolcott's awareness of the multiple configurations and social interpretations of economic deception is limited within the context of representation. Consequently, while the material disguise of the woman in the bathing suit at Miami Beach is momentarily deconstructed and judged critically by Post Wolcott, the political effect of such exposure is instantaneous and fleeting. In contrast to the appearance of the two maids, middle-class rights to disguise and deception are protected by economic privilege and social status. Conversely, Post Wolcott's images of migrant workers in Belle Glade present working-class people without the protective layers of materiality, and therefore they appear to be uncorrupted by the spiritually destructive desires marketed to the complacent inhabitants of Miami Beach. They are depicted as being positively naked and as being representative of a more innocent, preindustrialized, precapitalist facet of American culture, which was typically expressed by Post Wolcott in images of a fertile and nurturing landscape. In the social context beyond representation, however, economically and socially deprived people were not innocently naked, but dressed in the moral values and spiritual definitions of the middle-class viewer.[72] Furthermore, like Post Wolcott's images of the mining community in West Virginia, and as in her photograph of the two maids, working-class subjects were portrayed without the psychological space and physical means to present themselves as they might choose. The two maids are literally wearing their poverty: nonthreateningly, without confrontation, disempowered and apparently without a self-identity that might allow them to define their economic circumstances for themselves.

Marion Post Wolcott's representations of the power differentials specific to economic and social inequality in the latter years of the Depression inscribe a potentially more generous environment where such differentials do not exist. As such, her critique was grounded in the political and philosophical yearnings represented by her landscape images. Beyond her photographs of economic deprivation and racist social structures, she imagined a future for America that was abundant, innocent, and basically liberal. Unfortunately, her images portrayed this new Eden as an extension of a working-class identity that she presented as instinctively natural, physically preeminent, and sexually driven. As a result, within the context of the ideological direction of the FSA, and commensurate with the political demonstrations of middle-class radicalism, her images defined economic and social deprivation one-dimensionally—in a way that simultaneously satisfied the political conscience of the viewers, while offering reassurance of their moral and intellectual superiority. In contrast, the self-identity and self-expression of those on the other side of the camera remained well secured within the frames of her photographs.

3

Esther Bubley:
Revolutionary Spaces

Revolutionary Spaces

On January 4, 1943, *Life* magazine featured an article titled "Washington in Wartime." The brief text, expanding on accompanying photographs by Alfred Eisenstadt, described the "madhouse atmosphere" in the capital city during the post-Depression years entering the Second World War.[1] An influx of over 300,000 new residents had caused acute housing shortages, an overwhelming strain on municipal services, and an unprecedented demand for entertainment and leisure facilities. The *Life* feature focused on the "many thousands" of women workers who arrived in Washington from Texas, Oklahoma, Minnesota, Arkansas, and the Dakotas, seeking clerical positions in government agencies. At the beginning of the war, 10,000 arrived in Washington, D.C., every month. Eisenstadt chose six women to represent an exodus from farm to city that reflected the migration of the rural poor to California in the previous decade.

Superficially, Eisenstadt's images conveyed an ahistorical disconnection between these fashionably dressed, well-groomed, commercially skilled single women, and their 1930s counterparts. A closer analysis of the photographs reveals a certain continuity between the middle-class appearance of the women he photographed, and the dispossessed rural poor so famously documented in FSA images. The rural women who arrived in Washington in the 1940s—perhaps the sisters and daughters of migrant mothers—had not been forced to leave their homes. Rather, as the *Life* article suggested, they had been seduced by an imagined life of "glamour, celebrities [and] romance."[2] Generally unmarried, without children, and lacking any visible signs of poverty or hardship, these women seemed to possess none of the symbolic potential of their California-bound predecessors. As such, they were not noticeably separated from the perspective of *Life* readers, and Eisenstadt's portraits were not visibly intended to provoke a sense of social responsibility in the viewer. Instead, the women wear the same clothes as the women featured in advertisements elsewhere in the magazine: their hair is arranged in a

91

familiar style and their makeup is applied in a similar fashion. The appearance of material equality inscribed a sense of mutual identification between subject and viewer, which also alluded to the reasons why rural—mostly working-class women—migrated to urban centers during the war. Fundamental to their practical hopes for financial security and personal liberation was the belief that they could buy the lifestyle that was central to the wartime marketing strategies of commercial advertisements, popular culture, and publicity campaigns conducted by the Office of War Information. As John Morton Blum suggests, wartime patriotism was sold to the American public—and to women in particular—"as if it were fantastic gowns, flat silver, or bright red lipstick."[3] In stark contrast to the documentary campaigns of the 1930s, national unity in the 1940s was forged around an individual's desire to purchase consumer products.

The *Life* article goes on to describe the tenuous connection between nationally marketed consumerism and the women workers in a social context that was economically unequal. The urban woman of the 1940s eventually suffered the same disillusionment as the Californian migrant. Fifty percent of new employees left their jobs within six months of their arrival in Washington. Unable to afford rent, food, or transportation on their meager wages, the article concludes that "1,000 frustrated girls" returned home every month, their dreams for an exciting future ended in overcrowded coldwater boarding houses, loneliness, drudgery, and disappointment. In retrospect, then, Eisenstadt's images seem to refer to an ephemeral connection between the young working-class women in the photographs and a commercial image that was ultimately exclusive. Their aspirations appear to end in social, economic, and psychological displacement that echoed the experience of Depression-era rural poverty.

The women in Eisenstadt's portraits are photographed either at their waists or cut off at their heads and shoulders. They face the camera, either smiling nervously or awkwardly not smiling. They are all dressed in outdoor clothes; their hair curling around neat earrings, arranged in the fashionable style and brushed away from eyebrows precisely plucked into arches. The identical construction and the arrangement of the images in lines around a text that describes them as "cases" displays the women as subjects of a social investigation in a way that undercuts the individualizing effect of the captions. Similarities in clothing and style suggest a communality between these women, but this possibility is removed by their separation into a series of images photographed against the same background and posed in the same way.

Eisenstadt's uniformity in framing his subjects suggests the rectangular rigidity of an identification picture or an official document.[4] This construction suggests a production line sensibility, where each woman has a moment in front of the Capitol Building knowing that she could be easily replaced by another woman, who might stand there for longer, more passively, and for less money. Thus, the dehumanizing and alienating factory-like conditions that formed the foundation of a consumer culture during the early war years are obliquely represented in Eisenstadt's images. The resulting sense of social disconnection, which was so consistently portrayed in FSA images, is also apparent in these photographs. Posed somewhat uncomfortably in front of a national landmark, the photographs are suggestive of tourist snapshots. This visual association is made clear by the amateurish construction of the images. The women are all posed as if the Capitol were growing out of their heads! Furthermore, because the women are so oppressively foregrounded within the frame, they seem very flat in relation to the three-dimensional Capitol. The building is shown to be far more substantial than the women, so their connection to the city and its economic opportunities is portrayed as marginalized and temporary.

Visual equality between the subjects and the viewer of Eisenstadt's portraits is only sustained by the urban middle-class clothes and fashionable mannerisms the women display. Consequently, their inclusion within consumer-driven wartime representation is recognizable only as long as they can afford to keep up appearances. Despite these economic difficulties, however, the women in Eisenstadt's photographs continued to express a desire to attain the material possibilities signified by their appearance. In this way, their apparent willingness to suppress their rural working-class identities in order to be included in a system of representation that depended on economic advantage was fundamentally opposed to the views expressed by women who worked in manufacturing industry during the war. Contrary to the abstracted, narcissistic desires, represented in the photographs for *Life*, the women whose testimonies were recorded in *The Life and Times of Rosie the Riveter* emphasized communality and solidarity in support of interests that were defined as explicitly working class.

Rosie the Riveter is full of reassuringly positive accounts of female work experience in an environment that is described as having nurtured working-class consciousness among women workers. For example, Celia Yannish described her welding job as inspiring a sense of self-worth, confidence, and independence, which eventually enabled her to confront the potentially oppressive circumstances of her labor:

On the assembly line in 1936, I had to ask for permission to get up. There was an atmosphere of fear and discipline. Here people walked back and forth and talked freely . . . I loved that job because I produced something. I wasn't just putting a screw in a lock. I knew it was precision work that required a skill. It gave me a self-respect I didn't have before.[5]

Another female worker, Lola Weixel, described the powerful possibilities of union membership for women workers that led to a tangible sense of specifically female class identification.

Kaufsky's shop, well, it was an old dive. We were very good producers, but we were earning far less than the men who were doing the same work. Blanche and I went to United Electrical Workers Union; we started wearing union buttons, and Mr Kaufsky's face changed. He didn't like us anymore. We were no longer his girls.[6]

Furthermore, Margaret Wright, an African-American woman, related a growing sense of psychological unity among black workers—particularly women—who had generally worked as domestic servants before the war:

A lot of blacks that were sharecropping, doing menial work and stuff . . . saw how things were and how things could be. They decided they did not want to go back to what they were doing before. They did not want to walk behind a plow, they wouldn't get on the back of a bus anymore.[7]

Taken collectively, the words of these women working on factory floors, shipbuilding yards, and production lines counteracted the individualized acceptance of commodity culture seen in the images of clerical workers in *Life*. Arranged and edited under a symbolically unified title, *Rosie the Riveter* implies a sense of class unity and sisterhood among women workers, which resisted the ideological implications of the consumer ideology that was central to government campaigns. Reflecting this, antagonisms on the factory floor are described as having been mostly gender based, focusing on male ridicule of female workers, and finally concentrating on the expectation that women workers should leave their jobs as men returned from the war. Adding to the book's narrative assertion of a specifically gender-based working-class community, the text concentrates on common problems faced by the women workers. As a group, they faced everyday threats to their safety: industrial deaths in war plants rose to 37,660 between 1940 and 1944. Women workers also confronted the emotional problems of being working mothers. Demand for child-care facilities, shorter hours, and reduced night shifts are described as having been the central focus of female organization on the factory floor.[8]

Rosie the Riveter concentrates most specifically on union activity as a means of promoting self-awareness and class solidarity among female workers. The text states that, by 1945, union membership had risen to five times its number in 1939—from 800,000 to 4,000,000—and that, as a result, there were more wildcat strikes during World War II than there had been throughout all of the 1930s. One woman's comment reflects the generally uncritical appraisal of union activity in the book: "I guess some people can make deals with the boss to get what they need, but in the end an individual has very little power, a very small voice."[9] The additional pressures of racism faced by African-American women, and occasional disunity amongst the ranks of white women union members, are briefly referred to in *Rosie the Riveter*; but the discursive arrangement of the text, along with the suggested commonality of interests and validating personal reflections of individual women, creates a sense of self-consciously feminist and actively working-class solidarity among all women working in defense industries. In this way, Connie Field et al. were able to construct an image of working-class women employed in wartime industries that was radically different from the consumerist image referred to in Eisenstadt's images and advertised through government information agencies. The conflict between these apparently antagonistic definitions of working-class female identity in the 1940s is complicated further by Katherine Archibald's study of a wartime shipyard.

Archibald began her investigation of the Moore Dry Dock Company in Oakland, California, expecting to find the same sense of worker solidarity that is so clearly expressed in the testimonies of *Rosie the Riveter*. Instead, she was shocked to discover a workplace founded on a basis of interconnecting class, race, and gender conflicts. Immigrants from the Midwest were degraded and ostracized by the native Californian workers. Midwesterners, in turn, were vociferously anti-black, anti-Mexican and anti-Semitic. The position of African-American workers in the psychological hierarchy of the factory is described pointedly by Archibald:

Hatred of the negro was no simple product of chance perversity on the part of the white shipyard worker. It was rather an indispensable constituent of his sense of well being, and the very foundation on which his estimation of his own importance rested.[10]

White female workers—the majority of whom had been employed before the war—made up 20% of the labor force by 1943, and were regarded with resentful suspicion by male workers. Nonetheless, white women workers' regional prejudice toward migrant workers and racial hatred toward black workers was equal to that of their male counterparts. Archibald's observations attest to the multifaceted expression of such attitudes. One woman, a migrant worker from Oklahoma, was routinely victimized. As a rural woman, she was considered lazy, ignorant, and greedy by native Californian women, who were in turn considered uneducable and unorganizable by male workers. Archibald describes Beulah as being "abnormally sensitive to the ridicule which her origin brought upon her,"[11] and as a result considered her a ripe candidate for liberal enlightenment. Archibald pointed out the equation between class prejudice and Beulah's own vociferous racism. Beulah's reaction was emotional and telling: "She fairly shrieked in answer . . . 'But I'm no nigger! I'm not black!' And, sobbing in her now immense distress, she ran off to tell whoever would listen that I had said she was 'no better than a nigger wench.' "[12] This incident attests to the hierarchy that lay behind the facade of class and gender solidarity described in *Rosie the Riveter*. At the same time, Archibald's recollection of the incident reveals her own problematic position as a middle-class viewer of a predominantly working-class environment. Archibald was unable to fully comprehend Beulah's reaction to her well-intended lesson beyond concluding that she was hysterical and overemotional. Furthermore, although Archibald relates what she perceives to be the experience of racism, she does not interview any African-American workers directly. As such, the perspective of black workers is understood through the racial hatred of white workers, whose own social and economic victimization is misinterpreted through the observations of a middle-class woman. Further undermining the image of a united wartime work force, Archibald describes an antipathetic union at the shipyard, which far from nurturing solidarity among its splintered work force, precipitated divisions on the factory floor. At the Moore Dry Dock, both the American Federation of Labor and Congress of Industrial Organizations–affiliated unions—preferred to accept women members only on a temporary auxiliary basis, and generally denied African-Americans membership altogether, prejudicially reducing the unions' representative power at the shipyard by 40%. One observer noted the irony of such shortsightedness: "The union missed the bus, they completely missed the bus, and all you can hope is that if the chance comes again they'll know enough to do a better job."[13] Union indifference to race and gender diversity on the factory floor was predicated on labor leaders' complicit investment in the public image of harmonious commitment to military and economic victory. On a national level, the CIO's agreement to relinquish workers' rights to strike officially supported the government's long-term commitment to commercial capitalism. In the factories and shipyards, institutional dependency on obsolete notions of working-class identity being exclusively white resulted in divisive and violent hate strikes against African-American workers. A similar failure to organize white working-class women equally to men produced a female workforce that was physically excluded and psychologically indifferent to the benefits of unionization.

Each of these three studies present different—and conflicting—perspectives on the experiences of working-class women during the early war years. The women in Eisenstadt's images appeared to be middle class, whereas the women described in *Rosie the Riveter* were identified as working class. Furthermore, Eisenstadt was working for a commercial magazine, while Archibald's observations were intended to complicate representations of the industrial workforce. From a retrospective position, *Rosie the Riveter* was intended as a testimony that would present a politically informed history of women working in wartime industries. Adding to these differences in perspective, Archibald's study was sociological, Eisenstadt's photo-journalistic, and *Rosie the Riveter* was an oral history and also a film. Nevertheless, each observer arrived at a fixed image of working-class identity in the 1940s, which led the viewer/reader toward definite conclusions: that working-class women wanted to be middle class, or that working-class women were confidently unified, or that working-class women were hopelessly divided. None of these three representations portrayed working-class women in the early 1940s as complex individuals, capable of expressing their particular points of view from their own personal perspectives. Instead, each observer defined his or her particular style of representation in relation to an institutionally sponsored image of national harmony, equal sacrifice, and mutual economic benefit. Whether—as in Eisenstadt—the depictions are illustrative and basically supportive of the image, or—as in Archibald—they are set in dialectical opposition to the image, or—as in Field—they are revisions of the image, in each case self-identified, multifaceted working-class experiences were co-opted, misunderstood, and disguised to fit a one-sided discourse surrounding a system of institutionalized representation defined exclusively from a middle-class perspective. Ironically, it is this overall sense of unity—between studies that are apparently contradictory—that holds the most potential for expressing a self-identified working-class perspective within wartime representation. Each study takes up the subversive possibilities presented by the others. *Rosie the Riveter* undermines the middle-class artifice presented in Eisenstadt's images, while Archibald's study undermines the sense of unity in *Rosie the Riveter*. Moreover, Archibald's descriptions of the way working-class women defied punitive dress codes and male ridicule in the shipyard by wearing long hair, tight sweaters, and lipstick, suggest that working-class adoption of middle-class appearances in Eisenstadt's images could be considered a potentially radical position. In the following explorations of photographs by Esther Bubley, I want to examine the contradictions presented in these three representations of working-class women in the 1940s: revolutionary spaces that are uniquely and subversively explored in her images.

The Greyhound Bus Trip

Esther Bubley was born in Superior, Wisconsin, in 1921, where her father was the manager of an automobile supply shop. Before becoming a photographer, she studied painting at the Minneapolis School of Design. In 1940, aged nineteen, she moved to New York City where—through a connection with Edward Steichen—she got a temporary studio job with *Vogue* magazine. In 1941, she moved to Washington, D.C., to begin work as a microfilmer in the National Archives. Later that year she was hired by Roy Stryker to work as a laboratory technician for the Historical Section of the FSA.[14]

Even from these scanty biographical details, it is clear that Bubley's photographic apprenticeship was much different from those of Dorothea Lange or Marion Post Wolcott. Bubley's small-town, lower-middle-class background pales in comparison with Lange's teenage confrontations with the Lower East Side and her intrepid cross country adventures. Nor did Bubley have the advantage of Post Wolcott's bohemian education in Greenwich Village and Vienna. Bubley's pre-FSA experience was in commercial and fashion photography rather than in socially concerned documentation like Lange, or with journalism like Post Wolcott. Bubley did not even have a driver's license. Her photographic projects for the FSA were therefore usually confined to the Washington, D.C. area, and to the outskirts of Virginia. Also unlike her predecessors, when she traveled it was not for thousands of miles through the southern states solo with a hatchet in her car. Nor did her journeys take her across the Midwest and California consumed with a vision to reconstruct a social and economic history of agricultural production in the United States. Instead, Esther Bubley traveled from Washington, D.C., to Memphis on an overcrowded Greyhound bus. Consequently, her view of America in the early 1940s was not of an unobscured road heading west seen from the roof of her car, but looking awkwardly through the bus driver's windshield. She stood in the aisle, precariously balanced as the bus moved along, and tried not to get in the driver's way. As a result, Bubley's vision was a little lopsided and her view was not quite squarely framed.[15]

The apparent lack of clarity in Bubley's perspective appeared to be balanced by the subject matter of government photography in the 1940s which, according to Roy Stryker, was decidedly less complicated than had been the case in the previous decade. In memos to Russell Lee and Arthur Rothstein, he outlined what he saw as the new direction of the Historical Section, emphasizing a "need to air brush and uplift the file":[16]

We must have at once: pictures of men, women and children who appear as if they really believed in the U.S.A. Get people with a little spirit. Too many in our file now paint the U.S. as an old people's home, and that just about everyone is too old to work and too malnourished to care much about what happens.[17]

Stryker's insistence on portraying America in a more upbeat style as it entered the war nevertheless extended from his conception of the way rural poverty had been documented in FSA photography. His desire for representational continuity as the Historical Section's project was gradually overwhelmed by the Office of War Information was apparent in his letter to Jonathan Daniels, an administrative assistant to the President. Stryker noted that "out of America at peace grew the strength of America at war. This soil is the same soil and the people are the same people."[18]

Stryker's concern that the FSA file might be disseminated, or even destroyed, instead of being preserved as a complete record of the 1930s, also extended from a realization that his position as the head of the Historical Section was becoming increasingly compromised by the demand for images made explicitly for propaganda purposes. Gardner Cowles, the director of the OWI's Domestic Branch, maintained that documentary photography should be utilized as a facet of a massive advertising campaign, which would sell the concept of war to a recognizable audience of consumers.[19] As a result, Stryker's emphasis on creating an historical record—however misleading—was rejected in favor of what was termed a "positive approach, which quickly answered the instinctive human question, what is there in it for me?"[20] This milieu of commercialism alienated more scholarly participants in the OWI. Historians Arthur Schlesinger and Francis Brennan tendered their resignations from the department on April 14, 1943, along with a statement:

There is only one issue—the deep and fundamental one of the honest presentation of war information. . . . we are leaving because of our conviction that it is impossible for us, under those who now control our output, to tell the full truth. No-one denies that promotional techniques have a proper and powerful function in telling the story of war, but the activities of the OWI on the homefront are now dominated by high pressure promoters who prefer slick salesmanship to honest information. They are turning this office of war information into an office of war Bally-hoo.[21]

Unlike Schlesinger and Brennan, Stryker was less concerned with conveying the absolute truth about wartime activities than he was with maintaining his particular vision of the FSA. Thus, F. Jack Hurley's explanation of the reasoning behind Stryker's resignation as head of the Historical Section in 1941 seems somewhat understated:

The work for the OWI was often rather dull. The war agency required straight propaganda photographs: it had no use at all for the sort of thoughtful, probing, pictorial analysis that had become the hallmark of the historical section.[22]

Esther Bubley apparently agreed with this judgment. In an interview with Andrea Fisher she recalled that, after Stryker's departure, the scope of documentary photography was fundamentally "narrowed" with "the loss of his personal visionary breadth."[23] Despite these reservations, however, Bubley's photographic projects for FSA/OWI remained commensurate with the government's demands for a positive wartime image of mutual sacrifice and absolute faith that America would prevail against fascism. To this end, Bubley photographed crowds gathered at patriotic parades to celebrate Memorial Day and to cheer civil defense volunteers. She also documented high school students supporting their colleagues as they joined the armed forces, and as they studied in preparation for the bright future assured by the guarantee of American victory. In and around Washington, Bubley's images captured soldiers and their sweethearts visiting national monuments—a constructive combination that enshrined heterosexual love and family values alongside the symbolic constancy of American history. Bubley's photographs of women living in boarding houses while they worked in government offices and wartime industries also supported the OWI's reification of the family unit. Her images suggested that even while their husbands, sons, brothers, and fiancés were absent, visions of home and family could be maintained psychologically through women's support for each other.

Bubley's documentary contribution to the wartime image was nevertheless complicated by her trust in the photographic traditions of social documentation. She saw no essential difference between her own work for the FSA/OWI and the "classic" images of the 1930s. She believed that her photographs "stood proudly in the tradition of Dorothea Lange and Walker Evans,"[24] and so considered that her aim as a documentary photographer was to establish a personalized relationship between herself, her subject, and the viewer, in order to help the person she had photographed. As such, Bubley's practical means of approaching a subject reflected the methods of Lange and Post Wolcott. Katherine Dieckmann

notes that Bubley "chatted up a storm" with the people she photographed,[25] an observation that is compounded by Anne Adams, the
managing editor of Standard Oil's company magazine, *The Lamp*:

Esther Bubley's work had a great warmth to it as far as people were concerned.
I never think of Esther as just doing a scene. I think of people when I think of
Esther, and a great warmth and feeling for women, children and men. She was
interested in humanity.[26]

Anne Adams's appreciation of Bubley's photography in the 1940s
echoed compliments made about Dorothea Lange's apparently innate
concern and compassion for the poverty-stricken subjects of her Depression photographs. This appreciative equation added a further dimension
to the seemingly concrete patriotic nature of Bubley's assignments, and
should have meant that her work not only served the purposes of government propaganda, but also that her photographs should have significantly contributed to the historical record of the FSA. On the contrary,
Bubley's photographs were almost never reproduced in official documents or popular magazines in the 1940s and, as she suggested to Dieckmann, her "negatives were simply tossed into the file . . . unused."[27]
Moreover, Bubley's images also remain largely unexamined in the
FSA/OWI files at the Library of Congress. In stark contrast to Lange,
whose visual legacy became the historic iconography of the Depression
years, the symbolic value of Bubley's images has been generally
ignored. It is therefore imperative to ask what it was about Bubley's photographs that deconstructed the wartime themes she was required to document, and simultaneously transcended her self-conscious adherence to
the traditions of FSA photography.

Bubley's Greyhound bus trip began in September 1943. The distance she covered, beginning in New York City and ending in Memphis,
Tennessee, was reminiscent of the geographic scope of an FSA assignment. The various subjects of her images also reflected the general focus
of 1930s social documentation. She photographed women with their
children, old people, and people of different races. Moreover, since all of
these people were cramped together on the bus, she also depicted the circumstances of their economic disadvantage. Dieckmann notes that in
certain images Bubley focused on "waiting areas full of the bedraggled
and worried . . . standing in line for the 'free' bathroom."[28]As such,
Bubley focused on documenting poverty in its specificity, much as her
FSA predecessors had done. Also reflecting the work of Lange and Post
Wolcott, Bubley photographed people performing menial labor: unload-
ing baggage and cleaning the inside of the bus. Most obviously in line

with FSA tradition, however, Bubley made images of a population on the move—dozens of people crowded together on the bus, hundreds of them pushed together in station waiting rooms, restrooms, and platforms. Her photographs of the physicality of human movement implied a sense of visual association with the migrant populations photographed in the 1930s. This detailed portrayal of a fundamental historical continuity between the 1940s travelers and the class and race divisions of the previous decade also undermined the image of optimistic renewal and national unity that was fundamental to wartime representation.

Bubley's understanding of social and economic divisions within the positive veneer of OWI campaigns is clear in the representational juxtapositions she made between her various Greyhound bus images. In certain photographs, the passengers appear to be fairly happy with the circumstances of their journey. They share jokes and laughter, keeping up their spirits in the appropriate wartime manner. A similar optimism is displayed in a series of photographs Bubley made of the bus driver's home life.[29] His family pulls together, sharing household tasks and enjoying brief leisure time. Significantly, publicly sanctioned gender roles within the family are maintained in these photographs. The mother takes care of the house and children, while the father goes out to work in a job that is portrayed as being essential to the war effort. One image of the American flag emblazoned above a bus schedule enshrines this patriotic message. Significantly, the flag is placed at the center of the man's work environment. Consequently, the narrative progression of the rest of the photographs ensures that the value system signified by the flag in the context of war is brought home—naturally and traditionally—by the father to his loving wife and grateful children. Such patriotic images were fundamental to the OWI project and to wartime representation in general. The photographs of the bus driver and his family fitted nicely with an optimistic image made by Anne Rosener, for example, showing a woman in neat clothes and perfect makeup, cheerfully "saving waste fats and greases from which war materials will be made."[30] In relation to many other of Bubley's photographs, however, these appropriate wartime messages are so perfectly arranged, so brightly constructed, and so one-dimensionally optimistic as to appear almost surreal.

In this way, Bubley's photographs appeared somewhat incongruous to the images that were fundamental to OWI campaigns. In particular, she concentrated on official depictions of femininity that were central to government information. Recruitment drives designed to encourage women to take up wartime jobs promoted an image of self-sacrificing, nurturing motherhood to symbolize patriotism and national unity. Reflecting this formulation, war work was presented as an extension of a prescriptive female role. Manual labor was described as being commensurate with housekeeping; stamping machine parts was related to cutting cookies; welding was presented as being a "meticulous handicraft," akin to embroidery.[31] Furthermore, since taking on a wartime job was considered an expression of a wife's support for her husband or son and therefore her country, female patriotism was judged in terms of a woman's loyalty to her traditional position within the home. By placing female employment within a discourse of domesticity, it was therefore to be expected that women would return to their normal household duties after the war was over. As a result, the wartime work experience for middle-class women did not mark the beginning of increased female employment in the future. Rather, their experience compounded the traditional notions that subsequently informed the repression described by Betty Friedan in *The Feminine Mystique*.

OWI propaganda was thus clearly based on traditional notions of appropriately female behavior. This bias was more complicated, however, since the image of a loyal housewife cheerfully sacrificing her domestic purity for the benefit of her family and her country was directed specifically at white middle-class women, and so inevitably ignored the wartime experiences of working-class women, most of whom had been working in menial jobs before the conflict began.[32] As Leila Rupp suggests, the marginalization of working-class women as compared to middle-class women in government representation was such that "one would have thought it was the first time the factory gates had opened to women."[33] The absence of working-class women from official and popular portrayals of manual labor during the war years was therefore predicated on the invalidation of their historical contribution to the industrial economy. Working-class female identity was repressed further, since national concern about the moral safety of working mothers by definition referred exclusively to white middle-class women. As a result, marriage and motherhood were not publicly sanctified goals for working-class women. The visual outcome of this negative dialectic was a public image that reversed the symbolism of the FSA project. Unlike in the Depression when working-class people—particularly women—were made into icons of middle-class American values, during the war years representations of working-class women were systematically excluded from OWI campaigns. Undermining this middle-class bias in official representations of femininity, working-class women are subtly and subversively portrayed in Bubley's Greyhound bus images.

In one photograph, Bubley focuses on a woman cleaning the inside of the bus (fig. 3.1). Her body is constricted by the tight frame of the image, and she is also physically confined by the seats on either side of

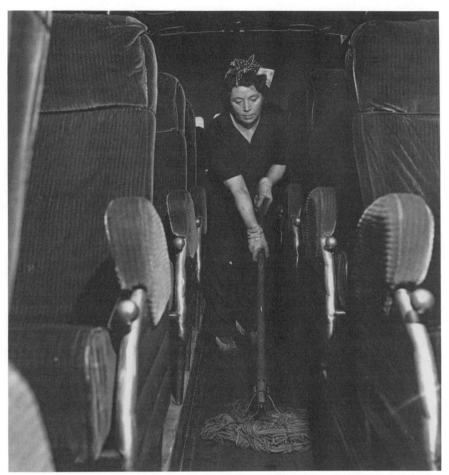

Fig. 3.1. Esther Bubley. Reproduced from the Collections of the Library of Congress.

the aisle. She pushes the mop in front of her as she moves toward the back of bus. From the viewer's perspective, the woman seems to be receding into the dark background while her mop and the seats she has cleaned appear huge in comparison to her ever-decreasing body size. In effect, the woman seems to be gradually disappearing into the center of the photograph. This sense of imminent absence is compounded in relation to the other bus images: of the station full of people waiting to get on the bus, or of passengers on the bus, all collectively participating in the conservation of fuel and rubber and, according to the imperatives of wartime information, visibly "doing their bit" for the war effort. By taking this photograph in such a context, Bubley establishes the essential but inevitably absent presence of a working-class woman within a system of representation that—almost exclusively—placed middle-class women at the symbolic center of OWI campaigns. At the same time, Bubley focuses on the light falling on the woman's arms as she pushes the mop away with a certain amount of strength and purpose. This action manifestly refutes the potential invisibility that is implied by the woman's backward movement, and which was compounded by the middle-class bias of government information. In capturing this oppositional dynamic, Bubley has enabled the working-class woman to quietly subvert and actively invade the physical space occupied by the patriotic passengers, a context that formed the exclusive foundation of OWI photography.

By photographing people who were systematically excluded from the visual rhetoric of government propaganda, Bubley drew attention to the one-dimensional artificiality of official imagery. In so doing, she was able to expose, deconstruct, and subvert a wartime image that presented American society as being positively unified and mutually supportive at a time of national emergency. To a certain extent, Bubley was able to do this by remaining true to the traditions of FSA documentary methods: that is, she was interested in highlighting economic and social disparities between the subjects of her images and the middle-class people who formed her viewing audience. Unlike other FSA photographers, however, who routinely photographed poverty and oppression in ways that were reassuringly other than those of the viewer, Bubley used the unifying rhetorical devices of OWI publicity ironically, to reveal the personalized proximity of economic and social inequity to every individual American. Thus, oppression and injustice in Bubley's images are not visibly received as exclusive "whites only" signposts, or as depictions of "the other side of the tracks," instead her images emphasize these experiences as being fundamentally intrinsic to the actual bodies and psychological sensibilities of both the subject and the viewer.

Bubley used the physical space of the Greyhound bus to emphasize this point. Passengers on buses were not easily separated into race or class hierarchies. Certainly, in southern states, African-American passengers were forced to ride at the back of the bus, and passengers were divided into separate waiting areas and bathrooms, even though such means were ridiculously ineffective. In reality, as Bubley's images reveal, all races and classes waited at the same platform and had to travel in the same small bus space. Even as a white photographer employed by the government, Bubley did not have the luxury of distance between herself and her subjects. She was not able to take her photographs and run if she was closed in on a bus. Rather, she was almost literally living and sleeping on top of the people she was photographing. The resulting sense of awkward closeness between herself and the other passengers was conveyed as an uneasy proximity between subject and viewer in her photographs. Her images manifestly reveal an experience of having one's space invaded, or at least temporarily intruded upon. Bubley compounded this claustrophobic construction by using the bus windows as internal frames that "allowed her to press her subjects together—or emphasize their inseparable distance."[34] Thus, despite the proximity of bodies, Bubley also focused on the ways individual passengers maintained their self-possession. She photographed them looking away from the camera, protecting themselves with arms and legs crossed, asleep or daydreaming. The passengers were portrayed as "a nation of zombies," their bodies connoting an underlying feeling of psychological inertia and individualized apathy.[35] Beyond this conclusion, however, Bubley's approach to her disassociated, somnambulant subjects had a distinctly political edge.

Bubley used the enclosed space of the Greyhound bus to highlight the ways in which white, middle-class—particularly female—bodies were closely guarded, politically protected spaces in American culture. This point was extended within the context of government propaganda in the 1940s, since white middle-class female identity became symbolic of the war's purpose. Men fought to protect America for their wives, mothers, and daughters, while women remained at home, loyal and chaste, so that the men could be welcomed home in a satisfying fashion. Punitive legislation was formed and enacted in order to reinforce this suggestively gendered, economically and racially specific, rhetoric. In particular, segregation was maintained through the politically enshrined notion of protecting white middle-class women from black men who were deemed to be sexually threatening. This assumption was most obviously manifested during the war in segregated work and social spaces, exclusive white and black regiments, and separate nursing corps for the exclusive treatment of wounded black soldiers. Segregation in the military even extended to an enforced separation of blood from black or white donors, so that white soldiers' bodies would not be contaminated by that of a black person. This kind of politically inscribed revulsion towards any kind of intimacy—physical or psychological—between different races who were supposed to be united as Americans, is clearly evident in many of Bubley's images for the FSA/OWI, but one photograph from the Greyhound bus series is especially resonant.

The photograph depicts a crowd of people waiting for a bus at the Memphis terminal (fig. 3.2). Since this is the same station that Bubley had photographed to emphasize a "Whites Only" sign, the station is presumably officially segregated. Nevertheless, there is one African-American man waiting there, standing alongside a crowd of white men and women, both soldiers and civilians. In relation to the visible signs of

Fig. 3.2. Esther Bubley. Reproduced from the Collections of the Library of Congress.

segregation, the black man is already labeled as a transgressor of social norms. As a result, in the racist South this man would be under threat from the white crowd surrounding him. Reflecting this possibility, the white people take up most of the space within the frame. In relation to the white group, the black man appears to be confined to a small space to the left of the photograph. He is also closely foregrounded, and with his heels hanging over the edge of the platform his presence within the frame is precariously balanced. There is a sense that if the white crowd were to advance slightly at any moment, he could be pushed forward and over. In this way, Bubley has constructed an underlying feeling of threat and danger toward the black man. As a reaction to his vulnerability, he seems to be poised in a defensive manner. He clutches his bag in a rigid arm, using it as a shield placed between his body and the white people. Having established this line of defense, his left hand seems to be relaxed in his pocket and he can look directly at the white woman carrying the fur coat, who in turn looks down, awkward and uncomfortable in the face of his poise and self-assurance.

In contrast to the black man, all of the white people appear nervous and self-consciously insecure. Although centuries of racist violence and institutionalized power protect their position, and despite the fact that even within the frame of this photograph they are in the majority, almost every one of the white people is looking away, with their arms crossed over themselves as if to protect their bodies. The young woman sitting on the platform holds her bag over her lap, and the small boy's hands are crossed over his groin. They appear to be huddled together as if in submission to the black man's potential power, not simply in an expression of a stereotypically perceived sexual threat, but set against his composure in relation to their discomfort, his direct stare in comparison to their uneasy down-turned eyes. Thus, his self-confident defiance of the racist threat they represent to him visibly overcomes their embarrassed self-consciousness of their own whiteness.

Thus described, this photograph might be considered alongside Post Wolcott's "Wendell, North Carolina" photograph as a representation of an everyday enactment of racism. Extending from this interpretation, however, Bubley has deliberately complicated the visual interactions between black subject and white viewer in her photograph. The African-American man has his back to the camera, but since his pose is so powerfully self-possessed in relation to the white people in the photograph, he is not devalued or exploited by his unawareness of the camera. In a sense, his obliviousness defies the viewer's perspective. Moreover, the only person making eye contact with the viewer is the white soldier positioned more or less at the center of the photograph's frame. His look is also a little defensive, but because he is a white man in uniform symbolically protecting a group of women and a child, his look appeals to the patriotic expectations of wartime representation. As a result, the white middle-class viewer is visually connected to the same sense of submission and guilt that is presented in the faces of the white people in the photograph. Furthermore, since her view is also obscured by the black man's strongly resistant back, Bubley's position as a white photographer working for the government is also associated with the white people in the image. Thus, her officially sponsored perspective, as well as the power of the viewer—both traditionally made concrete in the dynamics of documentary photography—are ultimately compromised by the construction of this image.

Most significant in relation to this photograph, however, is Bubley's direct reference to the manifest hypocrisy of OWI publicity. Super-

ficially, the empowerment of the black man in relation to the white passengers is compounded by his military uniform. Up to a point, this fact
makes the white people's diffidence more ironic, since the black man is
sacrificing his well-being for a country that violently excludes his race.
Also, the position of the white soldier at the center of the group of white
women is particularly compromised by his ignorance of the black man.
Wartime information projected an image of camaraderie and mutual
respect between military men that is clearly absent between these two
soldiers. At the same time, the black man commands indirect respect
from the white crowd because his black body is covered by a white uniform. His military costume is symbolically oppressive, and yet at the
same time it represents a means by which black people could gain self-
awareness and self-confidence in the face of institutionalized racism. In
this sense, the soldier's uniform is a powerfully protective disguise
against overt expressions of white racist violence. While he is wearing it,
the white people on the station are not able to recognize the black man
for what they want him to be. Relatively safe in his patriotic costume,
the white people's previously unrestricted power to judge him is confused. Nevertheless, the personal power and individual self-protection
that is afforded to the black man because of his uniform is shown by
Bubley to be only a temporarily equalizing phenomenon. Standing
behind the black soldier are at least three others, two of whom are
clearly white. This mixed-race group appear to be relatively at ease in
one another's company. Indeed, the black soldier and the white soldier to
the left of his shoulder are standing very close together, perhaps suggesting that they are traveling companions. Whatever might be the nature of
their relationship, the separation between the racially mixed group of
soldiers and the white civilians on the right of the frame is emphasized
by the presence of the stern-looking white soldier standing among the
white civilians. The opposition reveals the social and political realities
fundamental to official representations of soldiers, and the reassuring
images of traditional family life that were depicted as the symbolic
future that American men were fighting to preserve. In the middle of this
visual dialectic, the black man is permitted to associate on superficially
equal level with white men, as long as he is fighting to ensure the stability of an image from which he is racially excluded.

Thus, Bubley's construction shows that once the war was won and
family life was safely restored, white men could reclaim their socially
sanctified position as the protector of white women and children against
the threatening presence of the black man, after he had been stripped of
his military uniform. In this respect, Bubley's photograph simultaneously distorts fixed notions of racial identity, while critically decon-

structing the suspicious one-dimensionality of wartime representation. In so doing, she highlights the self-identity of the black man in a way that is challenging to a white audience but at the same time, her photograph places him in a social, economic, and political context that reveals the complicity of the viewer in ensuring his silence.

The National Gallery of Art and the Sea Grill Bar

Marjory Collins was a photographer employed by the OWI at the same time as Esther Bubley. In December 1942, she took a photograph entitled "Photographer's display on Bleecker Street, New York City" (fig. 3.3). At first glance, the photographs in the shop window—a series of simple portraits and a few wedding pictures—seem typical of any that might have been taken by a commercial photographer. Beyond the ordinary surface, however, Collins's photograph is very revealing about the ways gender identities were defined and constructed in official images during the 1940s. It is important to note that the traditional wedding photographs are set at the far right of the window at the edge of Collins's image, and that they are also smaller than the pictures in the other display. This difference emphasizes the additional resonance that was given to apparently simple wedding poses in the 1940s, a point that is made clear in the series of images placed at the center of Collins's frame. In these photographs, every man is dressed in a military uniform, and thirteen out of twenty show men in uniform without women. The rest of the photographs depict soldiers with their wives and families. A couple of these might be wedding pictures; two of the women are wearing corsages pinned onto white dresses, but their clothes are short and plain looking, deflecting the traditional focus of the wedding image away from the bride and onto the uniform of the husband.

Only one photograph shows a woman alone and she is dressed in an Uncle Sam costume. The juxtaposition of this image with those of the single men is particularly significant. In the images of individual soldiers there is an implied female presence. These pictures were most likely made for wives, mothers, and fiancées, to keep by their bedsides or hang proudly on their walls. The purpose was to remind the woman of her husband, sweetheart, or son, visually encouraging her to remain loyal, not only to him, but to the values represented by the uniform he is wearing. As such, a woman's emotional and sexual fidelity toward her husband was measured as an expression of her faithfulness to her country. Of course, it is likely that a faraway soldier would also carry pictures of his wife and family next to his heart but, as is clear in Collins's photograph, male fidelity was not a moral code institutionalized by government information. Indeed, in terms of official and popular representation

Fig. 3.3. Marjory Collins. "Photographer's display on Bleeker Street, New York City." Dec. 1942. Reproduced from the Collections of the Library of Congress.

the opposite was true. A soldier was expected to have sexual encounters while serving his country, as a way of maintaining his fighting spirits. On the other hand, female sexual expression—even for a single woman —was officially abhorred, hence the need for the single woman in Collins's photograph to be wearing an Uncle Sam costume. Her loyalty to her country is on full view in a uniform symbolic of American patriotism. Furthermore, because nationalism was signified in America through a male character, the fact that a woman is dressed as a man effectively negates her female sexual identity.

At the same time, however, the fact that a woman is wearing the costume of an archetypically male representation of American patriotism also highlights how national identity was forged around representations of female sexual identity. Collins's photograph identifies the ways in

which male and female sexuality and gender roles were defined according to the rhetoric of government information, but the image does not
explore how these roles might be successfully undermined by women
working on the homefront. Moreover, the men and women portrayed in
the photographer's window are presented as uniformly identical, suggesting that individual differences and oppositional definitions of patriotism were confined to sexual identity rather than economic and social
circumstances. In contrast, Esther Bubley's photographs are uniquely
radical: in her visual investigation of how fixed definitions of sexual and
gendered identity could be disrupted by women during the war, and also
by her portrayal of how economically and socially marginalized women
related to officially sanctioned images that defined femininity as exclusively middle-class. One way that Bubley began to do this was by visually undermining a system of representation that places the viewer—and
the photographer—in a position of power in relation to the subject of the
image.

The unique complexity of Bubley's perspective is especially clear
in one photograph taken in March 1943: "Soldiers taking pictures of a
girl on the steps of the National Gallery of Art on a Sunday afternoon,
Washington, D.C." (fig. 3.4). The photograph shows a single woman
standing against the wall of the huge building while two men in soldiers'
uniforms take her picture. One soldier stands with his camera poised at
his chest, while the other kneels slightly in a pose that suggests he might
be trying to frame his photograph of the woman although, because he
has his back to the viewer, it is not clear whether he has a camera or not.
Superficially, the photograph is fairly innocent. There are many such
images in the OWI files and in the pages of *Life* magazines from the
1940s. The photographs that illustrated articles like "Life Goes Boating
with Sailors and their Girls," for example, showed couples or foursomes
enjoying days out together, sometimes with the woman taking a picture
of her boyfriend, or of couples taking snapshots of each another.[36] Often
the couples would be pictured among crowds of other people, probably
families and tourists, posing in front of Washington's national monuments. The atmosphere between the men and women was usually one
of fun and innocence—maybe a little sexual interplay—but mostly
romance and mutual enjoyment, presenting the scene as a way women
could offer a little light relief to soldiers about to go into battle.

Bubley's photograph appears to be somewhat tense and atmospheri-
cally off-balance in comparison with these images of patriotic innocence. There is almost a tangible sense of danger in the connection
between the single woman in Bubley's photograph, pushed up against
the cold expanse of marble, and the two faceless men, who seem to be

Fig. 3.4. Esther Bubley. "Soldiers taking pictures of a girl on the steps of the National Gallery of Art on a Sunday afternoon, Washington, D.C." March 1943. Reproduced from the Collections of the Library of Congress.

dark and imposing in front of her. This vaguely threatening mood is enhanced by the way Bubley has framed the image so closely around the three people. Doubtless, since this seems to have been a sunny day in Washington, there would have been dozens of other people around, but Bubley chose to isolate this scene. As a result, the woman appears to be disturbingly alone with the two soldiers. Added to this, Bubley has captured the men as they seem to be moving in on the woman. This is particularly true of the man on the right. He seems to be poised where he might easily pounce on the woman. Moreover, if he has a camera, it must be positioned around his genital area and, allowing for an psycho-analytical interpretation of the image, the implicit sense of phallic power is enhanced by the marble columns that rise above each man and enclose the woman from behind. Freud notwithstanding, Bubley has rendered the act of taking a photograph with a certain amount of male sexual power that is directed at the female subject who is smiling nervously in response, her eyes lowered somewhat submissively, as the two soldiers enclose her with their cameras.

According to this definition of Bubley's photograph, the gender dynamics that were implied by the photographer's window display in Marjory Collins's image are symbolically revealed, but Bubley's radical position does not end with this exposure. Her perspective—together with that of the viewer—is aligned with the two men in the picture. Like the soldiers, Bubley is employed by the government for the duration of the war and, also like the soldiers, she is viewing and taking an image of the woman on display in this photograph. Indeed, the shadow that falls behind the woman, distorting the bland whiteness of the National Gallery's marble wall, could be taken as a representation of Bubley herself—and therefore the viewer—within the actual image. As such, Bubley has effectively "come clean" about the distribution of power between subject, photographer, and viewer in documentary photography. The woman is clearly subjected to the view of the camera in the image. Her position is constricted and her means of self-expression are repressed. She is routinely disempowered by the camera's gaze that is directed at her by the two soldiers in the photograph, and also by the underlying presence of the photographer acting on the instructions of the government, and on behalf of the expectations of her patriotic audience.

As well as revealing her own position as the photographer of this scene, Bubley's perspective in relation to the people portrayed also reveals the hierarchical social context that underlined official definitions of male and female identity in the 1940s. Bubley has taken the photograph from a position where she is looking up at both the soldiers and the woman standing on the gallery steps. From this point of view, the viewer is directed first upward at the soldiers and then—following their gaze—toward the woman who, in turn, is positioned above the soldiers. This construction establishes a symbolic hierarchy where the viewer's patriotism is measured against his or her deferential perspective in relation to the soldiers who, in the same way, have literally placed the woman on a pedestal, a position that metaphorically represents the reason for their military sacrifice. Furthermore, according to this construction, the soldiers—particularly the man on the right—do not seem threatening, but rather in awe of the woman's presence. The values that she symbolically embodies are also commemorated, since the kneeling soldier is depicted in a position that suggests the aspect of a traditional marriage proposal. The soldier with the camera might, therefore, be about to record the event for his friend to take away to war, an action that also memorializes the traditional family values that were deployed in government campaigns and concentrated on the symbolic potential of a female body.

By presenting female sexual identity as endangered and also worshipfully representative of American patriotism, Bubley has visually commented on the ways in which the male gaze was institutionalized by government information during the war years. At the same time, she also reveals the ways in which women were symbolically empowered under the auspices of official representation. The woman's position next to the National Gallery of Art enshrines her identity as representative of the democratic value system that was signified by Washington's monumental architecture.[37] The ideals that archetypically represented American society at its foundation are thus reinscribed and communicated to the viewer through the ideological import represented by the woman portrayed. Despite the apparent valorization of femininity in the picture, however, Bubley's visual investigation of gender identity in wartime representation also revealed the economic and social limitations of its symbolic appeal.

Karen Anderson has noted that a "renewed vigilance on female sexual conduct" became an integral part of official information campaigns in the 1940s.[38] This was particularly true in regard to working-class women. Anderson's study concentrates on a housing project in Seattle, where women were routinely arrested for prostitution under the auspices of the Social Protection Division of the Office of Community War Services. As Anderson notes, the SPD led a campaign intended to search for "incipient and confirmed sex delinquents."[39] Their powers extended to a broad definition of sexual misconduct applying only to women, which included "promiscuity: i.e. sexual activity without sincere emotional content; or, endangering moral safety or health: i.e. frequenting bars, loitering etc., without a male escort." The penalties for such crimes included mandatory testing for sexually transmitted diseases and a jail sentence while results were awaited, which in some cases could be for up to five days. Anderson concludes that as a result, between 1940 and 1944, there was a 9% increase in women charged with "moral violations."[40] In Seattle alone, three hundred women were detained every month.

There was a clear class bias in such moral judgments. Anderson comments that the sentences given to women arrested for sexual delinquency required them to "work, live a clean and temperate life, keep good company, and stay away from undesirable places."[41] The middle-class standards that underscored such statements are made emphatic in Anderson's study, since the threat of moral decline in Seattle was routinely blamed on the influx of migrant workers who lived in poverty-stricken housing projects while they worked in wartime industries. This point was made clear by the police chief's comment in a Seattle newspaper: "The area is flooded with war working families who have come here from the midwest. Parents are busy working and the kids run wild. The young fellows are making too much money."[42] His statement was compounded in an editorial that expressed the trepidation of the middle-class suburb of Denton toward the housing project, which they perceived as being a veritable hot bed of moral decline and misbehavior: "The young people in the housing project had access to liquor and throw promiscuous parties which would only admit girls if they had sex with all the men."[43]

Anderson concludes that such fears were generally unfounded. It is clear that they were fueled by an underlying need for established middle-class communities to maintain a psychological class hierarchy within a city that was supposed to be united by the war effort. Subsequently, the legislative effect of such fears ensured the victimization of working-class people—particularly women—by the government's morality police. Presumably, it was not only working-class women who took advantage of their husbands' absences, yet it was the working-class housing projects that were most vigorously policed, and it was working-class women who were left out of the loyal, hardworking, efficient, and capable image of female identity during the war. Thus, officially morally reprehensible female sexual expression was transposed onto the bodies of working-class women. The working-class equivalent of Rosie the Riveter or Mrs. Minniver was the Victory Girl.

A comment made by a soldier fondly remembering his wartime encounters with Victory Girls describes an image of female sexual expression that significantly opposed the tenets of official wartime representation:

Some of the guys could hardly wait to get to town and see some of those Victory Girls they had heard about from the permanent personnel on the base. The girls went out only with pilots, and each guy had to give them a picture for their scrap book. Some of the girls even carried little Brownie Hawkeyes or something like that to take their own picture.[44]

On the one hand, individualized female sexual expression was ideologically transferred onto economically and socially disempowered women who were easily marginalized from acceptable middle-class consciousness. In contrast, it was allowed that such women were performing a necessary wartime service for lonely soldiers. Initiation into the male world of the military included an outing with a Victory Girl. Sex with such a woman was a test of manhood, a rite of passage that a young draftee had to undergo so as to prove his macho potential for combat. Consequently, the soldier describes the Victory Girl as powerful, almost predatory: "They'd pick up guys at soda fountains or in the movie theater. Some of them took on four or five guys a night I heard."[45] These women were portrayed as voracious and insatiable. In contrast to Bubley's photograph at the National Gallery, the women in this context use their cameras as sexual weapons. As they collect images of their conquests, they take on a Medusa-like quality. Consequently, there is a definite element of fear to be inferred from this soldier's memory of sexual bravado. A young soldier might enter into a sexual battle with a Victory Girl, be taken prisoner, and then be lucky if he came back in one piece. At the same time, because female sexual power was presented as a natural facet of working-class identity, economically and socially deprived women were further removed from government representations of female identity. Working-class women were thus defined— and confined—by their officially unpatriotic amorality in opposition to a definition of femininity that symbolized democracy, family stability, individual freedom, and a wealthy future.

Bubley tried to work between these two fixed stereotypes: of the morally marginal, sexually available, archetypically working-class Victory Girl, and the mythologically pure, patriotically loyal, middle-class woman. In so doing, she often focussed on women whom she presented as not fitting either image and, as a result, simultaneously undermined the one-dimensional terms of official representation to reveal a diverse and complicated definition of female identity. Most revealing in this respect were Bubley's representations of women who defied their officially inscribed public roles. For example, in March 1943, she took a series of photographs at the Sea Grill, a restaurant bar in Washington, D.C. Bubley made several portraits of the barman and of the waitresses, as well as the many customers, both soldiers and civilians, but she focused on one woman in particular. The young woman is first photographed alone, and then later laughing and drinking with two soldiers. The first photograph of the woman on her own is accompanied with a caption, selected by Bubley from the young woman's own words:

I come in here pretty often, sometimes alone, mostly with another girl, we drink beer, and talk, and of course we keep our eyes open. You'd be surprised at how often nice lonesome soldiers ask Sue, the waitress, to introduce them to us.[46]

Bubley has also added the additional title "Girl sitting alone in the Sea Grill, a bar and restaurant, waiting for a pick up" (fig. 3.5).[47] The viewer

Fig. 3.5 Esther Bubley. "Girl sitting alone in the Sea Grill, a bar and restaurant, waiting for a pick up." April 1943. Reproduced from the Collections of the Library of Congress.

is not given a sense of the woman's age, marital status, background, or moral standards, but from her own words it is at least clear that she intends to meet a soldier, as she does on frequent nights, and (as the following photograph implies) ease his loneliness by showing him a good time. Whatever that might imply sexually, the woman is certainly making herself available for the attention of "nice lonesome soldiers."

In terms of government-sponsored representation, then, this woman is on the edge of what was defined as social acceptability. Indeed, in certain states she would have broken laws designed to maintain the moral unity of American family life. Even if her presence in the Sea Grill bar was not illegal in the District of Columbia, it was certainly made illegitimate by the rhetoric of government information. Nevertheless, Bubley's image subverts the moral oppositions that would normally define this woman as sexually promiscuous and thus, according to the rubric of government policy, displaying behavior that was pejoratively assumed to be typically working-class. The construction of the photograph detracts from any suggestion of seediness or moral suspicion. The atmosphere is certainly moody, but not in any way disturbing. Light falls on the woman's face making her seem beautiful, almost fragile. This feeling is enhanced by the way she looks away from the camera, perhaps in an expression of self-possession, but also of self-protection. Her legs are crossed and her arms are folded in front of her, placing her beyond the reach of the camera's gaze—and consequently the viewer's moral judgment. Her apparent obliviousness is compounded when one notes that there is a man's face behind the woman, looking through the window from the street, through the blinds covering the window, over the woman's head and, with one eye, apparently noticing and confronting the camera. Even from such a distance, the man seems to be more aware of being looked at than the woman. This contrast is made more ironic since from the woman's stated intention the viewer might assume that she wants to be looked at, that she has put herself on display and that, consequently, she deserves whatever action or judgment that display invites. However, in the construction and lighting of the photograph, Bubley has once again undercut the power of the viewer's gaze, and as a result, she has deconstructed the middle-class biases of official representation. At the same time, she has also undermined the mythology of sexual aggression that was assigned to working-class women. To this end, Bubley has used her training in fine art and commercial photography to complicate this woman's self-identity beyond predesignated social and political meaning.

Bubley's perspective is compounded by the way she has lit the scene to be clearly evocative of Edward Hopper's painting "Automat" (1927). There is the same sense of disaffection and social detachment. The woman is waiting alone in the corner of the booth while the rest of the seating space takes up almost a third of the frame. The distance between her handbag and the crumpled napkin beside her leaves an available space for somebody, but the sense of isolation is so profound that one gets the feeling that the void will never be filled. Indeed, when the photograph is interpreted using the Hopperesque visual language Bubley has evoked, the fleeting attachments made by this woman each night become infused with a sense of pathos and nihilism. In contrast to 1930s applications of painting to documentary photography, where the working-class subject's identity was submerged beneath the impositions of artistic misrepresentation, Bubley has used Hopper's work to reveal an emotional depth to this woman that the viewer might otherwise refuse.[48] Furthermore, by covering the image with the metaphysical aura of a painting, Bubley has enabled the woman—who is a real woman—to play the part of one of Hopper's "Nighthawks." Consequently, her real identity is never fully exposed to the viewer.

Bubley extends this sense of disguised identity further in the Sea Grill image. Although the woman's face is brightly lit, she is evidently sitting among shadows. This, together with her pose, her appearance, and the way she holds her cigarette, is consistent with the conventions of a film noir heroine. Indeed, Mary Anne Doane's description of a femme fatale's "most striking characteristic . . . the fact that she never really is what she seems to be . . . is not entirely legible, predictable or manageable"[49] provides a perfectly apt caption to Bubley's photograph. In the guise of a film heroine, the woman is able to transgress social codes and acceptable spaces that would have otherwise placed her in politicized sexual jeopardy. Following the narrative progress of the filmic language her appearance evokes, she is placed beyond the reach of official definitions concerning her femininity and her class identity. Like most of Bubley's photographic subjects, then, she can exist in between repressive wartime narratives, and beyond the conventions of documentary photography.

The Boarding House and Dupont Circle

Esther Bubley further explores the radical spaces presented between definitions of femininity and class identity that she negotiated in the Sea Grill Bar photograph, in a series of images taken at Arlington Farms, a residence for women who worked for the U.S. government, and at a boarding house in Washington. As suggested earlier, the majority of the women living in boarding houses and residence halls were lower-middle and working-class women, who had come to the city in search of well-paid clerical jobs, as well as for excitement and romance only dreamed of in their rural and midwestern homes. Often they would be disappointed and return home; otherwise they would stay, struggling to overcome depressed living conditions and exploitative work situations.

These women were the same women photographed for *Life* magazine by Alfred Eisenstadt as part of a constant stream of expendable labor, who aspired to an appearance of middle-class sophistication that proved difficult to maintain. In Bubley's boarding house images, the process through which this identity was constructed is explored. More significant, however, is her portrayal of the way these women lived beyond middle-class conventions of acceptability and appearance and created their own individualized senses of selfhood and personal expression.

In the first instance, Bubley is acutely aware that 1940s social construction of female identity in particular was an economically privileged process. An individual had to be able to buy a suitably middle-class appearance in order to be considered socially acceptable. In 1940s systems of representation, this was not simply a matter of accepting the vestiges of bourgeois snobbery but of being able to participate fully in an economic, social, and political context in which middle-class values, beliefs, and appearances were institutionalized and disseminated by the government. Bubley makes this clear in certain photographs. For example, in an image entitled "A girl looking at snapshots in her room, Arlington Farms," the woman is supposedly the central subject of the photograph, but she occupies only the bottom left hand corner of the frame. Instead, Bubley focuses on the clothes hanging out to dry all around the room's window, emphasizing the second half of her caption, which reads: "A typical room scene, since there is a shortage of space in the laundry and the authorities say that hanging the laundry outside will make the project look like a tenement."[50] Clearly, government regulations ordered a standard of appearances that judged the environments of a tenement building to be substandard, implicitly morally corrupt, and definitely undesirable. In this photograph, Bubley has portrayed the intimate effect of such institutionalized class bias as extending even through to how this woman cleaned and dried her underwear.

The connection between economic exclusion and the politicization of middle-class appearance is depicted more complexly in "Girls window shopping, Washington, D.C.," Dec. 1943 (fig. 3.6). In this photograph, three young women are gathered around a shop window looking at clothes displayed on a female mannequin.[51] The three women are visually similar to residents of the boarding house. Significantly, they are physically separated from the objects of their collective desire by a glass barrier. Since they do not have the means that would allow them entry, Bubley has established an economic division in this photograph. From this position, she has also constructed an element of social hierarchy between the consumer items on display in the window and the three women who remain outside. The mannequin is positioned close to the foreground of the frame, making "her" appear much larger than the real women, who stand to the left of the photograph's center. Almost two-thirds of the frame is taken up by the window display. Moreover, the mannequin's left arm is poised as if to move toward the three women. In contrast, the women stand close together, almost huddled, their hands crossed in front of themselves, eyes lowered without meeting the gaze frozen on the mannequin. This opposition endows the well-dressed mannequin with more physical space, more sense of movement, more height,

Fig. 3.6. Esther Bubley. "Girls window shopping, Washington, D.C." Dec. 1943. Reproduced from the Collections of the Library of Congress.

and even more self-possession, than the real women. What is more, the mannequin is better groomed, more attractively made up, and is dressed with more sophistication than the three women outside. The mannequin represents the manifestation of the middle-class appearance desired by the women, but because of their economic position, they are presented by Bubley as marginalized from the material and social power over which the mannequin presides.

Nonetheless, because Bubley has chosen to portray economic exclusion in the guise of a store mannequin, she is able to show the artificiality of middle-class identity. It is this sense of insubstantiality that allows for the possibility of imitation, infiltration, and possible subversion by the economically underprivileged women. Reflecting this possibility, it is not clear whether Bubley has taken the photograph from inside or outside of the shop window. The reflection from the glass cuts across the viewer's perspective and places the women in the artificial space occupied by the mannequin. From this point of view, the real women are empowered in relation to the mannequin, they now possess the ability to deceive the viewer's gaze. It is this power—to defy the viewer, and retain a sense of self-identity, despite ideologically inscribed notions of class position and aspiration, that is most radical and important in Bubley's boarding house images. She approaches her subjects in a way that removes them from the visual expectations of traditional documentary photography, and also from the narrative processes of wartime imagery and politics. Bubley captures the self-identified subjective processes in the boarding house women, and simultaneously complicates the visual connection between the viewer and the depicted subject. The women in Bubley's photographs construct their own personal narratives, despite their economic disadvantages, in such a way that their subject-hood excludes the middle-class viewer. The complexity of this construction is made clear in one image of a young woman looking out of her window, staring at a large house across the street (fig. 3.7). The photograph is captioned: "Boarders often speculate on the identity of the owner of the house across the street. They like to think it belongs to the president of a South American steamship line."[52]

In this photograph, the woman who is the subject of the image is portrayed in silhouette to the far right of the frame. Only her head and arms are visible to the viewer. To the left of the picture there are a few articles—a lamp, a bottle of water, and a newspaper, presumably belonging to the woman. At the top left and right corners of the photograph, there are some lacy curtains. But the central focus of the image is the big house outside the window, surrounded by trees and a manicured lawn. The house is certainly huge, with a stone pillar entrance, and a sweeping driveway with a shiny black car parked outside. The viewer makes the connection between the caption of the photograph and the house that is the central focus. This point is vital. What Bubley has photographed is not the woman, or her room, or the big house with the car outside of it but the daydreamed thoughts of the woman looking out of the window, or at least Bubley's imaginings of what the woman's thoughts might be. In either case, Bubley has given a mental process physical shape, and depicted the self-consciousness of the woman. Certainly, the caption offers the viewer some idea about what the woman is thinking, but Bubley's construction is more complicated than that. The viewer is provided with the material evidence of the woman's speculation about the big house, but the direction of her gaze leads beyond the house, and follows the road out of the frame of the image. This sense of unfixable

Fig. 3.7. Esther Bubley. "Boarders often speculate on the identity of the owner of the house across the street. . . ." June 1943. Reproduced from the Collections of the Library of Congress.

movement is compounded by the car which, from the viewer's perspective, is only halfway visible through the trees, but to the woman must be unobscured. The train of her reverie is accelerated in equation with the car, consequently, along with it, the woman's self-conscious individuality is allowed to exist beyond the frame of the image.

In her 1987 book, *Let Us Now Praise Famous Women*, Andrea Fisher labeled the element of psychological dynamism in Bubley's work "the drift of reverie."[53] I feel this analysis to be unconscious of the radical materiality of Bubley's photographs. Certainly, when taken individually, many of the images suggest a feeling of undirected dreaming, particularly in the boarding house series, which Fisher chose for her book.

However, when I returned to the OWI collection at the Library of Congress, it was clear to me that the self-conscious "look away" from the viewer's gaze had a precise political purpose. This is especially true of the images Bubley made on the streets in and around the Washington area, specifically in one photograph, "Children playing in a fountain, Dupont Circle, Washington, D.C.," 1943 (fig. 3.8).

The photograph shows three African-American children sitting under a statue of a goddess-woman. The white marble relates to the white summer dresses that the girls are wearing, visually connecting the children and the statue. Two of the girls sit at the feet of the statue, and the marble body seems to curve around them protectively. The viewer's eye naturally moves up the statue to the stone face that appears to stare

Fig. 3.8. Esther Bubley. "Children playing in a fountain, Dupont Circle, Washington, D.C." July 1943. Reproduced from the Collections of the Library of Congress.

down at the children with an expression of care. At the same time, the head is positioned in such a way that the goddess seems to be keeping one eye on the child who is standing apart from the other two. Bubley's composition echoes that of images made of mothers and children by FSA photographers in the 1930s, but at the same time, she adds a new level of irony and questioning to the emotional impact of maternal images that were typical of the FSA style.

Even though the connection between the mother figure and the children is clear in Bubley's image, the mother is obviously made of stone. The caring expression and protective stance are a facade. Consequently, the imposing white goddess becomes a symbol of the disparity between white middle-class-centered systems of representation, and the economically and socially marginalized subjects they sought to depict. In opposition, the African-American children are independently unmoved by the protective gaze of the statue, but the "look away" is not one of intimidation, defiance, or unfocused dreaming. Their averted gaze signifies a self-containment, and an existence and consciousness, that is separated from the white goddess in the photograph. The construction of Bubley's image allows each girl to establish a concrete presence and a self-identity that prevent the viewer from imposing a concrete narrative on the image. Further, the children not only reclaim their own space from the viewer, they also occupy the physical space that formerly represented the institutionalized traditions of wealth and power in Washington.

The statue was erected in Dupont Circle during an enthusiastic spate of monument building in the 1870s when Andrew Jackson, Admiral Farragut, George Washington, and Winfield Scott were all proudly memorialized in stone using a combination of private donations and congressional funds. The instruction for the Dupont Circle sculpture called for "a fountain, fifty feet in diameter, with a center piece of handsome design in marble or granite."[54] The structure was intended to decorate an area which, in the late nineteenth century, was inhabited by a "colony of millionaires."[55] By the 1930s and early 1940s, however, the economic profile of the population around Dupont Circle had changed considerably. Wealthy residents moved out of the city into Maryland and Chevy Chase, and as a result, their former neighborhood became home, first to middle-class families, and then gradually to poor whites and ethnic minorities. The process of economic change around Dupont Circle is clearly symbolized in Bubley's image. The statue metaphorically inscribes the exclusive wealth of the original residents. In opposition, the presence of the African-American children connotes the racial identity of the future population in Dupont Circle. Moreover, in relation to Bubley's other photographs of Washington's monumental architecture, which, according to the rhetoric of government information in the 1940s, represented democracy and freedom in exclusively middle-class terms, the African-American children are emphatically moving in on the viewer's privileged space. Furthermore, the trajectory of their "reverie" does not end in some unspecified, disassociated space, but is directed concretely at the material position of the white middle-class institutions where this photograph was placed. As a result, the political radicalism implicit in Bubley's photograph is given an historical continuity. The three African-American girls, who in 1943 were perhaps ten years old, look beyond the photograph's frame toward a future that is unknown to them but which, from a position of hindsight, anticipates the civil rights movement and Black Power, and from a 1990s perspective, the frustration of economic policies in the 1980s. Of course this is just speculation, but the vital point is that Bubley has photographed these three girls in such a way that the construction of their identities is given an historical imperative that was generally absent from FSA/OWI documentary photography. This portrayal effectively frees the three girls from their depicted subjecthood. They are visually removed from the political impositions of victimhood, heroism, or iconography. Unlike the white mother-goddess in this image, their identities are not fashioned in stone.

In comparison with other FSA and OWI photographers, Bubley was uniquely able to represent economically and socially oppressed people in ways that were potentially liberating and implicitly revolutionary. In the 1940s, she was able to work between the official images and narratives of wartime representation. In so doing, she exposed the class and race biases that were central to the rhetorical success of government-sponsored information. At the same time, she was acutely aware of her powerful position as a photographer employed to produce positive images for the United States government. In order to overcome this disparity, she found ways to expose, and thus to deflate, her own privileged perspective within the frame of the images she made. By doing this, she was able to create a space in her photographs for the self-identified presence of her subjects—but she did not expose them. She allowed them to create their own subjecthood, to disguise themselves, to hide, to confuse the viewer. Most significantly, however, the people she portrayed in her images do not remain within the frame. They are presented in a way that demands a dialectical process of narrative construction between subject and viewer beginning *from the subject's point of view*. As a result, Esther Bubley radically complicates not only what it meant to be the subject of a documentary photograph but what it meant politically, socially, and subjectively, to be female, African American, and working class in the 1940s—and beyond.

Part II

Working-Class Women

and Middle-Class Writing

Introduction to Part II

The grandmother went to an old candy box and took out the six old pictures . . . There was no mark on them except on the back, the name of the photographer . . . J. A. Edminston, Bushnell, Illinois . . . M. C. Stanley, Ann Arbor, Michigan, where they had stopped on a sunny day felt her need perhaps, the need of Penelope, not yet born, gone in sat down, had their heads vised, sat for a moment to make a mark of their passing which she now held in her hand. Who are you? What did you have to say? What did you know? And they made no answer, lost and dead, they would never tell, even if they knew.[1]

According to Mikhail Bakhtin an individual's sense of self is formed in a subconscious dialogue with an observed other. In Bakhtin's philosophy this is a social process, occurring continuously to create an open-ended historical dialogue of lived experience that is equally relevant to every member of any given community. His theory is politically complex, since the dialogical process of creating self-consciousness in relation to an observed other is fundamentally dependent on the position an individual might occupy in a society constructed hierarchically. Bakhtin illustrates his philosophy with a visual analogy:

The other human being whom I am contemplating, I shall always see and know something that he, from his place outside cannot see, himself: parts of his body that are inaccessible to his gaze. . . . are accessible to me but not to him. . . . This ever-present excess of my seeing, knowing and possessing in relation to any other human being, is founded in the uniqueness and irreplacibility of my place in the world.[2]

According to Bakhtin, then, although dialogic observation occurs from places that are socially disparate, the positions of viewer and viewed subject are nonetheless equally available and mutually experienced. Thus, the existence of an other, that is to say the experience of observing and being observed, is vital to the development of any individual consciousness whatever his or her class, race, or gender.

The fundamental egalitarianism of this aspect of Bakhtin's philosophy has proved an appealing device for some cultural critics. Such an interpretation of dialogism conveniently allows for an exploration of

131

"otherness"—which in an academic context means configurations of experience that are, generally speaking, nonwhite, female, and working class—while avoiding accusations of misappropriation or misrepresentation. Dialogism implies the possibility of an equal exchange between an articulate, materially privileged viewer, and an inarticulate, socially deprived subject. The notion of dialogue gives the "other" a voice that was previously refused and, furthermore, assigns an equal social power to that voice—at least in terms of the self-conscious construction of self-identity.

In these respects, Bakhtinian theory seemed an ideal methodology with which to continue this study. Having identified ways that working-class subjects might be photographed so as to disrupt and confound the ideological impositions of middle-class points of view, the concept of dialogue offered an ideal position from which to examine textual representations of working-class experience. Bakhtin presents a helpful continuity from observation to articulation, from seeing oneself to authoring oneself. Not only that, but socially and economically disadvantaged subjects are presented as able to engage in an aggressively self-conscious dialogue with their socially privileged viewers. Within this context, the working-class subject is then able to speak itself out of the frame of representation, and at the same time, is given the power to frame its middle-class viewers. Unfortunately, the easy philosophical transition from looking to speaking to dialogue proved decidedly less politically satisfying, upon closer examination of textual representations of working-class experience written by women in the Depression era. The extract from Meridel Le Sueur's short story "Our Fathers" that began this chapter is a case in point.

In Le Sueur's 1937 story, Penelope has become estranged from her rural working-class background. Despite memories of the emotional deprivation, social isolation, and economic oppression that led to her departure, she wants to recover her place within her family's history, and so be able to construct a sense of self-identity, which her separation has so far prevented her from achieving. An opportunity to begin this process arises when Penelope returns home for her father's funeral. She begins to search through some old photographs, looking for some understanding of what it meant to be a rural working-class person in her father's time, and from her grandmother's descriptions of the images, an explanation of what effect that history has had on shaping her own identity as a working-class woman.

The six photographs provide the only physical evidence of Penelope's family history. The experiences of the rural poor were not just absent from public records and official histories but were also left unwritten and unknown within individual households. The necessities of economic survival left no time to accumulate a written legacy; there are not even any proper letters. As Penelope realizes, "You cannot go over half a continent on horseback carrying letters, and if such letters said only 'We have arrived, all is well, hope you are the same' less reason to carry them at all."[3] Migrancy, instability, and illiteracy ensured that the least trace of working-class lives remained after their deaths. This historical absence is continued into the family's future: Penelope's grandmother rarely hears anything from her children, "only rumors whether they are alive or dead, had gone to this country or that, having from them only postcards of old journeys saying, 'Dear Mother, how are you, your loving son J. P.' "[4]

The silence of Penelope's personal history makes it impossible for her to achieve a fully realized sense of selfhood. She is able to look upon a photograph of her father and recognize herself "not yet born"[5]—but the questions she asks of her father's image—and therefore demands of herself—remain unanswered. She is able to picture herself within the frame of her family's history, but she is unable to extend that representation into a self-conscious articulation of her own self-identity. In other words, she can see herself as an image separate from her own consciousness but, in terms of Bakhtin's philosophy, she is unable to "author herself." As a working-class woman, she is removed from the dialogic process of her own self-creation: within the textual boundaries of Meridel Le Sueur's story, she is destined to remain a silent witness to her own life.

Meridel Le Sueur captures Penelope's unarticulated sense of being very effectively in "Our Fathers." Indeed, as a middle-class writer of radical fiction she would have felt it her duty to preserve, record, and politicize the lives and experiences of working-class women. In her own words, Le Sueur felt compelled to "mirror back the beauty of the people, to urge and nourish their vital expression and their social vision."[6] In this, Le Sueur's project has a specific dialogic purpose in relation to the distinction that Bakhtin makes between self-authorship—that is, the struggle to create a self-identity—and the kind of authoring that results in a work of literature. Bakhtin contends that an artist, in this case an author of radical fiction, has the ability to attain a privileged position in social dialogue, a perspective that Bakhtin calls "transgredience." From this point of "outsidedness," an author can choose whether to participate in a dialogic process with the characters in their text, and so can permit them to exist beyond the realms of textual invention, as it were.[7] Or, an author can maintain the privilege of his or her point of view and in Michael Holquist's words, "exploit . . . their characters much as a scientist exploits . . . laboratory rats."[8] In the case of "Our Fathers" Le Sueur draws attention to Penelope's inability to enter into a process of self-authorship, a silence that stems from the material circumstances of her class position. From this point, however, Le Sueur does not exactly detract from the responsibility of dialogic participation; instead she enacts a manipulation that effectively changes the focus of the conversation from Penelope's class status—which remains unarticulated beyond the frame of her father's image—to her femininity, which is given full expression by Le Sueur.

With the help of her grandmother, Penelope is able to reconstruct a selfhood that is specifically woman-centered. The grandmother is described as containing the record of the family's past within her huge body. She has preserved the testimony of dead relatives, and so is able to retell their stories as Penelope looks through the photographs and, at the same time she can pass on the memories for her granddaughter to keep. At the end of the story, Penelope understands the weight of this responsibility, presented as necessarily a woman's duty, and screams with recognition: "My father . . . our fathers, our fathers."[9] Her voice is weighted with the realization of her personal history, but is also directed at America's mythologized founding fathers. Le Sueur enables Penelope's voice to rail against official narratives of American history that have systematically excluded rural working-class people, but most important for Le Sueur, the angry interruption comes from a working-class woman, shrieking herself into history with a voice nurtured within generations of silent women, now powerfully emerging from Penelope's body.

The somewhat melodramatic conclusion of "Our Fathers" is emblematic in its revelation of the narrative tensions between Le Sueur's understanding of working-class identity, which derived from her observations of working-class people, and her radical insistence on a politicized female experience, which she believed to be common to women of every class and culture. In the story, Penelope's psychological silence is presented as a consequence of her class experience, symbolized by her father's image. Le Sueur is able to resolve the silence, however, by introducing a communality of experience between women—the women in the story and herself as its female author—that nurtures and symbolically "gives birth" to Penelope's voice. Consequently, the silence of her material situation is transcended by the rejuvenating possibilities of sensitivity, spirituality, and the transformation of pain into joy that is presented as inherent to a woman's body. Le Sueur gives this process a mythological dimension by evoking the story of Demeter and Persephone. Penelope's consciousness inhabits an underworld of silent, unresponsive ghosts until she is reborn, with help of many mothers, and guided by Le Sueur's narrative, into becoming a spiritually strong woman, able to express her anger at the essentially male gods of history, economy, and materiality.

Le Sueur's resolution of the dichotomy between class and femininity is typical of the way middle-class radical women presented working-class women in their fictions. Middle-class authors of fiction about working-class women effectively refused to participate in a problematic dialogue about a class experience that might have subverted their authoritative position. This marginalization of the specificity of class identity for working-class women has been continued in various studies of radical fiction written by women in the 1930s. Early investigations of radical fiction passed over the contributions of women radicals almost entirely. Subsequent feminist interpretations of the period have quite rightly criticized these generally male-authored analyses. Moreover, feminist critics of radical fiction have noted that, even when women authors are mentioned as contributors to the class analysis of proletarian fiction, such as in Walter Rideout's *The Radical Novel in the United States*, they have failed to "give attention to their inscriptions of gender."[10]

The first collection of radical writing from the 1930s to include short stories, poems, and reportage by women did not appear until 1987, with the publication of Paula Rabinowitz's and Charlotte Nekola's anthology *Writing Red*. The collection was intended to present radical fiction written by women as a site where left-wing politics and analyses of working-class identity intersected with experiences that Nekola and Rabinowitz defined as woman-centered, e.g., sterilization, abortion, sexuality, motherhood, and the feminist impulse among radical women, which, according to Rabinowitz and Nekola, was inherently antagonistic to the male-centered ideology of proletarian fiction. Subsequently, radical fiction written by women became a popular subject of study for feminist critics, particularly those who have identified themselves as historical-materialist or socialist theorists. Paula Rabinowitz continued her study of radical fiction in her book *Labor and Desire*.

Rabinowitz contends that "Leftist women's fiction of the 1930s rewrites women into the history of labor and labor into the history of feminism."[11] She illustrates this process by deconstructing what she sees as a textual dialogue between femininity, which in radical fiction is articulated by middle-class women, and proletarianism, which in a convenient opposition is symbolized by a working-class man. This focus on a dialogic opposition between vociferously rowdy male proletarians and subversively feminist writers is problematic. Rabinowitz offers a complex and challenging examination of what might be either the most potent or the most inclusive representations of working-class experience, but, in so doing she inevitably avoids analyzing the perspective of the working-class subject.

As Rabinowitz asserts, proletarian ideology insisted on a definition of working-class identity that was almost comical in its romantic machismo. In *New Masses* editor Mike Gold's words, a self-identified working-class author should be:

A wild youth of about twenty-two, the son of working-class parents, who himself works in lumber camps, coal mines, steel mills, harvest fields and mountain camps of America. He is sensitive and impatient. He writes in jets of exasperated feeling, and has no time to polish his work. He is violent and sentimental by turns. He lacks self confidence but writes because he must.[12]

Consequently, proletarian fiction typically took place in what Gold and his male colleagues considered to be the sites of working-class experience—the factory, the picket line, the boxcar—while the scenes of what female radicals thought to be working-class women's protest and struggle—the kitchen, the home, the children—were ignored. It seemed that, in relation to Gold's description, women were not physically equipped to be revolutionary writers in the accepted sense. As a result, feminist protest was consumed by male-centered class politics and, as Rabinowitz concludes, bourgeois middle-class expression—that is, literature that was individualistic, introspective, experimental, and in the proletarian sense unformulaic—was defined as feminine. In opposition to what Rabinowitz presents as an essentially patriarchal marginalization, radical women writers had to find ways to express their female identity while remaining true to the proletarian ideal. Rabinowitz suggests that in order to do this, radical women had to write about the lives of working-class women. Consequently, women writers utilized the only weapon that could logically oppose the male proletarian's brandished phallic pen: the womb.

In Rabinowitz's view, the radical woman writer's representation of working-class women was defined in almost exact opposition to Mike Gold's idea of a radical working-class man. The working-class woman was placed in a symbolically constricted home, rather than a field or a lumber camp. Rabinowitz notes that this confined situation defined the working-class woman as a "sexed body" rather than a "laboring" one.[13] Nevertheless, this representative working-class woman was able to nurture her potential for self-expression much in the same way that the proletarian man ejaculated his. In Rabinowitz's words, "[T]he tight economies of the working-class home constrict the daughter, closing in on her—as stifling to her imagination as they are to her body, yet providing a memory out of which to forge class consciousness."[14]

Occasionally, the imagined working-class woman came into conflict with the imagined working-class man and became the victim of familial violence which, according to Rabinowitz, reenacted "the violence of economic oppression."[15] Middle-class women radicals accepted —as does Rabinowitz, evidently—the image of a sexually aggressive working-class man, by representing in opposition a "brutalized" and "alienated" image of working-class female sexuality.[16] As a result, assertion of desire is described as a form of protest for working-class women in radical fiction. Essential to Rabinowitz's argument is the notion that working-class women come to revolutionary consciousness in radical fiction through an articulation of this desire, in defiance of moral codes imposed by social and economic ideologies to be sure, but most particularly in opposition to working-class men. This is a specifically feminist realization that, according to Rabinowitz, "reembodied the working-class woman within narrative and within history."[17]

By focusing on a textual dialogue between middle-class men and women, Rabinowitz uncovers an idea of working-class identity in radical fiction that is biologically essentialized and psychologically predetermined. Working-class women are confined to a subjective status presented as uncomprehending and inarticulate by middle-class women authors of radical fiction, an image that is defined in opposition to similarly reductive portrayals of working-class men. In both cases—and in Rabinowitz's study—a self-identified working-class point of view is circumlocuted in a discourse about class and gender defined almost exclusively from a middle-class perspective.

Ironically, Rabinowitz adds another dimension to the progressive silencing of working-class voices. In the course of her discussion she states that in texts written about working-class women by middle-class women, it is the radical woman author who is "doubly alienated."[18] The narratives of pregnancy and rebirth, which could easily define working-class women in radical texts, were apparently too narrow to contain the fictionalized personae of middle-class female intellectuals. Rabinowitz's conclusion is certainly logical since middle-class women were excluded as ideological concepts from the political discourses of proletarian fiction in the 1930s. Indeed, it would be a misrepresentation of Rabinowitz's work to suggest that her intention was to do anything other than recover and reconstruct the contribution of the white middle-class women authors within the history of radical fiction, and in so doing, to integrate radical politics within a middle-class feminist agenda. Reflecting this intention, the closing sentences of *Labor and Desire* state that "white middle-class feminist literature is foreshadowed by white women's revolutionary literature in the Depression decade."[19] Given this intention, it is only to be expected that the middle-class women authors discussed in *Labor and Desire* appear fully realized, historically contextualized, politically complex, and multifaceted, while the working-class women in their fictions—and, it has to be said, in Rabinowitz's examination—are represented merely as "elusive configurations."[20]

Although Rabinowitz's discussion of the political and ideological position of middle-class women writers within the discourse of radical fiction is ultimately convincing, her representation of working-class identity—both female and male—is disappointing. Her insistence on an anatomical sisterhood that transcends material circumstance indicates that her investigations of the ways class and gender, and feminism and materialism, intersect has proved irresolvable. Rabinowitz's removal of a self-identified working-class point of view from her discussion of radical fiction in the 1930s compounds Meridel Le Sueur's narrative avoidance of the complexities of working-class female identity. Like images of poverty in FSA photography, representations of working-class women in radical fiction are only half realized. Middle-class women authors and feminist critics have continued a dialogue that has excluded working-class identity from feminist discourse in the same way that proletarian discourse previously excluded women. It has been a discussion undertaken with good intention, no doubt, but it is a conversation to which working-class women have systematically been refused access.

My aim in the following pages is to reexamine radical fiction written by women in the 1930s so that a self-identified working-class point of view might be articulated. In this respect, my investigation of textual representations of working-class identity begins where my analysis of visual depictions ended. I have shown that working-class women can be represented as complex individuals, in ways that are politically and artistically challenging, by photographers who are middle class and who are employed by a government agency whose interests are fundamentally middle class. I want now to extend this project by showing how it is possible to write about working-class women in ways that enable them to speak for themselves in relation to political positions that middle-class writers have presented as proletarian or feminist.

My analysis begins with Le Sueur's image of Penelope looking at the photograph of her father. As such it is predicated by a theme that is fundamental to any investigation of working-class lives: silence. Le Sueur narrates over Penelope's silence, giving her a voice that speaks for her experiences as a woman but that leaves her working-class identity unarticulated. I have already shown how this feminist strategy has been continued in critiques of radical fiction. Most recently, feminist critics such as Paula Rabinowitz have employed Bakhtinian philosophy to insist that radical texts were the products of a dialogic process between middle-class women authors and their working-class subjects, set against a patriarchal definition of working-class identity. However, this valorization of textual complexity avoids the fundamental issue, which is that working-class women are prevented from writing about their own lives by their economic circumstances. For Bakhtin, self-creation in a psychological sense, and self-assertion in a social context, are fundamentally processes of articulation. But, as is clear in Le Sueur's story, socially creative dialogue cannot begin without self-awareness, and self-awareness cannot begin in a situation that is economically disadvantaged, materially underprivileged, and socially marginalized. This point is crucial to any investigation of texts written by women who are middle class but who claim to be speaking on behalf of working-class women.

By beginning here, I do not wish to suggest that working-class experiences cannot be written about by people who are not working class. To do so would be to repeat the ludicrous definitions presented by Mike Gold and others like him. Moreover, I want to avoid the trap of replacing one essentialized image with one more pleasing to my political sensibility, as has been the tendency of many feminist critics. Nevertheless my analysis works between the polarities of class and gender; as such, it is a investigation of a dialogic process, but it is one that is intended to articulate the position of the working-class woman subject rather than the middle-class woman author. It is my assertion that texts about working-class women should speak first for the history of working-class women. To reclaim these works only as an example of the diverse achievements of middle-class women writers is a double appropriation, which not only seems contrary to the intention of many of the authors, but which excludes working-class women from what amounts to an historical record of their lives in the 1930s, a history where, like Penelope in "Our Fathers," working-class women were not able to speak for themselves.

I concentrate here on work by women who have written primarily about working-class women in the Depression era. First, Meridel Le Sueur, who, as an active member of the Communist Party in the 1930s, wrote many stories, articles, essays, and reportage pieces about working-class experience for various radical publications. Her long career spans an identification with intellectual socialism in the 1920 and 1930s—inspired by her parents, a radical lawyer and an ardent feminist teacher—to her rediscovery as feminist writer in the 1970s. By examining her work, I want to show how her depiction of working-class women in the 1930s interacted with her feminism, which is more evident in her work of the 1970s.

In the final chapter, I will compare Le Sueur's approach with fiction about working-class experience written by Tillie Olsen. Like Le Sueur, Olsen was active in radical politics during the Depression and her short stories, poems, and reportage were published by the same left-wing journals. Also like Le Sueur, Tillie Olsen's work was rediscovered by feminist writers in the 1970s. Olsen was then able to complete a novel *Yonnondio: From the Thirties*, which she had begun as a young woman in the Depression. Olsen also wrote a short story collection entitled *Tell Me a Riddle*, in which she refers to the 1930s and related experiences that she had been economically unable to write about in the interim years. She wrote about her experiences in a critical work, *Silences*, which examines literary history from the perspective of authors who had been prevented from writing. *Silences* is not just a survey, however; it is a testimony to Olsen's own forty-year silence in which she struggled to find the means and the time to record her own life and the lives of others in similar situations, who would never be lucky enough to express themselves in ways that would be acknowledged in a literary context.

Tillie Olsen describes her effort to complete the novel she began in the 1930s as "an arduous partnership" between herself as "a girl of the thirties," and her adult self in the 1970s.[21] The success of *Yonnondio* attests to the resolution of Olsen's personal quest for self-identity. At the same time, her idea of partnership points to a wider context of political antagonism between class, gender, and race ideologies that have yet to be resolved. In my study of Tillie Olsen's fiction, I will show how these definitions might be expanded in order to include, support, and encourage a self-identified expression of the lives and experiences of working-class women.

4

Meridel Le Sueur:
Sexual Revolution

Alternative Images

The poet Delmore Schwartz once told a story of a well-known critic who, during the worst part of the Depression, arrived at the house of a southern friend for a visit, and had scarcely put down his suitcase when he asked, "Where are the sharecroppers?"¹ Despite Schwartz's patronizing tone, this anecdote presents a fairly accurate picture of "the intellectual in foreign parts, with a sense of mission at hand, and, for the first, and possibly the last time in American cultural history, a universal politics of class (or class conflict) to think with."² Schwartz's image of a cosmopolitan intellectual turning into an explorer when he reaches the unfamiliar southern states, eager to head out in search of the elusive sharecropper or tenant farmer in his natural habitat, shows how conversion to radical politics was often based on a desire to seek out a vicarious sense of what it was like to be poor and working-class in the 1930s. Voyeuristic experiences enabled middle-class intellectuals to feel engaged in a society that, in the Depression, seemed to be falling apart. By making an emotional alignment with what they perceived to be a working-class point of view, middle-class intellectuals could feel like they were actually doing something to change a capitalist society that was obviously in need of fixing. The real irony of Schwartz's image thus becomes clear. The deprivation suffered by rural and urban working-class people in the Depression provided an opportunity for middle-class intellectuals to readjust their political and emotional position in American society. The lives and experiences of working-class people provided a convenient new focus for their intellectual attention. In Schwartz's description, rural poverty provided an opportunity for middle-class intellectuals to expand their mental horizons and to experience new cultures; it also offered them the chance to become tourists, not just of a different state but of a different economic circumstance and, having seen it, to appropriate that "foreign" culture into a exciting new political perspective. Richard Pells describes the arrogance of these idealistic forays into the circumstances of poverty as opportunities for intellectuals to "escape from the political wilderness to which they had been consigned in the previous decade."[3] His statement is corroborated in a typically enthused comment made by Mike Gold, the editor of *New Masses:* "Whatever comes of it [the Depression]—it marks a great turning point in the consciousness of the American nation. It is the first time America has ever examined itself."[4]

Delmore Schwartz's image highlights the fact that, like most explorers into foreign lands, the radical intellectual's investigation of rural poverty was largely a self-referential expedition. At the same time it is clear that, despite their failings, radical intellectuals promoted a world view centered on the education and organization of working-class communities, while encouraging the revolutionary possibilities they considered inherent to working-class identity. This was a political position that had been absent from American culture before the Depression and, unfortunately, would never again be so visible. Moreover, Schwartz's comment alludes to the reasons why intellectual commitment to radical left-wing politics was so fleeting, and also why proletarian writing bore little relevance to, and drew virtually no enthusiasm from the working-class people it sought to represent.

The radical intellectual arrived in the South with a sense of "mission at hand," suggesting not so much a picture of a curious observer who might look and leave as it were, but of someone making a journey that had a certain evangelical purpose. In this way, a radical intellectual encountered rural poverty differently from a photographer working for the government. FSA photographers took pictures of sharecroppers and tenant farmers according to the predilections of government policy. They made images intended for display in congressional reports, departmental documents, and sociological journals. For the radical intellectual, however, the journey south was something of a pilgrimage, arriving at the actual site where the revolution might occur, a place from where he or she would return having had his or her radical will rejuvenated. Unlike FSA photographers, then, radical intellectuals did not simply record the details of rural working-class lives; they were witnesses to its political testimonies. Despite this difference in approach and purpose, however, the suggestion of an almost religious sense of commitment among radical intellectuals reveals an important connection between the government's official representation of rural working-class poverty in the 1930s and the radical response to it.

The physical and social effects of economic collapse, unemployment, migrancy, and dispossession in the 1930s were portrayed by the government as catastrophes of biblical proportions. Images of dust storms, floods, droughts, enforced exodus, and migrant mothers set out an iconography of the Depression that was entirely divorced from its historical and economic causes. The Depression was presented as "the work of an indifferent and impersonal God."[6] The government's response to the crisis was predicated on public acceptance of the pictures it disseminated. Consequently, even as the rural poor were reassuringly portrayed as "helpless yet unvanquished" victims, displayed for the benefit of a middle-class audience made nervous by God's apparent abandonment of America, the government continued policies designed to advance capitalist economics at the expense of working-class livelihoods. In short, the government responded to the Depression by extending the economic and social policies that had caused it, while simultaneously presenting an image of suffering wrenched from its historical and economic contexts.

Like the government's pragmatic (one might say calculating) response to the Depression, radical intellectuals understood and portrayed working-class identity in the same mythologized, iconic terms as official photography. Communist rhetoric was infused with religious metaphors and symbolism that were similar to those fundamental to FSA photography. The left-wing movement had created its own martyrs in its valorization of Sacco and Vanzetti and its subsequent appropriation of the Scottsboro Boys' defense. Of course, because Marx and Lenin served as secular prophets in radical circles, the Soviet Union was therefore a natural setting for Heaven. Also, since a trip to Moscow was the ultimate measure of intellectual commitment to radical politics, Bolshevik Paradise was simultaneously a mythological Mecca. In this context, the central task for radical intellectuals was to create their own set of dogmatic scriptures, edifying parables, and ritualistic prophecies that in the 1930s were known as proletarian literature.

Reflecting this background of radical religiosity, much of the literature written in support of the proletarian cause was predictable, repetitive, and one-dimensional in its representation of working-class identity. The relationship between the working-class subject of proletarian fiction and the generally middle-class audience who received it was similar to the dynamic between viewers and subjects of FSA photographs. The image of the heroic working-class man in constant conflict with the generalized "forces of oppression," whether on a picket line, in a migrant camp or on a factory floor, became the symbolic vessel through which radical intellectuals could achieve a "ceremonial catharsis for the middle-class audience unable to participate directly in the daily struggle of workers."[7] At the same time, proletarian literature was a textual site where radical intellectuals could atone for what they considered to be the sins of their self-obsessive predecessors. The individualistic introspection of writers from the 1920s was replaced by an emphasis on communal experience. The disaffected tone of experimental art was overpowered by a robust didacticism. A generation of writers and intellectuals noted for their nihilism and decadence were reviled by a group of radicals who were committed to a cause that they defined as morally correct. The voices of the Lost Generation were, metaphorically at least, found and born again in the pages of proletarian literature.

For middle-class authors of radical fiction, then, writing about working-class lives and the possibility of revolution that lay within them was a reassuringly redemptive process. Radical intellectuals had a distinctly "millennial approach" toward proletarian fiction; the idea that the revolution was at hand was guaranteed by its narrative progression. As a result, radical authors often "[exorcised] . . . the fear of the uncertain present by creating a hero so sure of the future that he can be outrageously improvident."[8] A revolutionary conclusion to proletarian fiction, poetry, and essays was therefore presented as an inevitable textual process as middle-class readers were assured of a reading experience that would satisfy their radical souls.

Since belief in the inevitability of a working-class revolution was an article of faith for the radical intellectual, any deviation from the narrative structure of proletarian fiction was condemned as an act of apostasy. A criticism by Whittaker Chambers, an editor at the *New Masses*, of Meridel Le Sueur's reportage item "Women on the Breadlines" (1932) was typical in its accusation of revolutionary heresy:

This presentation of the unemployed women, able as it is, and informative, is defeatist in attitude, lacking in the revolutionary spirit and direction which characterize the usual contribution to the New Masses. We feel it is our duty to add that there is a place for the unemployed woman, as well as man in the unemployment councils, and in all branches of the organized revolutionary movement. Fight for your rights![9]

Here, Le Sueur is chastised for undermining the official dogmas of proletarian fiction. The unemployed women in "Women on the Breadlines" do not follow the accepted narrative progression from poverty, isolation, and ignorance, to organization, enlightenment, and freedom. Le Sueur presents a picture of working-class women that appears to fall between the opposing discourses of radical politics and New Deal ideology. As a result, Chambers is compelled to add the required ending in an editorial note.

Considering this reaction to Le Sueur's work in 1932, it is surprising that in 1990 Constance Coiner described "Women on the Breadlines" as a reportage piece that conformed entirely to the "didacticism" of "official proletarian literature."[10] She criticizes Le Sueur for inadequately "penetrating the consciousness of the characters" and asserts that while "Women on the Breadlines" is a "valuable record" of working-class women surviving the Depression, it unfortunately lacks the emotional and psychological insight of Le Sueur's writing about "her own oppression as a middle-class woman and a member of the male dominated Communist Party."[11]

It seems ironic that Le Sueur's piece can be criticized first for not conforming to the ideologies of proletarian fiction, and then later for conforming too much. However, this paradoxical agreement between Chambers and Coiner occurs because they both approach the work from points of view that circumvent the perspective of the working-class woman subject. The official direction of proletarian literature was intended to construct a perspective that saved the working-class subject from the false prophecies presented by the New Deal government. This point of view was, as I have shown, largely an extension of a political commitment from middle-class intellectuals, founded on a one-dimensional image of working-class identity that was fundamentally disconnected from its historical and material context. Le Sueur's work seems to deviate from this official middle-class perspective in "Women on the Breadlines," apparently showing working-class women as individuals who, although almost paralyzed by economic deprivation, are still able to develop their own ways of subverting their oppressive circumstances.

Coiner criticizes "Women on the Breadlines" from the same middle-class point of view as radical intellectuals in the 1930s. Since Le Sueur was a woman writer in a Communist Party dominated by men and male-centered ideologies, her work is examined by Coiner for a subtextual feminist agenda. Coiner does not consider "Women on the Breadlines" to be a successful expression of Le Sueur's feminist consciousness, nor is it an adequate exploration of the feminist sensibilities of working-class women, in her estimation. Just as "Women on the Breadlines" does not work as proletarian literature for Chambers, it does not receive approval as a feminist subversion of that (middle-class) perspective for Coiner. In neither critic's opinion is the self-identified point of view of the working-class woman subject considered, even though Le Sueur seems occasionally to allow for that possibility in this particular piece of reportage.

The reasons for these apparently opposing, yet similarly motivated criticisms of "Women on the Breadlines" are fundamental to any discussion of Le Sueur's extensive body of work. Despite the criticism by Chambers, Le Sueur remained a loyal and productive contributor to proletarian literature. Indeed, despite Coiner's insistence on her marginalized position as a woman in the Communist Party, Le Sueur has described her sense of radical commitment in distinctly feminist terms: "Publishing you was love, nourishment, criticism. . . . Even when they neglected you, it's like your mother neglecting you."[12] At the same time however, Le Sueur's writing is often centered on a psychological interpretation of women's lives separated from their class identity. She is much concerned with reproductive rights, abortion, and sterilization; but more particularly she believes in a fundamental spiritual connection between mother and child. Also, her work often utilizes woman-centered mythology and celebrates an essentialized connection between women and nature. It is these elements in her work that revived her reputation as a feminist writer in the 1970s and 1980s, a role that she embraced, generally at the expense of her interest in class politics.

Le Sueur's work has spanned both feminist and Communist positions at different times in her life and critics like Chambers and Coiner have responded by concentrating on the ways either perspective has failed to be articulated, because of an uncommitted (for Chambers) or a suppressive (for Coiner) emphasis on the other. In the following pages I want to move away from this polarization between class politics and feminism that has proved to be a false opposition made from a middle-class perspective.

The Crisis of Class Identity

Meridel Le Sueur's commitment to Communist politics and proletarian causes was virtually a birthright. The left-wing credentials of her family history, and of her childhood in Kansas and later in St. Paul, Minnesota, were impeccable. Her mother, Marian, had been an active feminist and socialist before she married Le Sueur's stepfather, Arthur, a socialist lawyer. Both parents worked at the People's College in Fort Scott, Kansas, a school that was intended to educate and introduce poor farmers and laborers to radical causes. The Le Sueur house was a meeting place for left-wing activists of varying degrees of notoriety: "Wobblies, anarchists, socialists and union organizers . . . Helen Keller, Eugene Debs, Alexander Berkman and Ella (Mother) Bloor."[13] The list of infamously rebellious acquaintances was completed when, after Le Sueur left High School in 1916, she went to live in an anarchist commune with Emma Goldman.

Le Sueur's sense of commitment to radical politics was nurtured through the next twenty years of her life. She was an active pacifist during the First World War and in the 1920s campaigned on behalf of Sacco and Vanzetti. Her personal life also became a kind of radical statement when she decided to have a child, Rachel, in 1927. Her decision to become a single mother of two daughters—she had another daughter,

Deborah, in 1930—has been regarded by some critics as an early sign of Le Sueur's feminist position. However, at the time, Le Sueur defined her choice in distinctly Communist terms, citing Lenin's notion that "the primal relationship between mother and child is the only communality left in capitalist society."[14]

Le Sueur wrote continuously throughout the 1920s, but the radical tone of her work meant that only a few of her stories, poems, and essays were published. The social ostracism that resulted from Le Sueur's political activism and her single motherhood meant that she was often living on meager resources; however, her status as an educated middle-class woman meant that she was also able to traverse the social boundaries between political and economic marginality and bourgeois culture. As Elaine Hedges notes, Le Sueur occasionally wrote articles for mainstream magazines such as *Vogue* and *Harper's Bazaar,* "in order to make money."[15]

Fortunately for Le Sueur, as for many other 1920s radicals, the Depression decade represented a unique opportunity to combine literary skills with a sense of commitment to left-wing activism. The 1930s were a very productive time for Le Sueur. The Communist Party and John Reed clubs nurtured and encouraged her as a radical writer. Radical journals such as the *New Masses* and *Anvil* were welcoming places to publish her work. Social groups, political activities, and conventions, such as the American Writers Congress, provided a network of community support for Le Sueur and other like-minded artists. Le Sueur was even able to benefit from the cultural activities of New Deal agencies, working for a time as a contributor to the Writers Project of the WPA.

The importance for Le Sueur of having a visibly appreciative audience for her literary production was accompanied by a need to articulate a sense of political and emotional communality with the working-class subjects of her work. Proletarian writing demanded that authors should align themselves with the working-classes of America within a particular text, as on a picket line. A radical author—most often of the middle-classes—was not supposed to write *about* a strike, reporting the events objectively from the sidelines; he or she was supposed to convey a sense of involvement, of fighting not on behalf but in common with working-class people. Consequently, when Le Sueur wrote about a strike, she positioned herself simultaneously as a participant in the actual event, as a reporter of what occurred, as an interpreter of the political significance of the consequences and, most fundamentally, she imagined herself to be one of the strikers. More specifically, she felt herself become part of a single body of strikers, which she portrayed as a kind of organic whole rather than as a collection of individuals. In this sense, Le Sueur's experience of the Minneapolis truckers' strike in 1934 was much different from, for example, Dorothea Lange's impression of the San Francisco longshoremen's strike in 1933. Horrified and inspired by what she saw, Lange photographed the protests and demonstrations for an audience who were unaware of the longshoremen's situation. In contrast, Le Sueur wanted to move beyond Lange's point of view and become an intrinsic part of what she perceived as a collective working-class struggle. Le Sueur's description of herself standing outside the strike headquarters in a reportage article "I Was Marching" (1934), highlights her need to achieve this perspective:

For two days I heard of the strike. I went by their head quarters . . . I saw cars leaving filled with grimy men, pickets going to the line, engines roaring out. I stayed close to the door, watching. I didn't go in. I was afraid they would put me out. After all, I could remain a spectator. A man wearing a polo hat kept going around with a large camera taking pictures.[16]

From this position of photographic objectivity, Le Sueur begins a meditation on what role a middle-class artist such as herself, who was committed to radical left-wing politics, could take in a class struggle that by its very nature demanded action that was physically productive—that is, according to proletarian art, essentially working-class—rather than introspective:

I am putting down exactly how I felt, because I believe others of my class feel the same as I did. I believe it stands for an important psychic change that must take place in all. I saw many artists, writers, professionals, even business men and women standing across the street, too, and I saw in their faces the same longings, the same fears.[17]

According to Le Sueur, radical middle-class writers had to move beyond a viewer's perspective and position themselves within the body of the working-class subject. Only then could proletarian literature be truly revolutionary. She explores this process further in an analytical essay "The Fetish of Being Outside," which was published in the *New Masses* in February, 1935. In this essay Le Sueur chastises a fellow radical, Horace Gregory, for wanting to retain an objective view of working-class experience and for what she sees as his subsequent failure to integrate himself fully within the "dark passional world"[18] of working-class identity. She regards Gregory's equivocation as an expression of his middle-class status, stating that "joining has always been obnoxious to the bourgeois artist" who has historically made a "fetish" out of objectivity and individuality in literature.[19] This inherently middle-class perspective was taken always at the expense of communality, mutuality, and collectivism, which Le Sueur believed to be fundamental to working-class identity and of writing which expressed the interests of the working-classes.

As she makes these points, Le Sueur criticizes "bourgeois artists" such as Nathaniel Hawthorne, Edgar Allan Poe, and Gertrude Stein for what she considers to be their "infantilism and exhibitionism."[20] For Le Sueur, textual experimentation with language and narrative perspective were symptomatic of a middle-class culture that was disengaged from the dialectical process of economic history. Thus, artistic introspection, objectivity, and individualism were associated with competition, acquisition, and exploitation in capitalist society. Revolutionary artists must therefore abandon all such tendencies in their art in order to be able to participate in the "creation of a new nucleus of a communal society in which the writer can act fully . . . in a new and mature integrity."[21]

Paradoxically, however, although Le Sueur gives the notion of individual self-identity short shrift in "The Fetish of Being Outside," her description of her own psychological route toward radical identification with the working-classes begins with a distinctly personalized sense of dissatisfaction. She complains that "I do not care for the bourgeois individual that I am. I never cared for it. I want to be integrated in a new and different way as an individual and this I feel can come only from a communal participation which reverses the feeling of a bourgeois writer."[22] Le Sueur is able to overcome her anxiety by creating a psychological opposition between a middle-class and working-class self identity within her own consciousness. Her essay defines her middle-class side as intellectual, creative, and artistic, as well as fully contextualized within a cultural history that is separated from working-class people. In contrast, the facet of her identity that she defines as working-class is organic and romantically a part of the earth in a way that middle-class culture is not. As such, her conception of a political perspective that is working-class is fundamentally detached from the progress of economic history, being dependent instead on the elemental whims of nature. Also, whereas middle-class identity is self-expressive and literary, working-class culture is subconscious and inarticulate. Working-class identity is thus described by Le Sueur as naturally a feeling rather than a rational thought, as a "great body sleeping, stirring, strange and outside."[23] As such, working-class identity is expressed sensually and spiritually, in a way that is detached from the materiality of "the merchant world."[24] In Le Sueur's view, then, identification with working-class culture is a kind of therapy for the middle-class writer, requiring a fundamental reattachment to a primal (working-class) sense of selfhood, in order to cure a particularized feeling of psychological and emotional ennui. Revolutionary awareness is thus described in appropriately romanticized terms, as a longing to regress into a primordial state of bliss:

I feel, I, myself, have rotted and suffered and threshed in this element of the bourgeois class like an organism in a decaying pool with the water evaporating about you and the natural elements of your body and desires in stress and your hungers decaying and rotting and stinking to high heaven.[25]

According to Le Sueur's view in "The Fetish of Being Outside," a middle-class writer must resolve a politicized identity crisis in order to achieve a narrative perspective that is appropriately expressive of working-class identity. Ironically, however, this process is conceived wholly within the self-consciousness of the middle-class writer rather than the working-class subject of the text. Le Sueur has conceptualized working-class identity as ahistorical and inarticulate in relation to a middle-class identity that is self-expressive, although pejoratively "bourgeois." As a result, "unconscious" proletarians are entirely dependent on middle-class writers in order to give a voice to their experiences. Conveniently enough, Meridel Le Sueur has described a system of class politics in "The Fetish of Being Outside" that inscribes a satisfyingly active role for the radical middle-class intellectual, while simultaneously excluding the working-class subject from modes of self-expression that might be personally empowering and politically dangerous.

Events and Words

The internalized dichotomy between working-class and middle-class identity that formed the political consciousness of the radical intellectual was given full expression in proletarian writing. A successful piece of radical reportage or fiction depended on an effective projection of the author's image of working-class identity onto an event such as a strike or a protest rally. At the same time, the narrative process of the text was constructed to show how the middle-class author repressed a perspective that was "bourgeois," and was eventually converted to modes of expression that were defined in the author's mind as specifically working class. That is to say, the radical middle-class author moved from a narrative point of view that was objectively outside the action of a strike or demonstration and became physically a part of it within the text. As such, the middle-class author effectively became the subject of the work she or he was writing. Instead of simply describing events to the reader, the author appeared to be telling the story from the working-class subject's point of view.

In her reportage article, "I Was Marching," Meridel Le Sueur gives an apt description of how an objective, middle-class point of view might be transformed to a subjective and communal, and therefore more working-class perspective:

I have never been in a strike before. It is like looking at something that is happening for the first time and there are no thoughts and no words yet accrued to it. If you come from the middle-class, words are likely to mean more than an event. You are likely to think more about a thing, and the happening will be the size of a pin point and the words around the happening very large, distorting it queerly. It's a case of "Remembrance of Things Past." When you are in the event, you are likely to have a distinctly individualistic attitude, to be only partly there and to care more for the happening afterwards than when it is happening. That is why it is hard for a person like myself and others to be in a strike. . . .

Now in a crisis the word falls away and the skeleton of that action shows in terrific movement.[26]

For Le Sueur, the strike was important precisely because it is an action that she describes as de-individualizing and removed from a particular historical context. Moreover, it was an action that was emotional and instinctive rather than intellectual. Consequently, in order to attain a point of view that is working class, and therefore integrally a part of the strike, Le Sueur had to experience the event as a series of physical sensations rather than an intensely analyzed political process.

The strikers gathered at the headquarters in Minneapolis are described by Le Sueur as a collectively formed body, "dilated to catch every sound over the city."[27] None of them have names or individual identities. As Le Sueur serves them coffee, she does not see each man separately; instead, from a point of view that she decides is working class, she sees "the same tense dirty sweating face, the same body, the same blue shirt and overalls."[28] The strikers do not have feelings, responses, or even senses that function separately from one another. They eat at the same time; they get angry at the same time; if one is injured they are all injured; they move, in Le Sueur's description, like a "living circle close packed for protection . . . thickening, coagulating,"[29] like blood moving through a single, collectively formed body. The strike is an event that is experienced entirely within the identically formed, identically responsive, body of an undifferentiated working-class person. Consequently, Le Sueur considers it necessary to warn her middle-class readers that "if you are to understand anything you must understand it in the muscular event, an action we have not been trained for."[30] Thus, in order to understand a strike, a middle-class person such as Le Sueur, and the readers of her text, must learn not to think; they must simply feel.

In Le Sueur's opinion, at least in "I Was Marching," not thinking was something that came naturally to working-class people. This point becomes apparent when Le Sueur joins the women who are providing food and refreshments for the male strikers. She notes that "the kitchen is organized like a factory . . . each woman has one thing to do."[31] Le Sueur gradually joins the production line of pouring coffee, serving sandwiches, and washing cups. At first she finds the process strange, because, she says, "I have never before worked anonymously."[32] She finds the other women's indifference to her individuality disturbing and somewhat insulting, until she realizes that the women "don't see me because [they] only see what [they] are doing."[33] The working-class women at the strike commissary have been trained for their roles as endlessly efficient and tireless supporters of the strike action, after hours and years of working in the mundane, repetitious, crushing monotony of routine factory labor. In Le Sueur's view, however, their "organization and specialization"[34] at the commissary does not represent a subversion of production line work (although it must certainly have been so). Rather, she sees their work as an expression of the self-sacrificing nature of working-class women, who support their families' well-being whether on a picket line or working on the factory floor. From this perspective, the working-class women at the strike headquarters are not contributing their efforts out of a sense of independently minded political commitment. They are simply fulfilling the duties to which they are most suited —that is, performing mindless labor so as to ensure the survival of their families. Le Sueur confirms that this is her somewhat dubious opinion of the women in the kitchen when after one asks her, "Is your man here?" she feels compelled to lie in response; "peering around as if looking eagerly for someone," she replies, "I don't see him now."[35]

In the course of "I Was Marching," Le Sueur learns to become less middle class—that is, in her terms, less analytical, less rational, less thoughtful, and so more working class. She learns how to react spontaneously, without considering the political consequences or the historical significance of her actions. Instead, she instinctively knows, or rather feels, what is the right thing to do. At the end of the article, the strikers build a barricade and form a protest march. At first Le Sueur hesitates to join in; she still has a sense of middle-class reservation. As the barricade is built she asks, "What are they doing that for?" and receives no answer. Then, as she becomes more involved in the activity of the protest she feels, "suddenly on my very body, I knew what they were doing." Le Sueur's last question to the strikers is, "Could I march?"[36] As she joins the demonstration, she feels no need to speak or think or question the significance of what she is doing. Her response, which she describes as becoming fully a part of the politicized body of working-class identity, is experienced as a new awareness of her physicality and emotionality, separated from, and indeed overcoming, her rationality and her intellect:

The open mouth crying, the nostrils stretched apart . . .

I felt my legs straighten. I felt my feet join in that strange shuffle of thousands of bodies moving with direction, of thousands of feet, and my own breath with the gigantic breath. As if an electric charge has passed through me, my hair stood on end. I was marching.[37]

The separation between working-class identity and middle-class individualized intellectuality is made emphatic by the end of "I Was Marching." In accordance with Le Sueur's view of working-class identity, the strikers hardly ever speak; they never explain what they are doing, either to themselves or to her. There is no sense of how the strike was organized, or how it was negotiated or even why it occurred. Individual strikers do not explain why they joined the strike; there is no indication of what was sacrificed, or of what was at stake for any of the working-class families involved. Le Sueur does not question whether it was a difficult decision for the strikers either to stay at work and get paid, or to remain loyal to the union and the strike cause. Le Sueur apparently did not think it was important to ask what conditions were like at work before the strike, how little the workers were paid, or how long their days were.

These vital questions are irrelevant to Le Sueur's description of the truckers' strike, because her narrative position depends on a projection of an imagined opposition between working-class and middle-class identity that takes place entirely within her own self-consciousness. In order to present her view as a radical diversion from writing she considered "bourgeois," Le Sueur had to believe that working-class responses to a particular economic and social situation were politically innocent, and uncorrupted by thought processes that were abstract and therefore inherently middle class. In so doing, she diverts attention from the problematic fact that, because she is an articulate, literate, educated, middle-class author, she has the power to interpret and record the strike in a form that generally excluded a self-identified working-class point of view. This is not to say that radical journals refused work written by authors who were working class; in fact, the contrary was true, although that policy was largely unsuccessful. Nonetheless, working-class contributors could not have been encouraged by an image of working-class identity that was constructed from a perspective that was exclusively middle class. This experience was compounded for artists from a working-class background since this was an image where, as is clear in "I Was Marching," working-class subjects were systematically denied the ability to speak, to think, to analyze, to write, and to express themselves from a self-identified point of view.

Marginalization from the institutionalized dogma of proletarian fiction was the least problematic consequence of portraying working-class identity as an entirely intuitive and inarticulate event. In another reportage article written about the Minneapolis truckers' strike, "What Happens in a Strike" (1934), Le Sueur adds yet another level of exclusion from forms of literal representation that might have been individually and politically empowering for the working-class subjects of her work. This time, Le Sueur does not describe the strike as if she were a participant in the action. Instead, she describes the event as something real that happens in between, or rather in active defiance of, various textual interpretations of what has occurred.

In "What Happens in a Strike," Le Sueur describes the ways the truckers' strike was communicated to the strikers, to the employers, to the general public, to the government and the police, and to working-class people and union members elsewhere in the United States. Some of the publicity is negative and actively antagonistic to the strike cause. For example, the organization of employers in Minneapolis bought space in local newspapers and advertised the strike to the general public as an unnecessary and politically motivated action, designed to disrupt the consumer-centered life of the city. Having made that assertion, the employers' advertisement made a direct address to the strikers themselves: "Let them beware unless an outraged citizenry here take vigorous measures against them."[38] This unsubtle warning to the strikers also served as an incitement to those who were not directly involved in the dispute. The advertisement's dualistic purpose was intended to create an antagonistic opposition between the strikers on the one hand—represented by the employers as an unruly mob of Communist sympathizers—and the rest of the community, who were addressed by the advertisement as peaceful, fair-minded "citizens." As such, the employers' advertisement demanded that its readers take a side in the strike and, at the same time, offered a judgment on each reply. Consequently, the employers' advertisement misrepresented the progress of the strike—as Le Sueur notes, "the newspapers said that trucking was normal, in reality not a truck was running."[39] At the same time, the employers' financial control of the media meant that they could command the political and ideological dialogue that determined how the general public understood and responded to representations of working-class protest.

In opposition to what might be called capitalist representations of the strike that promised to serve the interests of middle-class Americans, Le Sueur relates the opinion of the union's daily newspaper, *The Organizer*. Here, the editorial line was intended to boost morale by stressing the unity of the strike in Minneapolis, while emphasizing the nationwide support of union members for the common interests of working-class Americans: "Fight like one man till victory. We are not fighting an isolated cause. Ours is the cause of the whole labor movement. Should we be defeated other unions would be chopped down one by one. Fight like one till victory."[40]

Unlike the employers' advertisement, *The Organizer* addresses a single audience of loyal union members. Consequently, the readership's response to the editorial's rallying call is already predetermined within the text. Loyalty to the strike, and to working-class protest in general, is always assumed by the article. In "What Happens in a Strike" Le Sueur aligns herself with the simplistic one-dimensional statement made in *The Organizer*'s editorial. Furthermore, although the progression of Le Sueur's article indicates that she is aware of the economic hierarchies that controlled how the strike was represented in the local media, rather than investigating the ways that such publicity might affect the unity and effectiveness of the protest, she simply dismisses the employers' advertisement as a "red herring."[41] From Le Sueur's perspective, and indeed from her representation of *The Organizer*'s editorial campaign, responses to the employers' advertisement merely constituted the irrelevant reactions of apathetic middle classes or, rarely, the treacherous working classes. In Le Sueur's opinion, because a fully realized, self-identified working-class response to a strike call must always be emotional and reflexive, an intellectual investigation of the multifaceted dialogue that surrounded the strike, and therefore constructed its meaning in the public imagination, was irrelevant. Le Sueur makes this point emphatically in "What Happens in a Strike," when she describes the full expressive power of working-class protest as being hidden behind "a barrage of words,"[42] a literal barrier that included "Conferences. With the labor board. With the employers. With the strikers. Cars speeding with ultimatums, with agreements, disagreements."[43] For Le Sueur, the negotiation processes were as misleading and irrelevant to the cause of working-class protest as the paid advertisements and the editorial interpretations of the employers' organization. Once again, rational analysis and political debate are presented by Le Sueur as anathema to working-class identity and self-expression. In her text, only bourgeois "liberal doctors and lawyers"[44] have faith in a positive outcome to official negotiations. Placed at an objectively bourgeois distance from what Le Sueur portrays as the sensual reality of working-class protest, middle-class sympathy with the strike is described as misdirected and essentially impotent: "Nothing can happen [they say] . . . this will all be settled square and above board. Why this is a civilized city! This will all be settled over the table."[45] In contrast, the working-class strikers are presented as being constricted by an unnatural reliance on rational discussion and negotiation. In Le Sueur's opinion, the strikers are incapable of expressing themselves in the terms defined by literate middle-class culture. Union negotiations and labor board conferences represent forms of communication that were apparently incomprehensible to the physical, emotional, and intuitive sensibilities of working-class people. Thus, a proclamation by the president of the union is particularly significant to Le Sueur: "I can't understand a word of these elegant negotiations. Speak in terms of bread and butter. I'm through listening to words."[46]

In Le Sueur's terms, working-class protest can only be given full expression when it occurs in defiance of middle-class dialogue; thus, the strike is most potent and most inspiring to Le Sueur when "words no longer have any meaning."[47] Furthermore, in order for the strike to end in a victory that is essentially working class, Le Sueur's narrative ensures a result where intellectual speech is defeated. Consequently, after the protest march ends in violence and disaster and "the words start again,"[48] the transcendent physicality of working-class action reveals these words "to be crawling with maggots, so rotten in the warp and woof murders come and go without detection."[49]

Le Sueur's textual sanctification of the bloodshed and death that resulted from the protest march is romantic, and might have served as a source of inspiration for any further confrontations with police authorities during the strike. Certainly, "What Happens in a Strike" fits the terms of class struggle as they were defined by the Communist Party, and the outcome—the creation of a working-class martyr after the recreation of a glorious battle—is an archetypical example of proletarian literature. However, in order to reach a successful political conclusion, the discursive progression of Le Sueur's text must also ascribe the capitulation of articulate working-class protest to the manipulations of capitalism, concluding, inevitably, with a working-class silence that is as emphatic as the middle-class words she condemns.

Le Sueur's celebration of action in opposition to words denies the necessity of working-class participation in the discourse that surrounded the strike, and subsequently refuses the possibility of a fully articulate form of working-class self-expression. As such, the employers' advertisement determined the construction of Le Sueur's essay in the same way that it set the terms of the strike as it occurred in Minneapolis. From a position of economic power, the employers were able to construct a view of working-class protest that could be easily detected and defeated by rational middle-class Americans. The progression of Le Sueur's article conforms completely to this perspective. The strikers are removed from the discourse about the strike—in accordance with *The Organizer* and the president of the union—and are placed by Le Sueur entirely within the action of the strike. As a result, the only form of self-expression available to the strikers is physical instinct. During the march the protesters were fired upon by the police and one of the men was killed. Le Sueur's estimation of the political significance of this event is measured, as I have shown, by the defeat of discussion about the strike, and is described most significantly in terms of the female body: "The skirts of the women had blood on them. The floor of the strike headquarters had blood on it."[50]

In response to the murder of the striker, the union arranged another demonstration at the victim's funeral. Ironically, *The Organizer* describes this event as some kind of victory for the union. Le Sueur notes the paper's headline: "WORKERS' BLOOD IS SHED. THE FIGHT HAS JUST BEGUN. THE FIRST MARTYR."[51] The conclusion of "What Happens in a Strike" celebrates the striker's death in the same way, as an event that paradoxically represented the ultimate expression of working-class protest. Naturally then, the dead striker, Henry Ness, is the only working-class person to be named by Le Sueur in her article. He has achieved the status of martyr and therefore he can be afforded an individuality and a personal history. The living strikers, in contrast, "have no names except the name of sorrow and the name of action."[52]

The conclusion of "What Happens in a Strike" highlights the dangerous futility of Le Sueur's insistence on defining working-class protest as an inarticulate event occurring as an intuitive response to a middle-class discourse which, because it is supported by the economic hierarchies of capitalist society, ultimately defines working-class self-expression. By disengaging working-class protest from the dialogue that surrounded the strike, Le Sueur's narrative leads inevitably into a silence, which however gloriously described, is literally dead. Even physical confrontation on these terms is proved ineffective. Significantly, the workers' final protest march at Henry Ness's funeral is described by Le Sueur as "a drama forming from deep instinctive and unified forces of real and terrible passion."[53] The power of working-class emotion and reaction has thus unfolded into a staged performance, choreographed "in meticulous order,"[54] which simultaneously reconstitutes the monologic power of capitalist middle-class discourse, transforming working-class self-expression into a ritualistic nonevent.

Bodies and Texts

The roots of Meridel Le Sueur's view of working-class identity as essentially illiterate, although positively intuitive, lie in the development of her feminist consciousness—a perspective that, like her socialism and literary radicalism, had its inspiration within her family history. Before she became a committed socialist, Le Sueur's mother, Marian, led an unconventional life for a woman. During an abusive first marriage, Marion realized that, as a woman, she had "no property and no civil rights"[55] under Texas state law. Likewise, her children were considered to be merely chattels of her husband's estate. In order to escape this situation, Marian, in Le Sueur's words, "kidnapped us in the night and fled North like a black slave woman."[56] Beginning a new life in Iowa and settling later in Minnesota, Marian Le Sueur's independent feminist spirit was supported by her new husband. However, Le Sueur's writing places her mother's inspiration, and the seeds of her own feminism, firmly within the cloistered body and steadfast mind of her puritanical, pioneer grandmother, Antoinette Lucy.

Unlike Marian, Antoinette's "feminism" grew out of moralistic religious commitment rather than from reading the words of Emma Goldman and Ellen Key. Like Marian, she divorced her husband, acting not in defiance of patriarchal law but in support of what she considered to be God's moral codes. Having vowed "she would die on the day of his death," Le Sueur's grandmother left her husband in response to what she considered to be his moral weakness, "because he was drinking up all the farms her father left her."[57] The protection of her property and her economic independence was thus an extension of her faith in Christian temperance.

Antoinette's fervent, gun-toting activities in the Women's Christian Temperance Union confirmed Le Sueur's presentation of her as one of the first wave of morally committed feminists. According to Le Sueur, Antoinette firmly believed that as long as women were pious and protected their virtue, they were naturally morally superior to men. This rigid dictate enabled Antoinette to escape an unhappy marriage and inspired her to survive as a self-sufficient woman until her death. On the negative side, she was, in Le Sueur's description, like a puritanical fortress. The only songs she knew were hymns. The only book she read was the Bible. Such was her fear of her own sensuality and physicality that she bathed only while wearing a voluminous petticoat. Reflecting this image, Antoinette appears often in Le Sueur's fiction as a forbidding but inspirational presence. Nonetheless, she was unimpressed and outraged by Le Sueur's literary activities. She often destroyed Le Sueur's work before she had read it, exclaiming: "All my life I've concealed the unsayable. Now you're going to destroy it all by saying it."[58] As a result, revealing what her grandmother had concealed—her body, her sexuality, any kind of emotional expression that did not lead directly and moralistically toward a puritanical God—became an integral part of Le Sueur's feminist project, a perspective that was intrinsically linked to her writing about working-class subjects. At the same time as her feminist moralism enshrined the superiority of women over men, Antoinette's puritanical fervor condemned the ethnic working-class members of the community—particularly the women—for their licentiousness. Consequently, from a young age Le Sueur was attracted to what she perceived as the liberating energies and sheer physicality of those cultures. While her grandmother's independence and strength of will was based on repression and constraint, the Irish, Polish, Norwegian, and Finnish rural working-class women seemed to embody personal freedom and sexual energy. As a child, Le Sueur took part in all the rituals and celebrations that were foreign to her. She describes herself as having been delighted by the "rich foods," the dance groups, and the marching bagpipe bands.[59] Le Sueur's response also links this spirited behavior with communal political activity: she remembers how, during a Saint Patrick's Day parade an Irish man, "three sheets to the wind," recited the last speech of Robert Emmet. As she listened, Le Sueur recalls herself as having been inspired to "a riotous temperament different from my grandmother's."[60]

In relation to this repressive piety, the communal sensibilities of ethnic working-class cultures in Le Sueur's town seemed to emanate from those activities her grandmother judged as being particularly carnal. Le Sueur describes, for example, dances "so colorful and varied . . . so sensual and beautiful. They freed me from severe puritan sexual rigidity, from relegating pleasure to guilt and sin."[61] Bowing to her grandmother's classist and racist opinion that bright colors were only worn by "Polish whores," Le Sueur was permitted to go to the dance only if she wore a white dress rather than a red or yellow one. Defying her, however, Le Sueur also "rubbed wet crepe paper on my cheeks and blackened my eyes with kitchen matches," so as to appear "voluptuous" for her partner: a farm boy with huge forearms.[62]

In contrast to Le Sueur, the girls at the dance are described as being emotionally and physically uninhibited. They laughed "too loud" and embraced each other just "to show how good it was to embrace."[63] Completely fitting her grandmother's image, Le Sueur describes the girls as colorfully dressed, drinking beer and moonshine, and as being unconcerned by men "feeling you up" as they danced.[64] In the final paragraph, Le Sueur recalls a simultaneous sense of horror and attraction to this behavior:

> As the night got deeper and the fiddlers hotter, we were flung into the men's arms, back and forth, a weave of human bodies. I couldn't tell one from the other. A girl took me outside with her. The girls lifted their skirts on one side of the field, and the boys stood with their backs to us on the other. I never heard such laughter or sensed such dangerous meaning in the night, in what took place in the woods, when the dancers returned with curious smiles and leaves in their hair. We seemed on the edge of some abysmal fire. But they seemed unafraid, plunging into the heat and the danger as if into a bonfire of roses.
>
> I was never the same again.[65]

Following one of the girls at the dance, Le Sueur is led to the brink of behavior she has been taught will lead inevitably to hell and damnation. Nevertheless, the realization that women could possess a sense of sexual bravado and emotional freedom without being punished was inspirational for Le Sueur, and since she was enlightened particularly by witnessing the behavior of working-class women, this perspective became linked inextricably with her representation of class identity. Consequently, the girls and boys at the dance are described in precisely the same terms as the women and men on the picket line in "What Happens in a Strike." Similarly, Le Sueur's enthusiastic participation is dependent on the same kind of perception and representation of working-class identity—at the dance, particularly working-class female identity—in her writing. The girls at the dance are described as an undifferentiated mass of human sexual energy, acting spontaneously without fear, knowledge, or understanding of the consequences of their behavior. The contrast between the pure physical sensuality of these women and the terror the body represented for Le Sueur's grandmother imbued Le Sueur's recollection with political—and feminist—significance. At the same time, it was the physical freedom ascribed to working-class women's bodies at the dance that to Le Sueur represented the inspiration for working-class protest as a whole. Thus, by placing working-class women subjects at the center of her radical writing, Le Sueur tried to write about feminism and class politics in a way that related to her own personal history. In so doing, however, the self-expressive identities of working-class women were often confined to the spontaneous reactions of their emotions and the physical demands of their bodies.

In Le Sueur's radical writing, the bodies of working-class women contain the testimonies of their lived experience, of their economic status and their material circumstances. Often, the resonant meaning she sees as being intrinsic to their physical appearance is the first thing Le Sueur notes about them. For example, in "Our Fathers," Penelope's grandmother is described as having a body that has been destroyed by years of factory work and by multiple pregnancies: "[H]er broken pelvis hung half to her knees from childbearing, from working in textile mills, from berry picking and tobacco-hoeing."[66] Despite this physical devastation, however, the grandmother's body is also a vessel that holds her personal history as a rural working-class woman. To this end, Le Sueur describes her as having "great flanks" and "thick flesh"[67] beneath which hides the story of a life that was indiscernible to Penelope, who asks herself: "What was buried there? What girl? What bright youth?"[68] Ultimately, the grandmother's story is never quite made tangible for Penelope or the reader. Le Sueur describes the grandmother's face as being "caught in the torso like a burr,"[69] unable to express fully the experiences and thoughts that lie buried in her desecrated body.

Occasionally in her early writing, Le Sueur retains this sense of incomprehension between the working-class subjects of her work and herself as a middle-class woman author. Notably, in "The Laundress" (1927), Le Sueur describes a young girl's view of Mrs. Kretch, an efficient and placid Polish woman who cleans her mother's house. Mrs. Kretch is portrayed as "stout," strong-armed, and despite her apparant satisfaction with her servant status, as having a "militant feminism in common" with the narrator's mother.[70] The gender connection between maid and mistress is described in outrageously classist terms by Le Sueur as a "peculiar devotion which often springs up between a very simple and vital woman and a complex intellectual one."[71] Elaine Hedges does not pick up on Le Sueur's patronizing tone; nevertheless she does point out that the portrait of Mrs. Kretch retains within it "some further secret meaning that she [Le Sueur] cannot grasp."[72]

The mystery of Mrs. Kretch's full identity is first described in physical terms, as a "foreign look" and "a secret air"[73] that seem to emanate from her appearance. Later in the story, the feeling of physical mystery is expressed more clearly in a dialogue between Mrs. Kretch and her daughter, Hilda. As Hilda sets the table, Mrs. Kretch tells the narrator that her daughter is an artist. She has painted some watercolors that are displayed in Mrs. Kretch's home. Having admitted her daughter's talent, she calls her in to explain her work. In so doing, the narrator feels that Mrs. Kretch "had uttered phenomenal secret words."[74] Her sense of curiosity is described by Le Sueur:

The girl came in and stood looking at her mother. They looked at each other, held each other secretly. I felt very near to solving the enigma of the woman and the girl. My heart beat, I felt excited for some unknown reason. Yet, it eluded me, and I came no nearer to the secret. I could not understand.[75]

Later, Hilda studies to be a graphic designer, and produces work where "colors and lines startled one unexpectedly, with something hidden and exciting, exactly in the same manner as the appearance of Mrs. Kretch."[76] Here, Le Sueur has identified a continuity between the secret silence of Mrs. Kretch and the creativity of her daughter. Although the exact nature of Mrs. Kretch's mysterious appearance is never made clear in the narrative, Le Sueur sets out a discursive space where the self-expression of a working-class daughter is nurtured by her mother in ways that are not immediately clear to the middle-class girl narrating the story, nor to the (generally middle-class) readers. At the same time, Le Sueur does not portray a form of self-expression that is defined as recognizably or stereotypically working-class. Instead, the mystery of Mrs. Kretch's identity and the strange beauty of her daughter's work provoke a response that is disturbing and challenging to a middle-class point of view, leading to a questioning about the circumstances of working-class lives, and the lives of working-class women in particular. Introducing the possibility of a dialogue that is represented as beginning from a working-class perspective, the narrator concludes her inquiry with an unanswered question: "Perhaps that was the secret thing. . . . One cannot with certainty trace these things, but surely great expression has somewhere a beginning, a vague and terrible budding."[77]

The radical position in "The Laundress" is undercut somewhat by the end of the story. Mrs. Kretch dies without ever fully articulating the secrets of her identity. The narrative concludes, rather, in the same way as the protest march in "What Happens in a Strike," with a coffin lid closing over Mrs. Kretch's face, the possibility of her self-expression entombed forever within her dead body. Conversely, as Hedges notes, Le Sueur continued her writing about working-class women so as to articulate "the ungraspable meaning"[78] that she had identified, and subsequently buried, in Mrs. Kretch's life. Thus, while the dialogic possibilities Le Sueur has inscribed in her narrative are closed off for the working-class woman subject, she, as the middle-class author of the work, can continue the narrative. Significantly, then, "The Laundress" ends with a statement: "[T]he body sinks into the ground it lies upon, the light fades within it, and there is nothing more visible."[79] This is an image that, even as it marks the end of Mrs. Kretch's life in the story, also highlights the perspective from which Le Sueur continued to write about working-class women subjects. In most of her work after 1927, working-class women were represented according to her own proletarian and feminist interpretations of the details of her subjects' visible physicality. As the conclusion of "The Laundress" shows, "bearing witness," as Le Sueur put it, was fundamentally about looking rather than interacting: if there was nothing left to see, there was nothing left to say about the lives of working-class women.

Following her mission to uncover and articulate the secret spaces that she portrayed as intrinsic to Mrs. Kretch's working-class identity, Le Sueur went on to write extensively about working-class women's lives. At the same time, in order to resolve the uncertainties in her representations of working-class women subjects, Le Sueur began to write about the bodies of working-class women, not as containers of a personal history to be uncovered, but as extrinsic symbolic expressions of their individual identities, their material circumstances, and their political points of view. For example, the eponymous "Eroded Woman" (1948) is described initially in terms of her broken-down body: "She was spare, clad in a kind of flour sack with a hole cut in the middle, showing the hulk of her bones and also the peculiar shyness, tenderness and dignity of a woman who has borne children, been much alone, and is still strong set against rebuff."[80] Unlike Mrs. Kretch, whose body was covered, almost disguised in layers of long black clothing, the eroded woman is naked except for a virtually transparent flour sack dress. Her body is exposed so that Le Sueur can decipher and explain the exact political meaning represented by her huge bones and sagging skin. From this first image, without the woman having uttered a single word, Le Sueur can establish that the woman is shy and tender, that she has borne numerous children, and also that her physical tenacity has ensured her future survival. The woman's home is similarly depicted, not simply as a symbolic reflection, but as physically a part of the woman's anatomy, an "extension of her gothic body."[81] The historical, economic, and political contexts that formed the foundation of her material circumstances are thus presented by Le Sueur as immediately tangible from the evidence of her physical appearance.

The eroded woman goes on to tell Le Sueur all about her family's struggle to establish a mineworkers' union; about her own working life raising ten children, traveling around the country in search of work, supporting and tending two husbands, both of whom died from diseases related to mining. Throughout the story, the woman defines her experiences in terms of her role as a wife and mother. She supported her husband's commitment to the mineworkers' union without a second thought, and without properly comprehending why. As she explains to Le Sueur:

"[M]y man always was a union man and I don't always rightly understant, but I am with him till the day I die and his thinking is my thinking."[82]

As the woman's history unfolds, the physical and emotional basis of her working-class identity is made increasingly clear. The woman describes her husband's long painful death from "chat hemorrhage" as ending, finally, when he inhaled and eventually drowned in his own blood. The woman's son recalls his father's death in the same way: "He held his breath and let his blood choke him and then he could lie down forever."[83] Significantly, the successful establishment of a mine-workers' union is described in similar terms by the son as "the right of our [that is, working-class] blood."[84] The difference between working-class oppression and working-class empowerment is defined by the eroded woman and her son as the difference between a flow of blood that coagulates and kills, and blood that circulates through the healthy, unionized body of mineworkers. Le Sueur's emphasis on images of blood as an alternately destructive and life-giving force relates directly to her representation of working-class identity and struggle as physical emanations from the politicized bodies of working-class women.

Reflecting Le Sueur's viewpoint, the eroded woman goes on to define her husband's death not only in terms of bleeding, but also in relation to the ways her work as a mother has been corrupted by her family's poverty. Her husband's life ends fatalistically, "like all the babies born so hard and dying early."[85] Her statement is compounded by her son who exclaims, "I'd kill a child of mine before he'd work in the mines."[86] For working-class women, the natural cycle of life, from sex to pregnancy to birth and nurturing, is corrupted in a murderous capitalist context. As such, the working-class woman's body is completely politicized in "The Eroded Woman," becoming the site where working-class identity is formed, and representing the place where working-class self expression is most politically resonant.

The limitations of representing working-class identity as purely centered on the female body are shown quite clearly in another reportage article, "Women Know a Lot of Things" (1937). Here, Le Sueur shows the physical, emotional, and sexual ways that working-class women formulate a political understanding of their material circumstances: "They pick it up at its source in the human body, in the making of the body, and the feeding and nurturing of it day in and day out. They know how much a body weighs, and how much blood and toil goes into the making of even a poor body."[87]

The opposition between textual expression and bodily feeling is emphasized by Le Sueur's later citation of the concerns of a young Spanish radical that after their recent enfranchisement, the "peasant women" of Spain might not vote for the left-wing United People's Front. Le Sueur dismisses these worries, asserting that the party would receive most of the vote, not because Spanish working-class women were able to understand particular issues and make politically informed choices between fascism and democracy, but because:

They voted with their hands, their feet, the knowledge bred and seeped in sun-drenched labor, in every bone and muscle, in grief in the night, and terror, of hours walking behind the plow, their sweat dropping into the furrows, birthing children on straw with only the priest to ease the pain.[88]

Since, in Le Sueur's view, the political consciences of working-class women were founded on pure feeling rather than intellectual thought processes, it was unnecessary to explain the political complexities of the Spanish election. Indeed, Le Sueur's image of politicized feeling and ideologized emotion within radicalized female bodies suggests that education and information might be detrimental to working-class interests. Rather, in "Women Know a lot of Things," the self-identified point of view of working-class women is literalized through descriptions of their biological experiences. Le Sueur presents the bodies of working-class women as texts to be read and interpreted in the same way as a government report or a newspaper article; thus, not only is female working-class identity contained entirely within her body in Le Sueur's writing, but that body is itself transformed into a series of politically resonant processes decontextualized from the material circumstances and the experiences of individual working-class women. Consequently, in "The Dark of the Time" (1956), a working-class woman's body is described by Le Sueur as being "like a great poem to read,"[89] and in "Women Know a Lot of Things," Le Sueur notes that for working-class women, "hunger and want and terror are a Braille that hands used to labor, and close to sources can read in any language."[90]

The complete textualization of working-class women's bodies in Le Sueur's writing enables her to conflate the tensions between proletarian politics and feminist consciousness in her narratives. As the middle-class author of rational, intellectual, articulate, political texts, Le Sueur was inevitably distanced by the pejorative class terms of her narratives. However, by assuming a perspective that was feminist as well as class conscious, Le Sueur could, by way of her biological communality with the working-class women subjects of her texts, understand and interpret working-class self-expression for a middle-class audience. By inscribing physicality, specifically female sexuality, pregnancy, birth, and motherhood at the core of working-class identity, Le Sueur was able to transcend the intellectual textuality of middle-class expression and write about class experience from an essentially female point of view.

Women on the Breadlines

Le Sueur's feminism was fundamental to her representation of working-class women subjects in her radical writing. Her insistence on politicizing women's lives was important, and in some ways subversive, within the frustratingly macho context of proletarian literature. The unique insight that her feminism provided is particularly evident in several of her reportage articles, notably "Women Are Hungry" (1934) and "Women on the Breadlines" (1932). In both of these essays, the insight that Le Sueur's feminism brings to her representations of working-class women reveals how economic oppression affected women's lives in ways that were specific to their femininity rather than their working-class identity. More important, Le Sueur tried to highlight ways that these women defied repressive and moralistic rules governing their behavior, and transformed them into tactics for self-empowerment and protest.

In "Women on the Breadlines," Le Sueur writes about working-class women who are struggling to find employment, money, food, love, happiness, and freedom in a city where municipal government and relief agencies colluded to deny, first, their poverty, and second, their efforts to express themselves as individual citizens. Unlike rural poverty, which was portrayed as a uniquely female experience in government photographs, poverty in the city was officially understood and treated as if it were a quintessential male problem. As Le Sueur suggests:

It's one of the great mysteries of the city where women go when they are out of work and hungry. There are not many women in the breadline. There are no flop houses for women as there are for men, where a bed can be had for a quarter or less. You don't see women lying on the floor at the mission in the free flops. They obviously don't sleep in the jungle or under newspapers in the park. There is no law I suppose against their being in these places but the fact is they rarely are.[91]

Against this background of silent invisibility, Le Sueur's project in "Women on the Breadlines" is to uncover ways working-class women survived what she calls the peculiar experience of "city hunger."[92] Away from the breadlines and hostels, the only place poor women could gather was at the Domestic Employment Bureau. They turned up each day knowing that there would be no work, and even though they realized that there would never be a job for any one of them, they will continue to turn up every day. All kinds of women arrive at the Bureau—married women, single mothers, young girls, old women, educated women and, in Le Sueur's words, "real peasants."[93] Each of them recognizes the futility of her daily ritual, but Le Sueur emphasizes the necessity of it. Waiting at the bureau each day is the only meaningful, vaguely self-assertive, thing that these women can do. The conspiracy of hope that exists between them disguises the relentless monotony of poverty. The whole of these women's lives, all of their physical, emotional, and psychological energies, is taken up with worry about what to do simply to survive their material circumstances, where the next meal is coming from, where the next dime will come from, where they are going to spend the night, how they are going to survive the winter, what was there left to sell. For the women sitting at the Employment Bureau, survival—physical and mental—is dependent on maintaining a facade of normality. So, they turn up each day hopeful that they will find a job. They try to look ready for employment. Their faces are "brightly scrubbed,"[94] they conceal their pale hungry faces with rouge, they mend the runs in their stockings— but, as Le Sueur shows, the quiet desperation that lies behind their thin disguises sometimes explodes. One day, a girl who like all the other women at the bureau has turned up regularly each day throughout the summer, finally cracks, "stamping her feet and screaming . . . You've got to give me something."[95] Her outburst is not only a sign of the realities of poverty that are concealed behind the polite atmosphere of repressed futility at the Employment Bureau; the reaction of the woman in charge also highlights the complicit necessity for the authorities to maintain the smokescreen that there is still hope for these women. Le Sueur notes that the woman in charge, who is normally set apart from the unemployed women by a wire cage, is also tormented by the pressure of repressing the realities of female poverty—so much so that she has had nightmares and "couldn't eat sometimes."[96] The young girl's "hysterical" outburst breaks through the wire cage that surrounds the woman in charge, destroying the flimsy appearance of hope and exposing the desperate situation that has engulfed these women's lives. The revelation lasts just for an instant. Both women face each other "in a rage, both helpless, helpless."[97] The woman in charge reacts first, not to acknowledge the young girl's exasperation, but to reconstruct the facade of normalcy, to reassert the necessity of "keeping up appearances": "Why don't you clean your shoes?" she demands, "We can't recommend you like that."[98] Le Sueur uses this exchange to highlight the ideological constructions that lay at the foundation of female poverty during the Depression. The woman in charge redirects blame, from institutional conspiracy and neglect, back onto the young girl, claiming that her poverty is her own personal responsibility, and that her inability to find work is the result of her own individual failure. Le Sueur makes this point emphatic as she shows how the young girl's outburst affects the rest of the poor women at the bureau. They are not awakened with realization, nor are they moved to express a similar sense of outrage and protest. Instead they "sat docilely, their eyes to the ground,"[99] quietly accepting their fate, and ashamed of their own complicity in its sealing.

In "Women on the Breadlines," Le Sueur appears to be describing an experience of poverty that is both class and gender specific. However, in another similar reportage article, "Women Are Hungry," she suggests that the ideological imperatives that force poverty underground in the city can cross class boundaries while still remaining an exclusively female experience. Nancy Sanderson is from a respectable, all-American, middle-class family. She had been working as a teacher but lost her job, so she has been forced to apply for relief work. Le Sueur explains that in order to get relief employment, a teacher had to prove to the state that he or she was destitute. Nancy Sanderson is destitute and starving, but according to official definitions, she does not appear to be. She struggles to maintain the look of middle-classness. She still goes to dinner with her friends, but "she eats so much . . . that it generally makes her sick afterwards."[100] She wears a lot of rouge so that she doesn't look hungry. When she goes to the state house she wears a "light Spring suit," all the time watching "to see that [her] elbows did not come through and that [her] last pair of silk stockings did not spring into a run."[101] Nancy Sanderson conforms to the standards of appearance required of a lady teacher when she arrives at the State House, but she does not look destitute: "[S]he looked all right. To look at her you would have thought she was alright."[102] Nancy Sanderson's middle-class appearance does not convince the man at the State House that she qualifies for relief employment. His hysterical reaction echoes the rage of the woman in charge of the Employment Bureau in "Women on the Breadlines," "You've got to prove it, don't you understand that, you've got to prove it . . . You've got to prove it."[103] The confrontation ends with Nancy Sanderson's fatalistic acceptance of an impossible situation. She leaves the office and "a silence followed her," an emptiness that is quietly acknowledged by the rest of the unemployed women in the office. Le Sueur concludes with a phrase that echoes the reaction of the unemployed women in "Women on the Breadlines": "[T]he people spoke to her in the common silence of hunger."[104]

The narrative similarities between Nancy Sanderson and the "hysterical" girl in "Women on the Breadlines" highlights the paradoxical communality between working-class and middle-class women, which Le Sueur portrays as their peculiarly female experience of poverty. The young girl in "Women on the Breadlines" did not look presentable enough to impress potential employers; she looked distastefully poor. Conversely, Nancy Sanderson did not look poor enough to qualify for a relief job. In both cases, social institutions and government agencies conspired to marginalize women's poverty, hiding the facts in an official discourse that excludes female participation. Le Sueur does provide another dimension to the continuing dialogue that actively denied the existence of poor women. Significantly, however, this avenue of protest and self-empowerment is presented as available only to the working-class women subjects of "Women on the Breadlines." While Nancy Sanderson leaves the relief office in a fatalistic silence that ends with her own self-destruction, the poor working-class women in "Women on the Breadlines" find ways to defy, reject, and transform the patrician rules and moralist codes that govern their behavior. They are able to act where Nancy Sanderson could only accept her fate, by following the impulses of their bodily desires.

The working-class women in "Women on the Breadlines" do not behave as "the virgin women who dispense charity"[105] demand that the "deserving poor" behave. Instead, some of the women seduce men into taking them to the movies, exchanging the pleasure of their company for an hour or two's warmth and psychological escape in the afternoon. Le Sueur notes that for some women, being pregnant and deciding to keep the child is the ultimate form of protest against a society that would prefer poor women be sterilized rather than have children they cannot afford to raise. Similarly, the same women react against the self-righteous advice of social workers who criticize poor women for not eating the recommended "oranges and one quart of milk a day"[106] required if a child is to be born healthy. Unable to afford such basic items, in "Women Are Hungry" Mabel decides to fulfill her desire for luxury in a situation that tries to enforce the impossible demands of practicality and correct behavior: she "[turns] down chicken dinners and [asks] for spice cakes."[107]

Le Sueur highlights this impulse for extravagance as one of the few ways working-class women could maintain a sense of pride, individuality, and creative self-expression. Also in "Women Are Hungry," some young women use all their free provisions to make cakes from recipes advertised in ladies' journals, "then they eat cake for a week and have nothing the next three weeks, but it is worth it."[108] Le Sueur describes an identical impulse among the working-class women in "Women on the Breadlines." In a passage that is unique in radical writing, Le Sueur describes how working-class women struggle to find a sense of self-identity in a consumer capitalist culture that generally refuses their existence:

No one saves their money . . . a little money and these foolish young things buy a hat, a dollar for breakfast, a bright scarf. And they do. If you've ever been without money or food, something very strange happens when you get a bit of money, a kind of madness. You don't care. You can't remember that you had no money before, that the money will be gone. You can remember nothing but that there is the money for which you have been suffering. Now here it is. A lust takes hold of you. You see food in the windows. In imagination you eat hugely: you taste a thousand meals. You look in windows. Colors are brighter: you buy something to dress up in. An excitement takes hold of you. You know it is suicide but you can't help it. You must have food, dainty, splendid food, and a bright hat so once again you feel blithe, rid of that ratty gnawing shame.[109]

Within the pejorative discourse that defines female poverty in "Women on the Breadlines and "Women Are Hungry," buying a hat, dressing in bright colors, eating fancy cakes, and going to the movies might be considered self-defining actions for working-class women. However, Le Sueur's interpretation of those acts presents impulsive purchasing and flamboyant defiance of middle-class morality as yet more examples of the way poor working-class women were seduced and corrupted by the circumstances of their poverty, and their subsequent struggle to survive in an urban, consumer-driven culture.

Working-class women's lives, and most important for Le Sueur, working-class women's bodies, were completely commodified by the demands of "city hunger." Women were forced to sell their bodies, their affections, and their self-consciousness in order to get by. Their actions sometimes seem innocuous, for example when Bernice asks men she meets in the park to give her a loan so that she can pay her rent. Occasionally, Le Sueur presents these situations as signs of a kind of solidarity between working-class women and men: "[S]ometimes a girl facing the night without shelter will approach a man for lodging. . . . I have known girls to sleep on a pallet without molestation and be given breakfast in the morning."[110] Le Sueur's insistent tone would seem to belie what must have been the reality of these apparently selfless acts. Certainly, her own portrait of the city as a dehumanizing urban jungle suggests that such generosity would have been the exception rather than the rule.

Most clearly, Le Sueur shows that working-class women left without jobs and shelter were forced to sell their bodies and their sexuality for money. Most notably in "Women on the Breadlines," when Ellen no longer turns up at the Employment Bureau, a friend reveals that she has found another, more lucrative, source of income. In order to get food, Ellen shows off her legs to cooks at various restaurants. In order to get money, she lifts up her skirt in front of "some men gathered in the alley";[111] they each throw down a coin in exchange for a closer look at her body. For this Ellen earns two dollars and a "swell breakfast" for herself and her friend.[112] Susan Sipple has suggested that Ellen's display constitutes a "transgressive" act, whereby her body "stands as a sign of the failure of capitalism and patriarchal control."[113] In Sipple's view, Ellen's display represents a "subversive action [that] has the potential to effect change."[114] This interpretation is useful in relation to this particular scene if it is taken out of context from the rest of Le Sueur's article, and indeed, the subversion that Sipple identifies would seem to corroborate the radical potential that appears to be evident in the other examples of working-class women's defiance I have already mentioned. However, Le Sueur's sees no positive value in Ellen's display, and her narrative ultimately refutes Sipple's claim. In Le Sueur's view, placed, as it is, for sale in front of an appreciative paying audience, Ellen's show is no more a subversive act in a capitalist culture than is buying a new hat or a beautiful scarf. Ellen is displaying herself in the same way that silk dresses and fancy cakes are displayed in shop windows in the city streets. She makes herself attractive in order to seduce potential customers. The captivated male audience can purchase a look at Ellen's body just as a poor woman can indulge in an impulse buy. For Le Sueur, both actions are elements constituting the facade of consumerism that prevents poor women from realizing the abject realities of their situation and, simultaneously, absolves economic, social, and political institutions from any blame. Selling one's body or choosing not to have children are not positive actions for Le Sueur; both are evidence of the emotional, physical, and sexual malignancy that poverty has enforced onto women's bodies. Even women's psyches are transformed into commercial products to be co-opted by consumer capitalism. In Le Sueur's novel, *The Girl*, for example, Clara's awareness of her economic deprivations and her physical deterioration is lessened by her addiction to the fantasies she finds in movies, cheap novels and ladies' magazines:

Clara says everybody can get along if they try. . . . She says though she will have enough money someday, and she will get married and sing in the choir and play bridge on Sundays with the best people. Or she might get a typewriter business in a swanky hotel and wear black dresses with white collars and cuffs and see that everyone comes to work on time.[115]

Similarly in "Women on the Breadlines," Bernice, a large Polish woman, is described by Le Sueur as suffering from loneliness and "lack of talk."[116] Bernice is capable of expressing herself beautifully, but in her poverty-stricken isolation no one will listen to her "magical" stories. When Bernice first came to the city she had many hopes and expectations; "She had dreamed of having a little house or a houseboat perhaps with a spot of ground for a few chickens."[117] Now her consciousness has been taken over completely by the commercial seductions to be found in the city. She goes window shopping and her mind is mesmerized by the city's bright colors and different sounds. She goes to picture shows, as Le Sueur notes, "Sometimes she goes to five shows in one day, or she sits through one the entire day until she knows the dialogue by heart."[118] The whole of Bernice's self-expression and identity is caught up in imaginary conversations she sees in the movies. In Le Sueur's opinion Bernice has been forced to sell her body, mind, and soul in order to survive the city's commercial culture.

In this context, then, the central image of female poverty in "Women on the Breadlines" is not, as Sipple suggests, Ellen performing seductive dances for money or food; nor is it the image of women dressing defiantly in bright colors. Rather, it is the description that follows immediately afterwards, a stark image of what it feels like for a poor woman to sell her clothes, and then, after everything is sold, her body:

Like every commodity now, the body is difficult to sell and the girls say you're lucky if you can get fifty cents. . . . Perhaps it would make it clear if one were to imagine having to go out on the street to sell, say, one's overcoat. Suppose you have to sell your coat so you can have breakfast and a place to sleep, say, for fifty cents. You decide to sell your only coat. You take it off and put it on your arm. That street, that has before been just a street now becomes a mart, something entirely different. You must approach someone now and admit you are destitute and are now selling your clothes, your most intimate possessions. Everyone will watch you talking to the stranger showing him your overcoat, what a good coat it is. People will stop and watch curiously. You will be quite naked on the street. It is even harder to sell one's self, more humiliating.[119]

This description suggests that no matter how a working-class woman tries to maintain a semblance of normality, or even express a small measure of protest, ultimately she is naked, exposed, humiliated, and alone. She has no friends. There is no sense of community between poor women. As Le Sueur notes, "[A] woman always asks a man for help. Rarely another woman."[120] Instead, the poor women try helplessly to recreate the secure environment of marriage, children, and family. Hence, the poverty in "Women on the Breadlines" is not just female poverty, but specifically the poverty of unattached women—single or else estranged from their families. Without evidence of starving children to accompany her, a working-class woman had no social significance, she made herself invisible, shutting herself in a room eating "only a cracker a day . . . as quiet as a mouse so there are no social statistics about her."[121] As a result, these women advance their own demise; in Le Sueur's words, "[T]hey are like certain savage tribes who, when they have been conquered refuse to breed."[122]

Significantly, then, the last woman to be described by Le Sueur in "Women on the Breadlines," Mrs. Gray, is the mother of six children. In the struggle to ensure her family's survival, Mrs. Gray has been reduced to an appearance that is less than human, more than naked—her entire body is an open wound, "a great puckered scar."[123] In such a state, according to Le Sueur, Mrs. Gray becomes "a living spokesman for the futility of labor"[124] even though she never says a word. Her appearance is sufficient testimony of the wasted, aborted significance of a life lived in poverty, unable to achieve the fulfillment and happiness that is—centrally, in Le Sueur's view—the ultimate expression of a working-class woman's identity. In this sense, in Mrs. Gray's decrepit body, the class politics of "Women on the Breadlines" are given their fullest, most exclusively feminist, expression. Alone in the city, separated from men—except as customers for sex—unable to fulfill the destiny contained in their bodies, condemned to "the suffering of endless labor without dream,"[125] their fate is, in Le Sueur's opinion, a life of work ending without the possibility of love, emotional stability, sexual fulfillment, and healthy babies.

The bodies of working-class women are co-opted and corrupted precisely because they live in an environment that ensures their silence and transforms their self-expression and protest into marketable commodities. Consequently, their poverty is defined by Le Sueur as specifically industrial and urban, in an environment that is unnatural, destructive, unproductive—reproductively speaking—and essentially inhumane. From this background, the favored site for the working-class woman subject to come to full fruition in Le Sueur's writing is inevitably the countryside rather than the city. Her preference is perhaps understandable, connecting her writing about class to her own rural upbringing. However, her choice also forms the basis of her feminist consciousness, and as such wrenches her working-class women subjects away from an economic context that was historically and materially specific. "Women on the Breadlines" discusses working-class women in ways that conflicted with the demands of proletarian literature as well as the ideological imperatives imposed by consumer capitalism. Unfortunately, rather than continue an analysis of working-class women subjects in an environment and culture that was realistic and politically complex, Le Sueur settled instead for a setting that was pastoral and spiritual and, in her view, fundamentally feminine, inextricably linking the fecundity of nature with the fertility of working-class women's bodies.

Sexual Revolution

The idea of representing femininity as a concept that emanated from the cycles of nature is evident in the earliest of Le Sueur's stories. In "Spring Story" (1931), a young adolescent, Eunice, gradually becomes aware of her sexuality in relation to the budding trees and the shrubs emerging from the fertile ground around her rural home. She is described first as a "green girl" awakened by the sensual feeling of the wind in her room, blowing upon her "cold, but with a strange fertile promise to it."[126] Enlivened to a new heightened awareness by the wind, Eunice looks out of the window into garden where she notices a tree, which Le Sueur describes in distinctly anthropomorphic language. "The top limbs looked as if they had begun to break open. they looked as if excitement were upon the branches. . . . She ran to the window and put her arms in the light. They looked white with little reddish hairs alight in the sun. Perhaps she too was going to burst into leaf and bloom."[127] In this paragraph, the processes of nature and the cycles of female sexuality are combined in a series of intertwined images. The girl holds her arms out like branches, her hairs are "reddish" like the tree, which is described as being surrounded by "a faint aura of reddish brown." Similarly, the tree's branches are described as "limbs." Moreover, at the end of the story, Le Sueur associates the majestic elm with Eunice's mother who, to help her daughter embrace womanhood, looks out into the garden "peering into the deep shadow that lay under the elm."[128] Reassured that her daughter is safe, almost protected, by the maternal energy that Le Sueur describes as intrinsic to the tree, the mother stands at the doorway for a moment, then returns to the house.

The mother's concern for her daughter is a reaction to Eunice's gradual realization that her awakening sense of sexual being is inevitably linked to male sexuality, something that she regards with fear and desire in equal measure. When she meets some young men in the street she flirts with one of them, but when he reacts with a smile she cannot reciprocate, "she felt like running as fast as she could."[129] The combination of terror and desire is expressed in terms of nature at the end of the story. Eunice returns to the garden, and looking up at her window she longs to recapture the innocent "moment of brightness and wind"[130] that she had felt that morning. Instead, she stays outside and stands in a bed of canna lilies, growing beneath the maternal elm tree. The cannas are described by Le Sueur as symbolically phallic, inspiring attraction, revulsion, fascination, and fear in Eunice. "She could see the white curved sprouts like scimitars just thrust from the earth. She put her finger on one of them and felt them hard and cold but with a moisture and this strong urgency, this upward thrust of power. They thrust upward, hard and single, awaiting their day of flowering."[131] In this image, Le Sueur shows that both male and female sexuality are an intrinsic part of the earth's natural cycles. Unlike female sexuality, however, which is described as open, yielding, nurturing, and full of a multiude of sensations, male sexuality is cold, driven by power, aggressively and violently thrusting out of the earth like steel blades. This symbolic opposition reflects Le Sueur's feminist philosophy that although men and women form an holistic, organic union with the earth, men—and specifically male sexuality—are a potentially destructive force. Male sexuality is driven by a desire to escape from the earth, which in Le Sueur's view is implicitly female: beautiful, fertile, and nurturing like a womb.

Le Sueur's notion that male sexuality drives men to sever and escape their organic connection to the maternal earth is explored further in another short story, "Holiday" (1930). Here, a young man, Peter, tries to alleviate the monotony, poverty, and misery of his life in the city by taking a day trip into the countryside. Living in the city has filled Peter with an overwhelming sense of anger and aggression. The only way that he can numb his violent emotions in an urban environment is to get drunk and beat his wife "until he felt better."[132] Walking into the countryside relieves Peter's bitterness somewhat. Away from the city, he can open up his body and senses to the elements, walking "until he forgot his sense of cold and threw back his collar and opened his shirt."[133] The purity of this physical sensation invigorates him, replacing the "bitter hatred that always lay like rotten fruit in him" with "good air that smelled of hay and horses."[134]

Unfortunately, the rejuvenating effect of a rural environment is corrupted by Peter's masculinity. His attraction to the material gains of the city—money, radios, automobiles—shields him from the redemptive power of the earth and nature. What he is seeking is numbness, desensitization, and protection from the oppression of city life, so that he can concentrate on achieving wealth, possessions, and personal power. Consequently, he also has to defend himself against the maternal forces of nature, so he has to stay as drunk in the countryside as he was in the city. Peter does not want to reawaken his senses and recapture the natural, rhythmic thrill of living. Rather, he wants relief from feeling. As a result, he is most happy when lying on the ground in a drunken slumber, when "the sense of his own body [goes] away."[135]

Peter's essentially male need for sensual numbness is fundamentally sexually driven. After drinking more wine, Peter becomes attracted to the tanner's daughter, Jenny. When she rejects him, he becomes violent, then apathetic. "He caught her dress and yanked it toward him, bringing her body up against his own with such force that she was knocked breathless. With a remote idea that she had struck him, he threw her away from him again and heard her fall on the ground which seemed far below him."[136] The aggression of Peter's sexual urge reflects his defensive inability to reconnect with a rural environment that would make him whole. The entrapments of the city and the violence of his job, accompanied by his desire for success in the material world, distance him from the rejuvenating possibilities inherent to a natural environment that Le Sueur defines as explicitly female. The hopelessness of this realization is made clear when, in the heart of the country, Peter completely rejects the opportunity for redemption offered by the natural, female world around him: "Nothing was going to get him," he exclaims. "He would not come near anything. If he could just stay isolated in the open field untouched and lonely."[137] Peter sees the countryside as a threat to his manhood; he has to reassert himself by striking out at a tree as he would beat a woman—his wife or Jenny—attacking the femininity of the earth as if it were a real woman:

Striking something also was a way of keeping alive. It was something to do. Like striking the ground, striking and striking as he had stood half the night striking the looming flesh of his old woman. He would like to strike her now, softly and incessantly on her flesh and swear. Thinking of it he sat up as if he had been thinking of love.[138]

According to Le Sueur, human connection to the earth is most fully expressed through sexual union between men and women. Often in Le Sueur's writing this union can be corrupted and made meaningless when sexual drives—always male—are misdirected toward money, self-interest, or power. Accordingly, in Le Sueur's work, socialism is an inherently female impulse, while capitalism is portrayed as a typically male desire. For example, in "Harvest" (1929), the transcendent purity of a newly married couple's relationship is threatened by the husband's infatuation with buying a new threshing machine, which will, in his estimation, make the couple "powerful people in this neighborhood."[139] The wife sees the new machine as a sexual rival, "an encroachment like another woman."[140] It is a machine that she believes will threaten the sexual unity they have found together—an energy that is described as elemental, attuned with the seasons, and expressing the rhythmic fertility of the earth around them. Le Sueur portrays heterosexual sex as inseparable from the earth's energies. In the woman's mind her husband's work in the field, ploughing, planting, and harvesting, is indivisibly a part of their sexual life together. For the wife there is no boundary between the earth's fecundity and her own fertility. Consequently, her husband's attraction to the thresh-ing machine inspires a jealousy that destroys the sexual, spiritual, and emotional equanimity of their lives together. The equality of the relation-ship is ruined, and she becomes economically enslaved to her husband's capitalistic desires: "It's your money," she says. "Do with it as you like. It's yours. You're the master of the house."[141] Inevitably, their mutual desire is also transformed into a matter of her submission to his sexual demands: "In an hour she went with him, prevailed upon by his physical power over her."[142] Her husband's misdirected desire for the machine also infects his wife's consciousness. The woman's jealousy distorts her feel-ings about her pregnancy—the new baby is not to share. She comes to think of it as her private property; "[S]he thought of the child now as a weapon."[143]

Significantly, although the woman regards her husband's attraction to the new machine with sexual jealousy, the machine itself is described in distinctly phallic terms, with "big knives thrusting back movement even in their stillness, and then on driving power."[144] The thought of her husband "mounting" and driving the masculine beast revolts the woman.[145] Her horror confirms Le Sueur's representation of heterosex-ual sex as natural and pure, implying that any other kind of sexuality is malevolent and perverted—as destructive toward the holistic, organic, socialistic relationship between men and women as industrialization and consumer capitalism.

In "Harvest," Le Sueur sets out the gender polarities that form the foundation of her feminist world view. Nature and the earth are por-trayed as essentially female/maternal forces. Consequently, women are the key to the transcendent purity that Le Sueur defines as central to het-erosexual sex. Men are also a part of the earth's life force; therefore sexual union with women is the most empowering and natural way that they can reconnect with their essential nature. Unfortunately, men are also attracted—helplessly it seems—to the seductive temptations offered by wealth and power. Men want to make money more than they want to make love. As a result, the institutions of consumer capitalism, corrupt industry, political neglect, economic disaster, social injustice, media pro-paganda, idleness, apathy, decadence, nihilism, female oppression, and class oppression are, according to Le Sueur, the result of an unfettered male desire spinning endlessly out of control.

This exploration of the roots of Meridel Le Sueur's political per-spective reveals how fundamental her feminist consciousness was to her writing about working-class people and working-class women in particular. The gender polarities that were set out in stories like "Harvest" and "Spring Story" correspond directly to her representations of working-class protest in "What Happens in a Strike," and are consistent with her portrayal of working-class women subjects in "Eroded Woman" and "Women Know a Lot of Things." Le Sueur's feminism begins with the assertion that the earth is a female force to which women are naturally attuned through their sexuality, and most obviously because of their biology. In opposition, those things that are destructive to the female earth are, naturally, defined by Le Sueur as essentially male. However, women are sometimes seduced away from their biological destinies by temptations that are inherently male. Thus, middle-class women in Le Sueur's writing are often attracted to the exigencies of capitalist culture. They gather possessions, they are vain and proud and, most important, they repress their sexuality in ways that working-class women almost never do in Le Sueur's writing. Consequently, middle-class women are more male, and thus less essentially female, than the working-class women subjects of Le Sueur's radical writing. By the same token, working-class men are tempted by capitalism in the same ways as middle-class women. As a result, according to Le Sueur's feminist logic at least, the most female subjects in her radical writing are working-class women. Of course, from Le Sueur's point of view, this is a positive representation. Working-class women are the most naturally socialist, the most naturally attuned to the earth, and so the most sexually expressive and biologically reproductive. Since, for Le Sueur, revolution was a fundamentally sexual process rather than a historical-materialist one, working-class women are the most self-assertive and politically articulate subjects in her radical texts. Unfortunately, her insistence on gender oppositions that inscribed working-classness as female and middle-classness as male simultaneously reduced working-class identity to an essentialized category removed from its historical and economic contexts. Subsequently, in Le Sueur's texts, working-class women subjects are silenced from two directions: their working-class status defines them as intuitive rather than intellectual, physical rather than rational, and able to express themselves best through action rather than discourse. This inarticulate, marginalized position is compounded further by Le Sueur in her depiction of gender, valorizing emotion over thought, biology over history, and nature over materiality. As a result, the fundamental feminism that underscores Le Sueur's writing about class reduces her working-class women subjects to one-dimensional representations, without identities beyond their bodies, and unable to express themselves within the textual and political discourses that ensured their silence.

5

Tillie Olsen:
An Arduous Partnership

The Korl Woman

Tillie Olsen first discovered Rebecca Harding Davis's short novel, *Life in the Iron Mills or The Korl Woman,* when she was fifteen. She came across the work in an old volume of *The Atlantic* that she found in a junk shop in her home town of Omaha, Nebraska. At the time she did not know who had written the story, which as she recalls in the notes to her biographical interpretation of Davis's work, came to mean "increasingly more to me over the years, saying 'literature can be made out of the lives of despised people,' and 'you too must write.'"[1]

The story of Hugh Wolfe, a laborer at an iron mill who carves beautiful sculptures from the waste products left in his furnace, appealed particularly to Olsen's working-class identity. She notes that in the green pastures and transcendent landscapes of nineteenth-century American literature "there were no dark satanic mills," and the only working-class characters to appear were unrealistically "clean handed Yankee mill girls."[2] In this context, *Life in the Iron Mills* presented a unique image of a creative, emotionally deep, and intellectually complex working-class man, while at the same time it provided an intricate social and political analysis of his material situation. In this way, for Olsen, *Life in the Iron Mills* was "immeasurably precious. Details, questions, visions found nowhere else [were] dignified into living art."[3]

Stories were published anonymously in *The Atlantic* in 1861, so Olsen did not find out who had written *Life in the Iron Mills* until 1958. Discovering "that the author was of my sex," she realized that her attachment to Davis's work was not solely a matter of identifying with the working-class subject of the text but also with its middle-class woman author.[4] This sense of gender affiliation inspired Olsen to reread *Life in the Iron Mills* from a more feminist point of view. In so doing, she highlighted places in the narrative where Hugh Wolfe's desperate attempts to express himself beyond the repressive social and material contexts of his working-class identity subtextually revealed the artistic frustration Davis felt as a middle-class woman trying to develop a cre-

179

ative identity without crossing the social boundaries prescribed by her gender.

Davis was born in the isolated, parochial, industrial town of Wheeling, Virginia, in 1831. Her father was a financially successful, politically conservative, gentleman who believed that "all literature ended with Shakespeare."[5] Rebecca was the eldest of five children and, in accordance with nineteenth-century middle-class propriety, was expected to fulfill the role that was designated by her sex. She attended a finishing school where she acquired the skills that would prepare her for a life of genteel domesticity. As she noted in her diary, she learned "soft attractive graces. . . . Enough math to do accounts, enough astronomy to point out constellations, a little music and drawing, and French, history, literature at discretion."[6]

Eschewing this prospect, Davis chose the only other way of life available to a woman of her standing. She withdrew from "society" and began a life of respectable spinsterhood, where she lived in her father's house and helped care for the rest of the family.[7] In her biographical essay, Olsen tries to imagine the difficulties that Davis must have faced as she tried to develop her intellectual capacities in a situation so strictly circumscribed by practical responsibilities, social convention, and psychological "narrowness."

A young girl in a cramped life, fiercely struggling to tame and bind to some unfitting work the power within . . . faced down the harm and maiming of her personal situation, the self-scorn, the thwartings, and—fitted in between tasks and family needs, in secret and in isolation, without literary friendship and its encouragement—developed an ear, a discipline, made of herself a writer, against the prevalent, found her subject.[8]

Although Davis listed the "outward facts" of her life in her diary, and occasionally mused on the political and social upheavals around her, she never referred to the circumstances of her creative development, except, Olsen suggests, through her subconscious, subtextual connection to Hugh Wolfe in *Life in the Iron Mills.*

The narrative intersection between female author and working-class subject is made at the beginning of the text when the narrator looks down from her library window at the industrial scene below her. At first her vision is obscured, and the mass of people trudging to the mill each day merge with the smog, soot, and grimy residue that covers their faces, their houses, and the stagnant river that flows past their route to work. The physical distance between the narrator in her secluded library and the millworkers in the street below is emphasized as the author addresses the sympathetic middle-class people she imagines to be the readers of her work: "What do you make of a case like that amateur psychologist?" she demands. "You call it an altogether serious thing to be alive: to these men it is a drunken jest."[9]

Having constructed a sense of separation between working-class subject and middle-class audience, the narrative progresses toward a point of view that is aligned with the Welsh puddler, Hugh Wolfe. Contrary to conventional middle-class supposition, Wolfe is not psychologically subsumed by the material deprivations of his working-class life. Despite living in a squalid "kennel-like" room, living off "rank pork and molasses" and working in an endless cycle of "incessant labor" at the iron mill, Wolfe can express himself as an individual rather than as a component part of a manufacturing process.[10] In this way, although his physical situation is "like those of his class," he is psychologically and intellectually separated from the rest of his community. Consequently, he avoids the activities that are presented as being a panacea for working-class life. Wolfe is "never seen in the cockpit, did not own a terrier, drank but seldom [and] fought sometimes."[11] He is castigated for his reclusiveness by his fellow millworkers, who also mock him for what they perceive as being his lack of masculinity. Wolfe is nicknamed "Molly" and is regularly "pommelled to jelly" in bar room brawls because of his physical weakness. Wolfe's psychological deviation from the social context of his working-class identity is thus condemned as a dangerously effeminate affectation within a community that is depicted as being exclusively macho.[12]

The gender specificity of working-class identity in *Life in the Iron Mills* directly reflected Davis's experience. Her need for personal and psychological space in which to develop her intellectual capacities compromised her social acceptability as a woman. Olsen notes that Davis was considered physically unattractive "for a girl." She is described as having a distinctly unfeminine appearance—"handsome . . . dark, vigorous, sturdily built [and] strong jawed"—at a time when women were prized for their physical delicacy.[13] Likewise, Davis's interest in politics, literature, and philosophy was considered an unhealthy preoccupation for a respectable woman. As a result, she was forced to repress her femininity in order to become a writer or else risk becoming a "social outcast."[14] Writing *Life in the Iron Mills* was thus predicated on Davis's transgressing middle-class definitions of appropriate female behavior. She was forced into a process of self-conscious repression that found expression in her narrative and which, according to Olsen's interpretation, was most symbolically resonant in the carved figure of the Korl Woman.

Wolfe's sculptures were made from the waste product left in the furnace after the ore had been smelted. The puddler's job was to clean the furnace and dispose of the korl, then to endlessly repeat the task in accordance with the rest of the manufacturing process. Instead, Wolfe transformed the effluence of capitalist productivity into works of art that expressed individual working-class experiences, and which also described a potential for creativity and intellectuality that had been systematically destroyed by economic oppression. Reflecting this intention, the Korl Woman's naked, muscular body and "tense . . . clutching hands" are poised in an expression of hungry longing—not for meat or whiskey as the middle-class visitors to the iron mill suggest—but as Hugh Wolfe explains, for "summat to make her live."[15]

At the end of the narrative Hugh Wolfe is dead, but the Korl Woman remains in the narrator's study, hidden from view except . . .

Sometimes—tonight, for instance,—the curtain is accidentally drawn back, and I see a bare arm stretched out imploringly in the darkness, and an eager, wolfish face watching mine; a wan, woeful face, through which the spirit of the dead korl cutter looks out, with its thwarted life, its mighty hunger, its unfinished work.[16]

Olsen links this closing paragraph with her biographical interpretation of Davis's life. The demands of marriage—when Davis sidelined her writing to support her husband's political campaigns—and later motherhood, prevented her from publishing any other work that reached the standard set by *Life in the Iron Mills*.[17] By the time of her death in 1910, Davis was unknown as the writer of the short novel that had earned her a national literary reputation in 1861. Her death was mentioned in the *New York Times* however, under a heading that read: "Mother of Richard Harding Davis dies at son's home in Mt. Krisco, age 79." Finally, her individual creative identity was enclosed within the confinements of a female role that she had spent her early writing years trying to rearrange. Moreover, it was an inauspicious ending that signaled the beginning of over a hundred years of literary obscurity. As a result, the silent, half-hidden desperation contained in the Korl Woman's gesture toward the narrator at the end of *Life in the Iron Mills* reflected the fate of the working-class subject of the text back onto its middle-class woman author. This narrative intersection is repeated by Olsen in her biographical essay:

From her work—like the figure of the mill woman cut in korl, kept hid behind the curtain it is such a rough ungainly thing—her epoch looks through with its thwarted life, its mighty hunger, its unfinished work.
It is time to rend the curtain.[18]

As well as highlighting the ways in which Davis expressed her own repression through the character of Hugh Wolfe in *Life in the Iron Mills,* the biographical interpretation also alludes to the personal, political, and economic distance between Olsen's own identification with Hugh Wolfe in 1927, and her feminist affiliation with the author in 1972. Thus, when the Korl Woman appears to reach out toward the narrator—textually connecting the life of the working-class subject with the experiences of the middle-class woman author—the action also symbolizes the place in the narrative where working-class identity and femininity intersect. The connection is emphasized by the words that the narrator supposes might have been uttered by the Korl Woman: "Its pale vague lips seem to tremble with a terrible question 'Is this the End?' they say, 'Nothing beyond?'—'no more?'"[19] Significantly, the Korl Woman's unspoken demand repeats the verse that is quoted at the beginning of the narrative: Is this the end? O Life, as futile, then, as frail What hope of answer, of redress?[20]

Hugh Wolfe's story—the story of a working-class man—is related in response to this first question. His creativity, his sensitivity and, most important, the symbolic korl figure, seem to testify to the possibility that working-class self-expression need not be confined within the repressive boundaries of material circumstance. Tragically, Wolfe's realization that he is psychically as well as physically bound by his economic situation seems to refute the possibility that Harding Davis has constructed in her text. However, the apparent reiteration of the question after Wolfe's death redirects the narrative back to the beginning and implies the necessity of a rereading, this time from the perspective of the Korl Woman in the subtitle. Moreover, the rephrased question capitalizes "End," indicating the closure of a book but, since the Korl Woman's question is left unanswered, the narrative progresses beyond the conclusion of the novel. This incomplete ending inscribes the possibility of a continuation from a perspective that symbolically represents the position of a working-class woman in *Life in the Iron Mills*. Consequently, the Korl Woman is also a manifestation of Tillie Olsen's dualistic relationship to the text.

Despite the symbolic relevance of the Korl Woman to Olsen's identity, the figure is most obviously a silent statue carved by a working-class man who is, in turn, the imaginative creation of a socially repressed middle-class woman. As such, the Korl Woman also represents a hierarchy of economic deprivation, social marginalization, and—simultaneously—gender and class restrictions, which systematically ensure the silence of working-class women. Consequently, the only working-class woman to appear in Davis's text is Hugh Wolfe's cousin Deb, who is alternately described as animalistic, uncomprehending, amoral, easily manipulated, simplistically fatalistic, and most significantly, "stupidly invisible," in relation to Wolfe's untutored creativity and the emotional appeal of his sculpture.[21] Paula Rabinowitz suggests that Deb's one-dimensionality, obliquely represented by the impassive Korl Woman, confirms the "undisclosed" nature of working-class femininity in *Life in the Iron Mills*; an absence that prefigures radical writing by women in the 1930s.[22] Apparently reflecting this assertion, while Olsen highlights the similarities between Davis and Hugh Wolfe's character in her biographical interpretation, she does not explicitly refer to the experience of the working-class women who constitute an indelible subtext to working-class masculinity and middle-class femininity in the text.

Contrary to Rabinowitz's view, however, as a woman writer from a working-class background, Olsen's connection to *Life in the Iron Mills* was fundamentally informed by, and extended from, Davis's presentation of working-class women in the figure of the Korl Woman. Olsen began her first novel, *Yonnondio: From the Thirties,* in 1932, aged nineteen, just after she first encountered *Life in the Iron Mills*. Davis's influence is particularly exemplified in a description of a mining accident. Instead of relating the incident in symbolic terms, however, Olsen derides aesthetic interpretation and presents the scene in its stark reality. In this reversal of Davis's approach, the experiences of the miners and their wives are not beautifully expressed through classical art but are revealed in opposition to the expectations of middle-class taste: "Surely it is classical enough for you—the Greek marble of the women, the simple, flowing lines of sorrow, carved so rigid and eternal. Surely it is original enough—these grotesques, this thing with the foot missing, this gargoyle with the face half gone and the arm."[23]

In contrast to Davis' valorization of Wolfe's individual creativity, none of the miners described in *Yonnondio* are miraculous artists. Rather, their identities are defined and circumscribed by "the artist, Coal [who] sculpted them."[24] Furthermore, while Davis presents working-class identity through a symbolically resonant and aesthetically appealing female body, in *Yonnondio* working-class women's lives are the least discernible from a middle-class point of view. Consequently, artistic representations of working-class women in *Yonnondio* are not huge, imposing sculptures that shine white against the black foundry. Instead they are portrayed as small, silhouetted, cameos, "dwarfed by the vastness of night and the towering tipple. . . . black figures with bowed heads, waiting, waiting."[25] By presenting them as broadly outlined, unrecognizable shadows "pinned to the aesthetic hearts" of middle-class readers,[26] Olsen shows how the experiences of working-class women were repressed and appropriated into configurations of male working-class and middle-class female identities. As a result, representations of women who were also working-class were barely visible and subsequently, almost never self-defined.

Yonnondio is a testimony to the economic circumstances and social marginalization that made the obscurity of working-class women inevitable. In relation to Olsen's own experiences, *Yonnondio* marked the beginning of a creative process that had been inspired by radical writing in the 1930s. Ironically, *Yonnondio* also represented the closing of her artistic life span. Poverty, and the demands of motherhood, meant that Olsen's literary career was cut off in 1934 until 1973 when her work was recognized as an important addition to a developing canon of feminist literature.[27] Despite the acceptance of *Yonnondio* within these two politically disparate contexts, its dualistic appeal also highlighted a fundamental antagonism between exclusively male definitions of working-class identity in the 1930s, and the repressive middle-classness of the feminist movement in the 1970s. Consequently, *Yonnondio* testifies to the marginality of working-class women both in radical writing and feminist politics. As such, the forty-year gap between the beginning and the publication of *Yonnondio* is the most relevant in relation to Olsen's perspective as a working-class woman writer and also to that of the women she wrote about. Therefore, in order to fully understand Olsen's writing it is essential to examine the historical, political, and economic circumstances that inspired her to write *Yonnondio*, and which simultaneously prevented it from being completed.

Individuality and Communality

Tillie Olsen was born in 1912 or 1913 in Omaha, Nebraska, the second of six children. Her parents, Samuel and Ida Lerner, had escaped Czarist Russia and fled to America during the aftermath of the failed 1905 Revolution, in which they had been active participants. The Lerners continued their radical political activities in the United States—Samuel was state secretary of the Socialist Party and ran for office during the 1920s—but the family was poor. Irregular employment in various jobs, from farming to paper hanging, could not support the family and Olsen remembers having to work outside the home, shelling peanuts, from the age of ten. Being the oldest girl, she was also expected to help her mother with housekeeping and with taking care of the younger children. As such, the intersection between working-class labor and female responsibility began at an early age for Olsen.[28]

Despite economic deprivations in the Lerner household, however, Olsen remembers her childhood as having been "rich . . . from the standpoint of ideas."[29] She was encouraged to read the revolutionary literature that lay around her home, and as a result became familiar with the radical fiction and art that was reprinted in the pages of *Comrade* and *The Liberator*. Olsen's political education was compounded by the regular visits of famous radical activists to Omaha. She recalls hearing Eugene Debs speak at a town meeting, and as having been the child chosen to present him with a bunch of red roses. Reminiscing to Erika Duncan in 1984, Olsen even remembered a phrase from Debs's speech that set out a vision of a utopian socialist future in America, where society "would be like a great symphony with each person playing his own instrument."[30]

The image of a community where every person contributed his or her individual talent to create an equal and just society had great resonance in the development of Olsen's creative and political identity. Her familiarity with radical texts led to a committed interest in all kinds of literature. She became a member of the local library, where she resolved to read the entire fiction section from A to Z. She also scoured secondhand book shops for cheap copies of classic works and began to collect the five-cent Haldeman Julius Blue Books that published fiction specifically for a working-class audience. At the same time Olsen began to write. She kept a journal from the age of sixteen in which she made lists of resolutions that would help her become a serious writer. She secretly composed poems, short stories, and brief character sketches that she would later use in her published fiction. This early work was introspective, romantic, and self-consciously adolescent. As Deborah Rosenfelt notes, Olsen's poems were "lyrical, full of the pain of lost or unrequited love, the anguish of loneliness and the mysteries of nature, especially the winds and snows of the Nebraska winter. Several express deep love and affection for a female friend, and one describes a bond with her younger sister."[31]

In her later journal entries, Olsen would criticize these early efforts for being too detached from the political and economic realities that defined her existence as a working-class woman:

The rich things I could have said are left unsaid, what I did write anyone could have written. There is no Great God Dough, terrible and harassing, in my poems. Nothing of the common hysteria of 300 girls every 4:30 in the factory, none of the bitter humiliation of scorching a tie, the fear of being late, of ironing a wrinkle in, the nightmare of kids at home to be fed and clothed, the rebelliousness, the tiptoe expectation and searching, the bodily nausea and weariness . . . yet this was my youth.[32]

Olsen attempted to resolve the antagonism between her developing creativity and her commitment to her community by using her literary talents to write songs and skits for her comrades to perform at Young Communist League and Young People's Socialist meetings. She also tried to write from a more politically conscious position, in ways she believed would be easily understood by the rest of her working-class community. In common with her friends, she was determined to remain loyal to socialist causes, even when such commitments conflicted with her individual literary aspirations:

They were my dearest friends, but how could they know what so much of my writing self was about? They thought of writing in the terms in which they knew it. They had become readers, like so many working-class kids in the movement, but there was so much that fed me as far as my medium was concerned that was closed to them. . . . It was not a time that my writing self could come first.[33]

Rosenfelt suggests that Olsen tried to reconcile her creative identity with her political consciousness through her radical writing. However, an incident from Olsen's personal history reveals wider social and political contexts that were fundamental to what Rosenfelt defines as an essentially individual dilemma.

As a teenager, Olsen was the only child from her neighborhood to "cross the tracks" from her working-class community and attend the exclusively middle-class Central High School in Omaha.[34] Olsen was an enthusiastic and talented student, but her recollection of the experience was decidedly mixed. While participation in an elite middle-class environment "stimulated her intellectually," her education separated her from her working-class community and thus "crippled her socially."[35] At the same time, as a working-class student she felt psychologically excluded from an institution—and a mode of self-expression—that was overwhelmingly middle-class. The contradictions between Olsen's working-class identity and her intellectual development were exacerbated by the economic requirements of her family situation. This—coupled with a disagreement with her formerly encouraging teacher—eventually led to her departure from Central High.[36]

Olsen's experiences at Central High School show that the dichotomy between creative self-expression and political activity in Olsen's writing was not simply a diametric opposition, as Rosenfelt suggests, but an extension of an hierarchically constructed social context where creativity and individuality were defined as exclusively middle-class, and communality and physical productivity were pejoratively circumscribed as working class. As a result, the dilemma that Olsen faced as a teenager—between rejecting her community identity in favor of middle-class education, or repressing her individual potential on behalf of her working-class comrades—was an inevitable consequence of her economic status. The exclusive privileges of middle-class education were internalized by

Olsen and expressed (from a working-class point of view) as a self-defensive, self-fulfilling prophecy.[37]

Olsen's negative experiences at Central High School were positively reversed by proletarian politics and radical writing in the 1930s. Within a representational context that defined working-class self-expression as communally identified and politically active, Olsen felt able to combine her personal literary aspirations with her working-class identity. In a letter to Philip Rahv, the editor of *The Partisan Review*, Olsen described her eagerness to fit her biography to the proletarian image of an heroic, self-consciously working-class, artist:

> Father state secretary Socialist Party for years.
>
> Education, old revolutionary pamphlets laying around the house, (including liberators), and YCL.
>
> Jailbird—"violating handbill ordinance"
>
> Occupations: Tie Presser, hack writer . . . model, housemaid, ice cream packer, book clerk.[38]

Despite Olsen's vociferous presentation of herself as a "pure working-class artist educated only in revolutionary literature and the school of life,"[39] her protestations belied a more problematic relationship to proletarian ideology. The image of working-class identity in radical fiction, although presented as politically desirable, was constructed from a point of view that extended the political and narrative terms of middle-class self-expression while simultaneously repressing the intellectual scope of working-class writers. Consequently, Olsen's position as an author of radical fiction was strictly delineated within an idealistic, romanticized, middle-class image of her own working-class identity. Furthermore, the restrictions placed on Olsen's position as a working-class author of radical fiction were extended into textual representations of working-class subjects. As a result, her radical writing reveals a fundamental tension between individual working-class identity and its collectively defined, physically expressive, innately emotional and irrational image. Moreover, unlike most other radical writers, she continuously drew attention to the distance between her privileged perspective as an author, and the point of view of the working-class subjects in her texts. This emphasis created a space between the narrator and the depicted subject that actively disrupted the dogmatic process of radical writing, while simultaneously articulating a working-class point of view that was politically identifiable and individually expressive.

In "The Strike" (1934), the narrative tension that reflected Olsen's dualistic perspective as a working-class author of radical texts was clearly expressed. Like Dorothea Lange, Olsen focuses on the long-shoreman's strike in San Francisco. In contrast to Lange's socially concerned objectivity, however, Olsen's approach veers between narrative isolation and intense political commitment. Her dichotomous position is made clear from the opening paragraph of "The Strike."

Do not ask me to write of the strike and the terror. I am on a battlefield, and the stench and smoke sting the eyes so it is impossible to turn them back into the past. You leave me only this night to drop the bloody garment of Todays, to cleave through the gigantic events that have crashed on upon the other to the first beginning. If I could go away for a while, if there were time and quiet, perhaps I could do it. All that has happened might resolve itself into order and sequence, fall into neat patterns of words. I could stumble back into the past and slowly, painfully rear the structure in all its towering magnificence, so that the beauty and heroism, the terror and significance of those days, would enter your heart and sear it forever with the vision.[40]

Olsen begins her narrative by comparing the events of the strike—the immediacy of its action, the intensity of its emotional expression, and its political vitality—with her own textual rendering of it, which she describes as neatly ordered; progressing logically from its beginning to its conclusion; and as having been composed from a privileged distance of hindsight, physical separation, and peaceful contemplation. By emphasizing the textual distance between intellectually individualistic writing and intuitive, explosive action, Olsen appears to be conforming to the usual tenets of radical writing. Reflecting this, she seems to assert a fundamental difference between modes of expression that were designated as "bourgeois" or "working-class" in proletarian writing, and accordingly aligns herself with the latter. In common with the style of radical reportage, Olsen also renounces middle-class objectivity and places herself, as she claims in the opening sentence, literally "on a battlefield." At the same time, however, Olsen constructs a position within the opening paragraph of "The Strike" that reveals her narrative complicity with middle-class forms of textual expression. She removes herself from the sensual immediacy of the strike and refers to the action in the past tense. Beginning from a conscious literary distance, she describes the strike as a poetic, aesthetically powerful event that depicts working-class struggle as being beautiful and heroic. At the same time, the physical demands of political activism disallow the possibility of intellectual interpretation, and so she is forced to continue her description from a predictably radical perspective that seems to preclude the intervention of a middle-class perspective. Toward the end of the text,

Olsen complicates this conventionally proletarian opposition and describes the strike from the relatively secluded distance of union headquarters:

I was not . . . down by the battlefield. My eyes are anguished from the pictures I pieced together from the words of comrades, of strikers, from the pictures filling the newspapers. I sat up in headquarters racked by the howls of ambulances hurtling by, feeling it incredible the finger like separate little animals hopping nimbly from key to key, the ordered steady click of the typewriter feeling any moment the walls would crash and all the madness surge in. Ambulances, ripping out of nowhere fading police sirens outside, the sky a ghastly gray, corpse gray, an enormous dead eyelid shutting down on the world. And someone comes in, words lurch out of his mouth, the skeleton is told and goes again. . . . And I sit here making a metallic little pattern of sound in the air, because that is all I can do, because that is all I am supposed to do.[41]

In this passage, Olsen is physically separated from the site of working-class activism, but her presence at the union office ensures her political and emotional allegiance with the strikers. This dualistic perspective allows her to psychologically participate in the action while maintaining a semblance of textual distance. Moreover, the separation between Olsen's writing and the physical events of the strike is continuously emphasized. As such, the metaphorical eye, which in the opening paragraph was clouded by smoke and debris, is now closed. Removed from the action, Olsen maintains an objective, individualistic, almost photographic distance between herself and the protesters that is intermittently interrupted by the explosive sounds and violent emotions of the strike scene. From here, she can write about the demonstration in a clear, analytical, sophisticated way; but her detachment from the working-class subjects of her text also imbues her individual, intellectual perspective with a sense of political impotence and introspective insignificance, which was commensurate with the decadent self-involvement of "bourgeois" writing. By deliberately framing her article in this way, Olsen effectively reverses the usual progression of radical narratives where the author begins from an archetypical middle-class perspective and moves steadily towards an epiphanic working-class conclusion. More subversive, however, is the way Olsen confuses the traditional polarization between individual self-expression and communal identity in radical writing to reconstruct the narrative from the point of view of its working-class subject.

Proletarian literature most often represented working-class identity as inarticulate and fundamentally separated from a defining middle-class

perspective that was rational and literate. The working-class protesters in
"The Strike" defy this prescriptive standard. At the beginning of her article, Olsen describes the action through the words of an individual striker,
Jerry (who, unlike the protesters in Meridel Le Sueur's equivalent piece,
is named). Olsen extends this individualized point of view by connecting
Jerry's assertion—"WE'LL BE OUT, and then hell can't stop us"—to the
events that lead up to the longshoremen's mass demonstration.[42] Significantly, Jerry's words are not subsumed by the progression from an individual opinion to a collective activity. Instead, Olsen maintains a working-class perspective within her narrative by using the phrase as a way of
communicating the physical events of the strike. As a result, the strikers'
demonstration is not simply an expression of an intuitive, communally
experienced protest, but a textual construction that literally spells out
Jerry's words: "H-E-L-L-C-A-N-T-S-T-O-P-U-S. . . ."[43] Working-class identity
is thus depicted as an advancing textual force, actively invading, rather
than silently retreating from, a narrative discourse usually defined from
an exclusively middle-class point of view.

The narrative progression from physical action to individual speech
is extended in "The Strike," when the protesters take over a public meeting where they are due to be addressed by the shipyard owners and the
mayor of the city. At this point in Olsen's article, the amassed voices of
working-class protest are confronted by the middle-class rhetoric of institutionalized power. At first the strikers act collectively, physically taking
over the San Francisco Auditorium as a group. Olsen's description, using
conventionally proletarian language, reflects this archetypically working-
class behavior. She marches alongside the strikers, united with them like a
single "flame, a force" in mass defiance of their capitalist opponents.
They sing choruses of union songs and collectively applaud their communal achievement. From a narrative position that she describes as being
aligned with her working-class comrades, Olsen creates a palpable sense
of "solidarity weaving us into one being" that allows the strikers to invade
physical spaces that previously excluded them: "[T]wenty thousand
jammed in and the dim blue ring of cops back in the hall was wavering,
was stretching itself thin and unseeable. It was OUR auditorium, we had
taken it over. And for blocks around they hear our voice."[44] Unlike most
radical reportage, which would have ended with this inspirational conclusion, Olsen transforms the strikers' physical presence into words she sets
against those of Mayor Rossi. He attempts to address the crowd through a
barrage of boos and jeering protest: "Remember, I am your chief execu-
tive, the respect . . . the honor . . . due that office. . . . don't listen to me
then but listen to your mayor . . . listen."[45] The discursive arrangement of
the mayor's speech reveals the institutionalized power that supports capi-

talist rhetoric. Having exposed this oratorical facade, Olsen then introduces the words of the strikers that interrupt the mayor's proclamations with insistent questions: "Who started the violence?" "Who calls the bulls to the waterfront?" "Who ordered the clubbing?"[46] The strikers' questions are unanswered, rather than ignored, by the literally silenced mayor, and the verbal confrontation culminates in a significant expression of working-class identity: "Shut up, we have to put up with your clubs but not with your words, get out of here, GET OUT OF HERE."[47]

The strikers' textually symbolic victory is extended as Olsen's narrative continues. The strike proceeds, but it is described not simply as a demonstration of working-class collectivity and physical force but as an actively articulate trajectory within the text. Removed from the institutional site of its power, middle-class speech is transformed into meaningless, inhumane, and animalistic action in comparison with rational—socially legitimated, in Olsen's text—working-class self-expression. Consequently, the mayor's voice is described as reptilian, and the brutal "Citizen's Committee" he organizes in response to the strikers' assertive voices is thus naturally reflective of his innate amorality.[48]

Olsen emphasizes the way literal power is appropriated into working-class self-expression by intersecting newspaper headlines that proclaim that "LAW AND ORDER MUST PREVAIL," with the personal experiences of individual strikers.[49] In so doing, she establishes an alternative interpretation of the strike that can be read and understood by people outside of the events. One man who has witnessed the violent demonstration at the waterfront watches "with horror, trying to comprehend the lesson the moving bodies were writing."[50] Olsen notices that, faced with this physical text, "in an hour all the beliefs of his life had been riddled and torn away."[51] Without the institutional security that has supported his middle-class identity, he struggles to interpret a point of view that is presented as fundamentally working class:

Listen, he said, and he talked because he had to talk. . . . Listen I was down there, on the waterfront, do you know what they're doing—they were shooting SHOOTING—. . . . shooting right into men, human beings, they were shooting into them as if they were animals as if they were targets, just lifting their guns and shooting. I saw this, can you believe it, CAN YOU BELIEVE IT? . . . as if they were targets as if. . . . CAN YOU BELIEVE IT? and he went to the next man and started it all over again.[52]

In this way, Olsen not only constructs a self-consciously working-class interpretation of the strike in opposition to capitalist media depictions, she also disturbs simplistic proletarian definitions of how that working-class point of view was expressed. The strikers are therefore able to figuratively write their own text within Olsen's in such a way that her own position as the author of the article is exposed. Realizing the political inadequacy of her perspective, she returns to the strike scene. The demonstration is over and only a few flowers are left scattered on the waterfront, marking the place where several of the demonstrators were shot by police. In this significantly unpopulated scene, Olsen picks up a leaflet that reads:

OUR BROTHERS

Howard S. Sperry, a longshoreman, a war vet, a real MAN. On strike since May 9th, 1934, for the right to earn a decent living under decent conditions. . . .

Nickolas Bordoise, a member of Cooks & Waiters Union for ten years. Also a member of the International Labor Defense. Not a striker, but a worker looking to the welfare of his fellow workers on strike. . . . [53]

Olsen's narrative exposure is compounded by this intersection of detailed descriptions of the two dead strikers. As a result, toward the end of her article, Olsen is unable to continue writing from an essentially middle-class point of view:

Listen, it is late, I am feverish and tired. Forgive me that the words are feverish and blurred. You see, If I had time, If I could go away. But I write this on a battlefield.

The rest, the General Strike, the terror, arrests and jail, the songs in the night, must be written some other time, must be written later. . . . But there is so much happening now. [54]

At the end of "The Strike" then, having established a textual basis for working-class self-expression, Olsen appears to negate the possibilities she has created in relation to her own working-class identity. Torn between individual self-expression and collective action, Olsen chooses the latter and leaves her ambiguous position at strike headquarters to return to the unequivocally working-class "battlefield." The ironic result of this pragmatic decision was manifested in the rest of Olsen's career as radical writer in the 1930s. She published only two other prose pieces: "Thousand-Dollar Vagrant" in *New Republic* and "The Iron Throat" in *The Partisan Review*; and two poems: "I Want You Women Up North to Know" and "There Is a Lesson" in the *Daily Worker*, all of which appeared in 1934.

The paucity of Olsen's literary output as a radical writer reflects Rosenfelt's assertion that Olsen put her "activist self" before her "writer self" in the 1930s. [55] More fundamentally, however, her relative silence in relation to other radical authors reveals the difficulties of her economic situation—problems that were exacerbated by the birth of her two children, one in 1932 and another in 1937. Furthermore, Olsen's inability to continue speaking and writing from a perspective that reflected her identity as an individual working-class woman highlights her ambivalent position within a literary and political movement that asserted the predisposition of working-class people toward communal activism rather than individual creativity; and which simultaneously defined that active power as being essentially male. As a result, the complex narrative structure of "The Strike," which enabled the working-class subjects to successfully subvert proletarian orthodoxy, simultaneously compromised Olsen's acceptability as a working-class woman author of politically radical texts.

Class and Gender in Radical Writing

Olsen's subversive portrayal of working-class identity in "The Strike" was complicated further by her introduction of a specifically female point of view. During the strike march, it is the female protesters who lead the advance into the literal spaces of capitalist power. Olsen notes that the message "hell can't stop us" was a particularly female message, carried by "the lines of women and children marching up market with their banners."[56] Despite placing women at the forefront of working-class protest, however, their presence is defined by Olsen as an extension of their role as the supportive wife and defensive mother within a male-centered family. Accordingly, the women march, together with their children and alongside their husbands, exclaiming that "this is our fight, and we're with the men to the finish."[57] Reflecting this assertion, the strike is depicted metaphorically by Olsen as an act of wifely and maternal love. Consequently, the days leading up to the demonstration are described as being "pregnant" with anticipation and revolutionary portent. This is an image that is reiterated at the end of the narrative when, after the violent march is over, leaving two male strikers dead, one woman remains at the scene: "There was a pregnant woman standing on the corner, outlined against the sky, and she might have been a marble, rigid eternal, expressing some vast and nameless sorrow."[58]

Here, Olsen portrays working-class protest as symbolically centered on an iconographic female body. As such, the female perspective in "The Strike" seems to reassert the disparate narrative terms of radical writing by presenting working-class self-expression as a fundamentally biological emanation rather than an intellectual assertion. At the same time, however, Olsen undermines her essentialist stance by concentrating on the pregnant woman's face—which, Olsen notes, is "a flame" of animated emotion—rather than the statuesque quality of her body.[59] The woman's look of psychological disturbance is compounded with a statement: "We'll not forget that. We'll pay it back . . . someday."[60] Her identification with the strike cause detracts from her gender identity and also reveals an antagonistic intersection between working-class self-expression and female experience in the narrative. The opposition also reflects Olsen's dichotomous position within a proletarian discourse where working-class identity was defined as male from a middle-class point of view. Olsen examines the social and political contexts that informed her dualistic perspective in a deceptively dogmatic article, "Thousand-Dollar Vagrant," published in *The New Republic* in August 1934.

"Thousand-Dollar Vagrant" refers to a law that was utilized by the police in San Francisco to arrest and detain left-wing political activists. Olsen wrote the article in response to a request by the editor of *The New Republic*, which she uses as an introduction to her narrative: "It was Lincoln Jeffers who commanded me to write this story. " 'People don't know,' he informed me, 'how they arrest you, what they say, what happens in court. Tell them. Write it just as you told me about it.' So here it is."[61] The article was thus conceived in classically proletarian terms: as an account from the arena of struggle, describing the dangers of political activism and the fearlessness of those who participated. Moreover, it was written as a reflection of a spoken recollection, giving the piece an emotional immediacy that was central to radical reportage.

Olsen begins her narrative by setting a scene of industrious political activity: "I would have left at nine thirty, but Billy came in with a thrilling story of how out in Filmore the telephone poles had been plastered with leaflets, with stickers: 'the Communist Party lives and fights'"—when suddenly, the air of earnest idealism is violently interrupted by "ugly voices" shouting, gangster-movie style, "Hold it, hold it, or we'll plug you."[62] The policemen's action inside the building reflects their dramatic entrance. They search the house, "flinging up curtains, peering in the garbage can, looking in the stove, ransacking the drawers."[63] Olsen adds rhetorical flourishes in grandiose proletarian style, imagining that "I wouldn't have been surprised if they had ripped out knives or irons and started torturing us, if their revolvers had been pulled out and gone off."[64] Set against this brutal, draconian behavior, the communist activists appear cool, rational, and logical. Faced with the shouted demand, "You a communist? . . . This country's not good enough for you huh? You don't like our constitution huh?", one of the party members replies calmly, "Yes. . . . that's legal isn't it?"[65]

Despite these excesses, Olsen describes her confrontation with the police from a specifically female point of view. During the raid, the officers order Olsen out of the room where they are interrogating the male activists. Their order physically separates her from the confrontation between institutionalized capitalist power and radical politics simply because she is a woman. Nevertheless, Olsen's marginalized position enables her to eavesdrop on the scene without placing herself in physical danger: from the corridor she can hear "questions [followed by] a thud of something soft on a body."[66] Ironically, this relatively empowered perspective is reversed by the policemen who question Olsen, not about her individual political affiliations but about her personal relationships with the male activists. They ask: "You married?" . . . You're Jack Olsen's girl aren't you? . . . Aren't you?"[67] For the policemen, Olsen's femininity means that her connection to political activism must be sexual, or at least emotional, rather than intellectual. This assumption allows the policemen to assert their masculinity and claim that their actions are intended to protect Olsen from the deviant behavior of the male communists: "You know what would've happened if we wouldn't have come. You'd probably be raped. Don't you know these guys aren't any better than niggers?"[68]

The gender polarities that Olsen establishes at the beginning of "Thousand-Dollar Vagrant" are made more emphatic after she and her comrades are arrested and imprisoned. The jail is divided into a "women's side" and a "men's side." The inmates of the "women's side" are mostly prostitutes who tell Olsen "it's the nicest city jail in the United States."[69] In keeping with this judgment, Olsen describes the female wardens as polite and apologetic as they search her pockets and shoes. The wardens' respectful attitude is reflected in the attitude of the man who takes Olsen's finger prints. She recalls that the "finger print guy . . . was the first one who hadn't refused to believe anything I said."[70] However, his conciliatory response is expressed in a paternalistic speech that echoes the sexual aggression of the policemen who arrested Olsen:

He asked me to tell him—honestly—if I believed in this communism, didn't I know it was all anarchy, rape and bloodshed? Didn't I know it was controlled in Russia? Didn't I realize how it would ruin my life to be mixed up with such a bunch—here I was fingerprinted, down for life as a criminal etc.[71]

The fingerprint man construes Olsen's political commitment to be an expression of her feminine weakness rather than a rational choice. He implies that, without realizing it, she has been led astray from an acceptable image of ladylike behavior toward a life of salaciousness and decadence. The fingerprint man's attitude is reflected in the punishment that is administered to the female communists. One woman, Marion Chandler, is quarantined by the judge and given tests for syphilis and gonorrhea. Her sentence is made especially ironic by Olsen's description of

Marion Chandler as "the wife of a communist active in the unemployed movement."[72] Mrs. Chandler is found guilty because of her marriage, and is punished as if this relationship were a sign of sexual—rather than political or ideological—deviancy.

By highlighting a specifically female perspective in "Thousand-Dollar Vagrant," Olsen extends the context of radical writing to include politicized definitions of working-class identity being exclusively male and femininity as an essentially middle-class experience. Thus, Olsen and the other women in "Thousand-Dollar Vagrant" are measured against an image of working-class masculinity that is judged as prurient and animalistic, and an acceptable model of female behavior that adheres to repressive middle-class values. Olsen attempts to define a self-consciously working-class—and positively female—point of view in her radical writing from between these narrative polarities. In so doing, she investigates the gender disparities within left-wing politics, as in "Thousand-Dollar Vagrant," while at the same time asserting the economic divisions between women, as she does in her poem, "I Want You Women Up North to Know."[73]

"I Want You Women Up North to Know" is addressed at the middle-class women who buy intricately embroidered clothes for their children without acknowledging the economic circumstances of the women who make them. Olsen examines the geographic distance and the economic disparity between middle-class northern women and working-class Mexican women by contrasting the rhetorical facade of consumer capitalism with proletarian representations of the Mexican women's lives. In the first verse, San Antonio is described ironically as a place "where sunshine spends the winter," rather than as a city where the workforce is systematically degraded and exploited to satisfy the demands of the female consumers "up north."[74] The fashionable women shopping at "macy's wannamakers gimbels marshall field" purchase the pleasant image and ignore the economic reality.[75] Their complacency is perpetuated by the shop assistant who translates the "blood [and] wasting flesh" of the female workers into an attractive sales pitch designed to appeal to the customer's maternal pride.[76] Reflecting this transformation, in the second verse Olsen contrasts the capitalist emphasis on "exquisite pleats . . . .exquisite work" with the everyday realities of the Mexican women's lives.[77]

The delicate stitches of the children's clothes are echoed in the drops of consumptive blood that "embroider the floor" of Catalina Rodriguez's room. Ironically, her desecrated body, "shrivelled to a child's at twelve," assumes the shape of the wealthy children who wear the clothes she makes.[78] Olsen describes Catalina as having being consumed by the economic process that defines her narrow existence. Nevertheless, the physical effects of her material circumstances are transformed into an insubstantial, aesthetically pleasing image, by the words of a "bourgeois poet":

> White rain stitching the night. . . .
> white gulls of hands, darting, veering,
> white lightening, threading clouds,
> this is the exquisite dance of her hands over cloth,
> and her cough, gay, quick, staccato,
> like skeleton's bones clattering,
> is appropriate accompaniment for the esthetic dance
> of her fingers.[79]

Olsen presents the politically impotent, poetically introspective, archetypically middle-class language as being a component part of the consumer image that has concealed working-class identity in this poem. At the same time, the insidious effects of capitalism have been internalized by the Mexican women. In particular, Ambrosa Espinoza whose "trust in god," Olsen suggests, ensures her blind acceptance of her deprived situation:

"Todos es de dios, everything is from god," through the dwindling night the waxing day, she bolsters herself up with it—
but the pennies to keep god incarnate, from ambrosa,
and the pennies to keep the priest in wine, from ambrosa,
ambrosa clothes god and priest with hand-made children's dresses.[80]

Ambrosa Espinoza's religious faith is presented as an integral part of the economic hierarchy that perpetuates her poverty. Her commitment to God therefore has far-reaching effects beyond her individual situation. Ambrosa's brother leaves San Antonio after being laid off from his job on the railroad. In a clichéd proletarian incident, he loses his grip jumping a freight train and severs his leg. Ambrosa continues to sew children's dresses in order to financially support her crippled brother. At the same time, she is convinced "that he prays and dreams of a another world, as he lies there, a heaven," to which Olsen adds the traditional communist non sequitur, "(which he does not know was brought to earth in 1917 in Russia by workers like him)."[81] In this way, Olsen highlights the essential masculinity of revolutionary activism, which she sets against a rhetorically constructed image of woman-centered capitalist exploitation. However, this traditionally proletarian framework is complicated by Olsen's concentration on an essentially female connection between proletarian dogma and "bourgeois" self-expression.

Olsen portrays economic exploitation as a purely matriarchal process in "I Want You Women Up North to Know." The wealthy mothers' psychological enclosure within the security of consumer discourse reflects the Mexican women's helpless acceptance of their exploited circumstances. Olsen presents each group of women as being manipulated by capitalism. The women up north are seduced into expressing their maternal impulses through their purchasing power, and their ignorant and apathetic actions precipitate the degradation of the Mexican women. Similarly, the Mexican women are forced to work in oppressive conditions so as to ensure the survival of their children. In both cases, maternal instinct, biological capacities, and sexual self-expression are corrupted by a hierarchical economic process that Olsen presents as being centered on the female body.

Reflecting this assertion, Maria Vasquez has been forced to sacrifice her potential for motherhood because of the economic circumstances that define her existence. She has never been married or had any children, so instead "for fifteen cents a dozen [she] stitches garments for children she has never had."[82] Her embroidery is presented as an expression of a female identity that has never come to fruition. Similarly, "two thousand eight hundred ladies of joy" choose to become prostitutes rather than spend their lives sewing children's clothes. As Olsen suggests, their decision is an empty one made between different kinds of physical exploitation: "[C]lap and syph aint much worse than sore fingers, blind eyes, and t.m."[83] For these women, desire and sexual expression have been transformed into marketable property by a system of economic exploitation that is perpetuated by the commodification of motherhood for the women up north. Olsen examines the intersection of economic processes and women's bodies—and thus working-class identity and femininity—in the third verse of her poem.

Catalina Torres is a "mother of four" who, like the other female workers, "embroiders from dawn to night." However, Olsen's suggestion of a biological affinity between the women up north and the female workers in San Antonio is undermined by her comparison of their respective children's bodies:

> Mother of four, what does she think of,
> as the needle pocked fingers shift over the silk—
> of the stubble-coarse rags that stretch on her brood,
> and jut with the bony ridge that marks hunger's landscape
> of fat little prairie-roll bodies that will bulge in the silk she needles?[84]

Olsen's description concentrates on the unavailability of fabric for clothes big enough to cover the scrawny and starved Torres children. In contrast, the luxurious silk that Catalina Torres stitches is abundantly able to clothe the spoiled fat children of the women up north. This fundamental material difference between experiences that are presented as being biologically identical is made emphatic at the end of verse:

(Be not envious, Catalina Torres, look!
on your own children's clothing, embroidery,
more intricate than any a thousand hands could fashion,
there where the cloth is ravelled, or darned,
designs, multitudinous, complex and handmade by Poverty herself.)[85]

Olsen's ironic tone detracts from the unrefined beauty of the clothes worn by the Torres children. Consequently, she avoids making a simplistic suggestion that, in comparison with the women up north, the poor Mexican women love and care for their children in a way that is uncorrupted by consumer ideology. As such, while "I Want You Women Up North to Know" concentrates on female identity, and particularly its expression in motherhood and sexuality, Olsen does not idealize biology as an innately nurturing and socialistic force that can undermine an exploitative—logically male—economic structure. Instead, she constructs a female point of view between proletarian narrative perspectives that define working-class experience as one-dimensionally masculine, and present capitalism as an effeminate expression of bourgeois identity. In so doing, Olsen attempts to examine femininity as an integral part of both capitalist economics and working-class experience. This is a narrative position that is central to her only novel, *Yonnondio: From the Thirties*.

The Mine

Paula Rabinowitz notes that *Yonnondio* is "perhaps the most widely read novel by a woman from the 1930s."[86] Similarly, Erika Duncan describes the book as an "on the road" for that decade, focused on, in Olsen's words, "the very early days of the Depression" before socially concerned politicians, artists, and writers began documenting the circumstances of poverty.[87] Nevertheless, *Yonnondio* transcends its 1930s context. Most of the events in the novel take place in the 1920s and, as Duncan suggests, the Holbrook family "never even arrive into the onset of the era that [the book] claims to be about."[88] Despite the fact that *Yonnondio* begins before the Depression, Olsen establishes a symbolically rendered continuity between the interminable heat and the suffocating fog that enclose the Holbrooks' lives in the late 1920s and—as Deborah

Rosenfelt notes—"the great droughts and dust storms of the 1930s."[89] This historical trajectory also extends into the 1940s and beyond. Olsen explained the scope of her vision in response to a question asking "why John Steinbeck had turned away [from working-class subjects] after the Depression." "She told me that the struggles of the farm workers went on just as dramatically in the Salinas Valley throughout the 40s, 50s, 60s, 70s, and still, only Steinbeck and others were not watching."[90]

When Olsen began writing *Yonnondio* in 1932 her vision was confined within the limited context of radical literature and politics. As such, the original plan for Olsen's novel conformed to narrow proletarian standards. Jim Holbrook was to either abandon his family in a desperate expression of his personal failure or, more heroically, he was to be blacklisted after leading a violent strike. In another version, Anna, the long-suffering mother of the Holbrook family, was to commit suicide. Orphaned and abandoned, the Holbrook children were to set off on a classically proletarian journey, riding freight trains and living like hoboes. In yet another plan, Maizie was to escape this fate and attain an education that would enable her to work as a schoolteacher for poor children.[91] Despite these emphatically proletarian scenarios, a diary entry written during the 1930s suggests that Olsen was becoming increasingly disillusioned with the polemical formulas of radical writing. Referring to the points in her narrative where she had interjected a didactic note of political prophecy, she wrote: "[N]ow it seems to me the whole revolutionary part belongs in another novel . . . and I can't put out one of those 800 page tomes."[92] Instead, as Deborah Rosenfelt notes, Olsen became "more and more concerned with showing how people came to class consciousness in an earned way, a bone way."[93]

Contemporary critics have focused on Olsen's divergence away from the traditional rhetoric of radical writing in *Yonnondio* as an expression of an emergent feminist perspective. Such interpretations have generally concentrated on the relationship between Maizie Holbrook and her mother, Anna. Typical of this point of view is Marilyn Yalom's contention that there is a fundamental connection between the working-class subjects of Olsen's text and its apparently entirely female readership: "[Olsen] was one of the first in the past quarter century to bring a consciously gendered voice to literature. That voice did not go unnoticed by members of the women's movement who recognized in Olsen a precursor for their own literary endeavors."[94] Similarly, in 1992, Elaine Orr's complicated analysis established a sharp gender division within the Holbrook family. Orr suggests that Maizie and Anna occupy identical and interchangeable narrative positions in *Yonnondio*, which enable a female reader to approach the text from a positively feminist point of view. Emphasizing what she sees as the maternally centered message of *Yonnondio*, Orr concludes that "Olsen insists readers become textual daughters (i.e., subjects knowing a likeness to the maternal) thereby closely hearing the mother and respeaking the text from a place nearby."[95]

More helpfully, Erika Duncan describes Olsen's concentration on the relationship between Maizie and Anna as a narrative "fugue and counter fugue," where Maizie's hopeful wondering at the beginning of the book is balanced by the bleak depression she perceives in her mother's life.[96] In contrast, toward the end of the novel, Maizie's increasing sense of apathy is set against Anna's steadfast retention of hope. This opposition is maintained throughout *Yonnondio*, extending beyond the mother-daughter relationship identified by Duncan, to include a similar tension between Olsen's depiction of Maizie's developing self-awareness in relation to material circumstances that are out of her control. The subsequent disparity between individual development and social context is central to Olsen's narrative perspective, as she has explained to Deborah Rosenfelt:

My vision is very different from that of other writers. . . . I don't think in terms of quests for identity to explain human motivation and behavior. I feel that in a world where class race and sex are so determining that has little reality. What matters to me is the kind of soil out of which people grow, and the kind of climate around them, circumstances are the primary key and not the personal quest for identity.[97]

Olsen's focus on the connection between economic circumstances and self-identity is fundamental to *Yonnondio*, and is centered specifically on a six-year-old working-class girl, Maizie Holbrook. At the beginning of the text, Maizie lies down on the ground—"between the outhouse and the garbage dump"—and recounts a list of the things she knows, starting with her name: "I am Maizie Holbrook. . . . I am a knowen things. I can diaper a baby. I can tell ghost stories. I know words and words. Tipple. Edjication. Bug Dust. Supertendent."[98] The tension between individuality and economic circumstances is evident in Maizie's speech, where every assertion of self-knowledge is countered by a statement that confines her potential within her material context. Thus, although Maizie is proud of her grownup abilities, her sense of personal empowerment is set against a suggestion that her gender and her economic situation force her to perform adult household tasks, like change a baby. This dichotomy is compounded by Maizie's mother, who worries that material deprivation has made her children "old before their time," especially Maizie, who, Anna notices, "for all her six and a half years was like a woman sometimes."[99]

The specifically female connection between Maizie's individually assertive speech and Anna's earlier recognition of the psychological affects of physical oppression is extended by Olsen to include the perspective of Maizie's father, Jim Holbrook. As Maizie recounts the words she knows, her speech progresses discursively from "supertendent" to a boast: "My poppa can lick any man in this here town."[100] Maizie's association between the person who represents the oppressive capitalist system and her father's macho prowess highlights how working-class men were also psychologically constricted by the demands of their physical circumstances. The conflict that Maizie identifies is echoed later in the narrative when, rather than answer Maizie's questions about material inequality, Jim imagines himself as a playful, strong, and generous father. Instead of admitting the economic power held over him by the mine bosses, he tells his daughter "an elaborate story of three dogs he fought, each big as a horse, [and finishes] triumphantly, 'Now do you think anybody could lick your daddy?' "[101]

From the outset of *Yonnondio* then, the psychological experiences that define Maizie's femininity and her working-class identity are fundamentally connected to her material circumstances. Consequently, although she can feel secure and self-confident lying on "the one patch of green in the yard" looking up toward the sun, she is also subconsciously aware of the dark chasm of space beneath her:

Bowels of the earth, she shuddered. It was mysterious and terrible to her. Bowels of the earth. It means the mine. Bowels is the stummy. Earth is a stummy and mebbe she eats the men that come down. Men and daddy goin' in like the day and comin out black, and he spits from his mouth black—Night comes and it is black.[102]

The coal dust covers and invades Jim Holbrook's body—a blackness that, in Maizie's mind, relates directly to darkness at night when "everything becomes like underground" and hides the nurturing sunlight.[103] Reflecting this, Olsen depicts Maizie's potential for "learning" in relation to a limitless blue sky, which is nevertheless symbolically rooted in the destructive and repressive darkness of the mine. Consequently, Maizie's soliloquy concludes with a statement that makes the connection between her self-identity and her material circumstances emphatic: "Mebbe I am black inside too. . . . The bowels of the earth. . . . The things I know but I am not knowen. . . . Sun on me and bowels of earth under. . . . "[104]

The psychological fragmentation that extends from Maizie's physical situation is reflected in her parents' relationship. Both Jim and Anna are connected to the mine through their gender-specific labor. Every day, Jim sets off to work at the coal face in a futile attempt to provide for his family. Similarly, Anna describes her female role as an extension of the manufacturing process at the mine. She supports Jim by making his wages stretch as far as possible and by preventing the children from disturbing his self-defensive equilibrium. Most important, however, she bears children who will become future workers in the home and in the mine. As a result, while Olsen places human sexuality at the center of working-class protest, it is a strategy of resistance that is ironically self-destructive, as Anna explains to Jim:

She [Maria Kavertnick] says that she wants the girls to become nuns so they won't have to worry where the next meal's comin from, or have to have kids. . . .

She says she doesn't want 'em raising a lot of brats to get their heads blowed off in the mine.[105]

The physical continuity between Jim and Anna is expressed through a hierarchically constructed cycle of violence that Olsen presents as being commensurate with their respective connections to the mine. Maizie notices that her father is covered with a black grime that reflects "the menacing light" that encloses the Holbrook family. As he washes the coal dust away, Maizie senses Jim's "alien sweetness," lying beneath the external layer of blackness, but, as Olsen suggests, "the coal dust lies too far inside; it will lie there forever, like a hand squeezing your heart, choking at your throat."[106] Internally engulfed by his physical circumstances, Jim Holbrook is unable to express himself except through anger, frustration, blind drunkenness, and violence toward his wife and children. Anna is also physically possessed by the mine. Maizie notices that her "momma looks all day as if she thinks she's going to be hearin something."[107] Anna's senses are constantly focused on waiting for the whistle that signifies an explosion or accident down the shaft. Moreover, her physical weakness in comparison with Jim means that she has to suffer the consequences of his self-defensive repression—a violent continuum that she extends toward her children: "[I]f they did not obey her instantly she would hit them in a blind rage, as if it were some devil she was exorcising."[108]

The cycle of aggression that enables Jim to assert himself—albeit violently and fatalistically—over his wife and children, is countered by Olsen's concentration on the self-expressive powers of the women in her text. At the beginning of *Yonnondio*, Marie Kavertnick describes the endless cycle of exploitation and death at the mine poetically. Anna recalls that "she talks about the coal. Says it oughta be red and let people see how they get it with blood."[109] Anna can articulate her fears about the mine and for the future of her children in a way that is disturbing for Jim. His aggressive response to Anna's words is to assert his physical power over her, but his irritated comment, "Quit your woman's blabbin,'" also establishes individual self-expression and psychological power as specifically female in the narrative.[110] Consequently, Anna can appreciate the importance of education for her children as a way of escaping the oppressive circumstances of the mine. In contrast, Jim can imagine nothing beyond his immediate situation. When Maizie asks him, "Pop, momma says I'm gonna get an edjication and my hands white. Is that a story, Pop?" He reacts with anger toward his wife for "[f]illin the kid's head with fool ideas." Psychologically paralyzed by the circumstances of his labor, he cannot express his hope that Maizie "could become a teacher"; instead he encourages her with a fantasy that is an extension of his futile image of himself: "Sure you are. You'll go to college and read books and marry a . . . doctor. And . . . eat on white tablecloths."[111]

Jim and Anna are alternately psychologically and physically constricted by their respective gender identities in *Yonnondio*. However, the sexual separation that Olsen depicts as central to the Holbrooks' consciousnesses is presented as a symptom of their economic circumstances rather than as a fundamental cause. In this way, Olsen's text confounds theoretical suggestions that self-identity is constructed psychologically, in a way that prefigures an individual's material situation.[112] Moreover, while women's speech is expressed poetically in *Yonnondio*, and is often presented by Olsen as being commensurate with physical experiences that are specifically female, Anna, Maizie, Marie Kavertnick, and the other working-class women in the text are not empowered by their expressive abilities. They are not able to transcend their material situations simply by articulating their sexual identities in a way that might undermine male social power. For Olsen, individual self-expression is determined by economic circumstances rather than gender hierarchies. Consequently, Jim's physical power and Anna's psychological freedom are equally reflective of working-class identities that have been restricted, confined, and crippled by their material situation. Reflecting this perspective, Jim's repressive silence is expressed by Anna as she wonders whether men care about the daily cycle of death and poverty in the mine. Significantly, her internalized thoughts are spoken out loud in "a deep man's voice . . . moaning over and over, 'God, God, God.'"[113] In the same way, the mine is described by Olsen in symbolically female language.

Moreover, the undifferentiated ways that both male and female psychological development is corrupted, restricted, and often destroyed by economic deprivation are made clear when Sheen McEvoy abducts Maizie and tries to throw her down the coal shaft.

Sheen McEvoy has been driven insane after an explosion in the mine burned off his face. Significantly, his madness enables him to articulate the thoughts that Jim and Anna have repressed. Psychologically detached from physical reality, McEvoy uses the same symbolic language that Olsen uses to describe the incarnate possession that leads Anna to strike her children. The "letters of fire dancing a devil's dance" around the mine are also a manifestation of the fantastic stories Jim creates to assert himself against capitalist power.[114] McEvoy sees "ghosts hanging from the cross beams . . . living in the coal swearing revenge when their homes were broken into."[115] McEvoy's ability to insanely express Jim's fantasies and Anna's worries extends from his psychological detachment from the economic context that destroyed his identity. Ironically, the explosion effectively released McEvoy from the material circumstances that repressively defined him. Consequently, when he looks in the mirror expecting to see his face, "he thought now some ghost in the coal was wearing it."[116] This perversely acquired freedom is compounded in relation to Anna who, unlike McEvoy, constantly has "the look of a mask" that prevents her from expressing her fears and, inevitably, her hopes for the future.[117]

Like Anna, Sheen McEvoy sees the mine as a destructive continuum of the reproductive process where pregnancy, birth, and motherhood are transformed into fear, danger, and death. At the same time, like Jim, McEvoy perceives the mine as a place where men are exploited and physically endangered in order to fulfill the economic demands of their families. From this dualistic perspective, the mine is symbolic of masculinity and femininity and, in the same way, is representative of an economic process that destroys both male and female bodies. Nevertheless, McEvoy perceives the mine as a devouring female presence that can only be satiated by returning a "little child pure of heart" to her barren womb.[118] In this way, Olsen portrays female identity as a subterranean presence that extends from the mine rather than a domestic setting, as most feminist critics of *Yonnondio* have suggested. Consequently, working-class women are not disempowered by a separation of labor that mysogynistically devalues women's work in relation to men's. Instead, Olsen suggests, male and female identity is fundamentally delineated by the economic context that the mine represents. As such, working-class men are identified—and marginally empowered—within the limited space of their physical labor. Conversely, working-class women remain hidden at the bottom of an economic hierarchy that does not recognize them as workers, and that simultaneously prevents them from assuming a domesticated female identity that middle-class women had already rejected as being wholly repressive. From this perspective, Maizie's association of the mine with her father's body is extended to include her mother's body, and therefore becomes a physical manifestation of her working-class femininity in the text. In this way, Maizie's abduction represents a point in Olsen's narrative where gender intersects with a definition of class identity usually defined as male. The clear delineations that Maizie has made between her father's physical power—"strong and tall, so far away"—and her mother's imaginative freedom subsequently become confused.[119] Internally, Maizie pleads, "Make it a dream, Momma, Poppa come here, make it a dream," but the simplistically engendered framework that has supported her is destroyed when she realizes that her mother's identity is determined by her economic situation in the same way as her father's.[120] Without a positive image of either her working-class or her female identity, Maizie cannot speak: "no words would come." Inarticulate and physically exposed, Maizie remains silent until she looks into the mine shaft that symbolizes the fundamentally uncontrollable material context that defines her as a working-class woman: "Maizie saw down, but there was no bottom. Her scream sounded now."[121]

The realization that is signified by Maizie's incoherent scream is reiterated in Olsen's text as an individual narrative space that exists between Jim Holbrook's physicality and Anna's psychological self-expression. Reflecting this textual opposition, Jim and Anna are shocked out of their antagonistic perspectives after Maizie's abduction, and begin a logical, rational conversation about the future. They agree to leave the mining town and move to a farm where the family can work together and the children will be revitalized by the natural environment. Despite this optimistic dialogue, however, Jim's and Anna's hopes are subsumed by the noise from Maizie's room: "crying, tossing, calling out fragments of sentences, incoherent words."[122] Maizie's interjection becomes more forceful as Anna and Jim decide to "make it a new life in the spring." Her interruption verbally symbolizes the economic realities that circumscribe the Holbrooks' lives. Having confronted a future where endless possibility was transformed into an empty chasm of potential destruction, Maizie expresses the unspoken knowledge that is the subtext of Jim and Anna's conversation with "terrible laughter, mocking, derisive, not her own. Anna and Jim, hearing it mix with their words, shuddered."[123]

The Farm

Initially, the journey towards the farm in Dakota reflects the positive narrative that began with Jim and Anna's conversation. The Holbrooks travel joyously and hopefully through a landscape that offers possibilities apparently so limitless that the sky seems to be "invisible."[124] The tangible sense of optimism is centered on the unity between Jim and Anna. Sitting alongside her husband on the wagon, Anna "felt like a bride"; their voices are harmoniously conjoined as they sing childhood songs together.[125] The sense of wholeness and harmony allows Anna to think back to the time before the mining town experience that seemed to engulf her. Having reclaimed a previous image of herself, Anna is then able to imagine a new one of the future: "School for the kids. Jim working near her, on the earth, lovely things to keep, brass lamps, bright table cloths, vines over the doors, and roses twining."[126]

For a brief interlude, Anna's hopeful reverie is reflected in Olsen's narrative. The natural beauty and nurturing elements at the farm give the Holbrooks a positive physical environment to expand and express themselves beyond the confinements of their working-class identity. The self-sufficient, naturally reproductive, and communally supportive work on the farm nurtures a fundamental sense of individual well-being and personal dignity that is presented in sharp contrast to physically debilitating, psychologically confining labor at the mine: "You're browning, children. The world is an oven, and you're browning in it. How good the weariness—in the tiredness, the body may dream. How good the table, with the steam arising from the boiled potatoes and vegetables and the full-bellied pitcher of milk."[127] The nurturing environment at the farm also temporarily incorporates Maizie's perspective within the optimistic trajectory of Jim and Anna's dialogue. Consequently, a positive female connection between daughter and mother is revealed. Maizie watches her mother dancing at the midsummer barn dance and is able to project her own future self onto her mother's beautiful and energetic body. Maizie's engendered aspiration toward her mother is reciprocated from Anna's point of view, when she recklessly buys "[identical]. . . . bright ribbons for Maizie and herself" to wear at the dance.[128] This newly supportive context nourishes Maizie's burgeoning sense of self-identity, and also allows her to develop the expressive skills that appeared to have been destroyed after her experience at the mine. She attends school for the first time, and displays an enthusiastic—although undeveloped—talent for reading and writing:

"eight years old and can't read yet, you'll have to go in the first grade with your brother Will["]. . . . Yet the lessons came easy—the crooked white worms of words on the second-grade blackboard magically transforming into words known and said, although they were still stumbling over the first-grade alphabet.[129]

However, the individuating power that is inherent to Maizie's education is measured by an accompanying sense of social exclusion. Insensitive comments from the schoolteacher make Maizie ashamed of the economic circumstances that prevented her from going to school in the mining town. This feeling of personal inadequacy is ironically compounded by an increasing sense of self-awareness. For the first time, Maizie realizes that her working-class identity differentiates her from her classmates. She becomes "acutely conscious" of her appearance—"her scuffed shoes, rag-bag clothes, quilt coat"—in comparison with other, economically privileged girls she has noticed "sitting high and proud in [their] buggies, ribbons in their hair blowing a long streamer in the wind."[130]

Maizie's dichotomous experience at school tempers the utopian atmosphere of the countryside that Olsen had set against the unremitting, claustrophobic, repression of the mine. The individualized potential that was nurtured by the natural beauty, "good earth," and nourishing sunshine on the farm might have allowed Maizie to escape the material confinements of her working-class identity. Unfortunately, her intellectual capacities are countered by the exclusivity of economic privilege. Thus, when Maizie recognizes the material difference between herself and her classmates she internalizes her marginalization, "[drawing] herself together to make herself nothing, to lose herself in the faded grey dress on her body."[131] In an action that reflects Olsen's own experiences at Central High School in Omaha, Maizie metaphorically deconstructs her identity and conforms to the expectations presented by her working-class status. Furthermore, the hierarchically constructed economic context that determines Maizie's self-defeating action negates any potential for positive progression beyond the idealistic space at the farm. This is an inevitability that is centrally inscribed in the text, but which is tragically incomprehensible from a working-class point of view.

The fatalistic optimism that is inherent to the Holbrooks' life at the farm is made clear by the incorporation of a sympathetic middle-class perspective within Olsen's narrative. Elias Caldwell is a college-educated, middle-class man, who has chosen to leave the "softness and ease" of his former life in the city and work on a farm.[132] His educational privileges enable him to explain the unspecified, unpredictable, apparently predestined unhappiness and poverty that enclose the Holbrooks' lives. He tells Anna about the economic system that controls profit, ensures exploitation, and represses human potential in the countryside:

When I came out, a man had some chance. The only thing against him was nature, locusts and drought and late frost. You took your chance. That was all you had to fight. But now that hardly matters. There's mortgage, taxes, the newest kind of machinery to buy so you do as good as the other fellow, and the worry—will it get a price this year.[133]

Caldwell's perspective also allows him to recognize Maizie's individual potential. He tries to encourage her to see beyond the restrictions of her working-class identity, past the exclusivity of middle-class expression, and into a place where knowledge and understanding are uncorrupted by capitalist economics. Maizie is inspired by Caldwell's stories about the constellations in the night sky, which before had seemed infused with memories about the mine. But Caldwell is an idealist; his wealth, his education, and his intellect have enabled him to reject the privileges of his middle-class identity and choose a life among "hard, bitter and strong—obscure people, [with] the smell of soil and sweat about them—the smell of life."[134] His choice makes him disdainful of his college education. He tells an uncomprehending Anna that "My education began after I got out of college."[135] It is a statement that is left unanswered by Mrs. Holbrook, for whom education is an almost unimaginable dream.

By introducing a sympathetic middle-class perspective, Olsen again emphasizes the economic determinants that define Maizie's working-class identity, and ensure her barely intelligible, mostly silent responses to Caldwell's gently encouraging words. An economically privileged perspective gives Caldwell access to the stories that are represented in the night sky. From Maizie's perspective, the stars signify possibilities that light up a darkness that had its working-class equivalent in the mine. Unfortunately, because Maizie is economically excluded from Caldwell's point of view—he is able to look upwards instead of relentlessly down—she can only imagine being able to recognize the constellations of stars, or having the knowledge to read a book with ease. The economic realities that determine Maizie's working-class identity make Caldwell's vision of an individualistic, idealistic place, where she will be able to understand and express her "wondering" incomprehensible. Consequently, Caldwell's well-intended lessons leave Maizie figuratively suspended between her working-class identity—which as Caldwell notes, is rooted in her material circumstances—and her individual desire for knowledge and self-expression:

[She sat] with a sense of nonbeing over her—of it being someone other than she sitting timeless, suspended in a dusky room, feeling a voice gathering around her, kind still hands of sound flowing into words meaningless and strange, meaningless when one tries to understand, but meaningful for a fleeting second.[136]

This moment of psychological stasis, where repression and possibility are simultaneously visible in Maizie's consciousness, is almost immediately undermined by the intervention of the economic context that fundamentally determines the narrative progression of *Yonnondio*. Jim has tried to delay the inevitable continuum of poverty and exploitation that defines his family's existence by concentrating on the immediate present, keeping his mind "motionless on the now, not on the past or what might come."[137] His attempts to psychologically distance himself from physical reality are eventually subsumed by the oncoming winter, which reflects an equally elemental realization that the landlord will take any profit he has made on the farm, leaving him "owin them after working like a team of mules for a year."[138]

The gradual reintervention of material circumstance into the utopian space that Olsen had created for the Holbrooks on the farm also determines the development of Maizie's identity. Once again, her individual potential is undermined, and eventually commodified, by capitalist economics. Her father sells the books that Caldwell gave to her after his death: "[the] fairy tales, Wilde's, and the Dickens and Blake" and, most significantly, "[the] book of Greek myths" that might have helped Maizie understand the stories behind the constellations in the night sky.[139] The books earn Jim fifty cents. From Olsen's perspective, that is the price capitalist society places on education and individual self-expression for a working-class girl.

Olsen describes the ceaseless economic process that metaphorically overwhelms the Holbrooks' lives as the winter closes in on the farmhouse. The snow is too deep for the children to be able to go to school, and storm clouds cover the previously limitless sky making the days seem "dim and short."[140] The family is confined to one room, gathered around the stove, where any distance beyond is "enormously magnified."[141] In their psychological and physical restriction, the harmoniously expressed hope for a new life and positive future at the farm is irrevocably destroyed. As a result, the disparity between Jim and Anna reemerges in Olsen's text. Jim is driven crazy by the unrelenting "closeness, the inaction" that reflects the closure of possibility for himself and his family.[142] He expresses his frustration physically, by uncontrollably lashing out at Anna and the children. In contrast, Anna—now pregnant—sits in mysterious self-involved silence, "her hands over her belly, a half smile of wisdom on her mouth."[143] Her psychological withdrawal is as insidious as Jim's violence is destructive. She neglects her children, does not clean the house or cook, and speaks only when the antagonism between herself and Jim is articulated as a renewed gender opposition in the text. Jim's violent outbursts are centered on Anna. He accuses her of failing in her roles as wife, mother, and housekeeper. In opposition, Anna's silence is broken only to remind Jim of his inadequacy as a man: "[F]ine bargains you make, fine bargains. . . . Anybody can cheat you out of anything. Can't even make a livin. Fine bargains—how to starve your wife and kids the quickest. . . . Oh sure it was all going to be fine. A new life, and you made one alright. A new way to keep in cold and wanting."[144]

The destructive dialogue between Anna and Jim is internalized by Maizie. Significantly, when she tries to reconstitute her sense of identity by pressing her body in the soft earth, she is reminded of "a face like jelly pushed against hers."[145] The memory of Sheen McEvoy reestablishes a frighteningly destructive image of working-class womanhood in Maizie's consciousness. Her fear is exacerbated by Anna's psychological retreat into her own body. Maizie can no longer recognize her future self in Anna. The disconnection between daughter and mother is described symbolically as Maizie looks around at the landscape that had once been fruitful, nourishing, and beautiful—like her mother dancing. Now the hills and trees seem to reflect the unyielding ugliness of Anna's pregnant body, and also reveal the accompanying threat of Jim's destructive presence. The trees seem "fat with oily buds," and the prairie looks like "swollen breasts."[146] More important, the sky that was once so expansive and lit with stars that reflected Maizie's consciousness is now filled with clouds that look like "bellies, swollen bellies, black and corpse gray, puffing out baggier and baggier, cloud belly on cloud belly till at the zenith they pushed out vast and swollen."[147] This distorted image of female identity further corrupts Maizie's ability to express herself: "She could feel words swollen big within her, words coming out with pain, bloody all clothed in red."[148] The literal destruction of Maizie's speech into what she perceives as an impenetrable, malignant, and abused female body initiates her into a cycle of unrecognizable, misdirected, ultimately destructive expression. She represses her fear and instead "begins to hit Will, hard, ferocious."[149] Her violent eruption is concluded with a futile repetition of a nursery rhyme that helps her forget the limitations of her knowledge.

Maizie's confrontation with childbirth is equally reminiscent of her previous encounter with the mine. She tries to dream herself away from the physical reality of the birth by focusing on the time she saw her mother dancing, but the sight of her mother's body, now contorted with pain, her face no longer animated and joyous but "set like a mask, purified, austere," reminds Maizie of Sheen McEvoy's face "[curtaining] over everything."[150] Running away into the barn, she tries to recollect the stories about the constellations, but the promise that they represented is obscured "half-drowned, blurred like through tears."[151]

Ultimately, Maizie is forced to let go of the hopeful reverie she had immersed herself in at the farm. The inevitable realities of her economic situation, which are signified by the overwhelming memory of the mine, are now combined with a physical recognition of her gender identity. Reflecting this, the Holbrooks' experience at the farm, which began so positively, ends with an expression of their failure projected through the female body. In this way, Olsen's narrative is precipitated from a feminized perspective, but is simultaneously constrained by the Holbrooks' material situation. The distorted development of Maizie's identity as a working-class woman consequently progresses between these disparate points of view, continuously deconstructing the harmony between Jim and Anna. Repeating the scene before the Holbrooks left the mine, Jim and Anna create an image of resistance and hope in a conversation where, significantly, their "two figures blur into one." Simultaneously, they announce their intention to leave the farm:

> Very low he says: "You're shivering. Cold?"
> "Awful cold. Lets go. Now."
> "But you cant take it lying down—like a dawg. You cant Anna."[152]

The City

The Holbrooks arrive in Omaha to face an urban scene that is presented in stark contrast to the optimism manifested at the farm. Anna and Jim grew up in the city, the streets are "old and familiar . . . to them, the scenery of their childhood rearranged."[153] The faint hope that initiated their return is thus immediately undercut by a narrative trajectory that effectively moves backwards to a place where they felt undefeated by the economic deprivations of their lives. Reflecting this beginning, at the end of the text, Anna looks up into the smog-filled sky and imagines seeing "a white bridal wreath, [remembering] when she was a girl. . . . Oh when she was a girl. . . . The life she had dreamed and the life that had come to be."[154]

The underlying sense of futility that accompanies the Holbrooks' arrival in the city is temporarily repressed as Jim and Anna try to reestablish a sense of normality and acceptance that might detract from the dilapidated state of their surroundings. When they arrive at their new house, Jim urges Anna to look away from the heat and stench and focus on the modern conveniences that represent the materiality of urban life:

"It's got a yard for the kids. They won't be runnin out in the streets to play, anyhow. And just think, running water with a faucet and a toilet inside the house. . . . And electric light. . . . And electric lights if we want."[155] Leaving her disappointment, frustration, and shock unspoken, Anna's weary rejoinder echoes Jim's pathetic hope that they will be able to participate in the acquisitive economy of the city. She dismisses his vociferous protest—"I know this aint no palace, but you ought to see what other folks are livin in for what we're paying"—with an assertion of her support for his masculine pride: "Sure, Jim, I know it's a real find. Guess I'm tired, that's all."[156]

Jim and Anna's apparent submission to consumer capitalism is predicated on a simultaneous suppression of their working-class identity, a negative dialectic that is continuously emphasized in Olsen's narrative. Working-class expression is presented as a silent subtext to the economically privileged discourse that dominates the city. Consequently, "the nameless FrankLloydWrights [sic] of the proletariat," who have built their homes out of "flat battered tin cans, fruit boxes and gunny sacks, cardboard and mother earth," have articulated their individuality not as a form of resistance to the economic deprivations that define their existences, but as a manifestation of their capitulation to their material circumstances.[157] For Olsen, the creativity displayed in these "wondrous futuristic structures" is a tragic expression of human potential systematically repressed and constrained by capitalist society.[158] Reflecting this, when the working-class children living in the city lie on the ground— like six-year-old Maizie at the beginning of *Yonnondio*—their self-consciously constructed reveries are not directed toward the sky, but are engulfed and corrupted by the degrading, fetid environment around them: "They lie on their bellies near the edge of the cliff and watch the trains and freights, the glittering railroad tracks, the broken bottles dumped below, the rubbish moving on the littered belly of the river."[159]

The discursive progression from material deprivation to psychological restriction is compounded in Olsen's narrative as the children adapt to the city environment. Maizie and Will turn away from an exclusive educational system that has labeled them as "dummies" because of their underprivileged backgrounds, and defensively—ultimately self-defeatingly—create their own individualized spaces:

Children—already . . . condemned as unfit for the worlds of learning, art, imagination, invention—plan, measure, figure, design, invent, construct, costume themselves, stage drama: endlessly—between tasks, errands, smaller children to be looked after, jobs, dailinesses—live in passionate absorbed activity, in rapt make-believe.[160]

Excluded—and disengaged—from the institutionalized privileges of middle-class education, these apparently self-defined working-class perspectives are easily commodified. Will becomes addicted to the movie adventures of cowboy Bill Hart. This obsession gradually invades his consciousness, seducing him away from the realities of his economic situation and insidiously narrowing his identity:

Subtly into waking and dreaming into imagination and everyday doings and play, shaping, altering them. Even outwardly: Will's eyes are narrowed now, his mouth drawn up at the corner, his walk—when he remembers—loose for the rest of his life he will grin crooked: Bill Hart.[161]

Will's fantasy offers him immediate sensual gratification that allows him to temporarily escape the heat and stench of the Holbrooks' house. However, his inclusion within the mythologies of American individualism and pioneering western adventure is circumscribed by the distance between himself and the one-dimensional image on the screen. He is rewarded with a decontextualized, imitative fantasy of participation, which simultaneously ensures that as a working-class man—barely possessing the ten cents price of admission—he will always remain outside of the reality. The desensitizing commodification of Will's consciousness is extended as his interest in cowboy movies develops into a fascination with gangster films. He and his friend Smoky, already having cultivated a reputation for petty crime, stand outside the Palace theater staring at movie stills: "A crook picture," Will says longingly.[162] His curiosity is precipitated by his poverty and an acquired knowledge that crime apparently pays—at least on the screen. Will's psychological connection to the cinema not only reflects his marginalization from middle-class capitalist America, it also reveals his possible future: presenting an apparently attainable image of success, economic power, and individual acquisitiveness that will lead inevitably to his destruction.

Maizie is also fascinated by the movies, particularly the romantic obsessions of her friend "Ginella," who delights in the tacky passion of films such as *The Sheik of Araby, Broken Blossoms, Slave of Love, She Stopped at Nothing, The Fast Life, The Easiest Way*.[163] In opposition to the machismo of gangster movies and westerns, however, Ginella and Maizie are entranced by an emotionally expressive, idealistically beautiful, and sexually desirable image of femininity. Ginella's enticing reenactment of a scene from *The Sheik of Araby* presents an image of women that undercuts the ugly, oppressive, wholly destructive view of the female body that Maizie has experienced thus far in her life. The frightening memories of her mother's blood and the symbolically engulfing blackness of the mine shaft are gradually erased as Maizie and Ginella repeat the dialogue from *The Sheik of Araby*, creating between them a hazy "lilac time": safe, dreamlike, and psychologically separated from the physical reality of working-class femininity.[164]

Olsen presents this fantasized discourse as a textual expression that subsumes material reality in *Yonnondio*. Ginella's "text" allows her to transform the impenetrable, claustrophobic heat of her home and of her job washing pots in a diner, into a sultry desert or a spacious palace where she can be "elegant, idle and served and cool."[165] Her imagination permits her to transcend her working-class identity, specifically her poverty and her Polish immigrant heritage. Instead of being Gertrude Skolnick with "red knuckled hands [and] broken fingernails," she can become the beautiful Ginella possessing "slender white fingers with talon nails."[166] Mass-produced and widely disseminated images of rich, desirable women make Ginella ashamed of her working-class circumstances and her ethnic identity. Ginella and Maizie associate their working-class identity with ugliness and undesirability. Consequently, material status— like furs, jewels and servants—appears to be dependent on submission to a sexual economy that, for working-class women like Ginella and Maizie, suggests a future of exploitation, degradation, and humiliation.

The cinema enables Will, Maizie, and Ginella to reconstruct themselves, temporarily allowing them to transcend their economic situation while simultaneously detaching them from material reality. The separation of psychological self-expression from physical circumstance is a dangerously distracting substitute for creativity in Olsen's text, and is encouraged by an ideology of consumer capitalism that is dependent on maintaining ignorance, apathy, and fatalism in working-class people. The inextricable link between individuality and material equality that is made clear in Olsen's comparison of Will's, Maizie's, and Ginella's metaphysical "texts" with the macabre nursery rhymes recited by the Holbrooks' younger son, Benjy.

Not yet old enough to construct a self-defensive distance between himself and his material situation, Benjy expresses the isolation and fear that invade his consciousness through "terrible texts" related to his baby brother Jimmie:

> Plaintively, as if understanding its meaning:
>
> Ol' clothes to sell, ol' clothes to sell'
> If I had as much money as I could tell
> I never would cry ol' clothes to sell.

And desolately:

Mother, Mother, I am sick.
Call the doctor quick, quick, quick.
Doctor, Doctor, will I die?
Yes. You will. And so shall I.[167]

Maizie recognizes the meaning of Benjy's words and tries to cover them with a distracting text of her own. She gathers the children around her and quickly sings "Hoopde Dooden Do Barney Google with the Googlygoogly Eyes, I'm Dreamin Now of Hally."[168] She also encourages her father to participate in her semantic game, asking him to tell Ben and Jimmie some stories of "when you were little." But Jim cannot respond. The overwhelming physical exhaustion of his work has silenced him, "thieved his text," leaving him unable to retell the tales that had intermittently comforted and protected Maizie and Will.[169] Similarly, Anna, engulfed by her household work, finds there is no time for the kind of fantasy that might allow her to temporarily escape from the endless routine of her female labor. Significantly, Olsen concludes that by the time working-class children reach adulthood, "it is already too late for texts."[170]

Jim's and Anna's silence is described as gender specific by Olsen, but also as being rooted in the same economic context that defines their working-class identities. Thus, Jim rails against an image of masculinity that systematically degrades and exploits him. Working in a sewer, Jim and his co-workers are berated for their failure to comply with impossible-to-attain productivity targets. The supervisor calls the men a bunch of "women" who would rather "suck titty all day instead of working like [men]."[171] Significantly, Jim's reaction to the speedup process at the sewage works is that "it cant be done" if the workers are to "stay human."[172] Initially, this response places his own experience within an alternative context of morally acceptable labor and living standards, and connects his individual exploitation with the experiences of the rest of his workmates and of his family. However, Jim's rational and holistic reaction is undermined later, when he goes to a bar and gets drunk in an attempt to forget the humiliations of his day. Jim's inebriation, like his children's obsession with the cinema, allows him to reconstruct his identity in such a way that he can believe he has some control, and equally, some power to change his life. Consequently, he focuses on his physical superiority over his wife and children and convinces himself that his degradation is a direct result of his role as a husband and father. This misguided belief is evidently compounded when he compares his apparently emasculated position with the freedom of his unmarried colleague,

Jim Tracy, who has been able to walk out of the sewer job without regret or responsibility. Jim's frustration at his economic position is subsequently transformed into a fierce and uncontrollable sexual anger. Inevitably, he transposes his sense of disempowerment onto Anna whom he imagines avariciously "counting his pay money," in an image that logically progresses to his justification of physical violence toward her: "Goddam woman—what's the matter with her anyhow? Dont even have a wife that's a wife anymore—just let her say one word to me and I'll bash her head in."[173]

Jim's violence is presented by Olsen as the distorted result of his economic exclusion from the ideological structures of consumer capitalism. This assertion is emphasized as Jim's thoughts are continuously interrupted by symbolically resonant phrases that connote the rhetoric of the American Dream. Jim therefore interprets Tracy's independence as a naive action of a man who has not yet realized his marginalized position: "He believed the bull about freedomofopportunity and achancetorise and ifyoureallywanttoworkyoucanalwaysfindajob [*sic*] and ruggedindividualism and something about pursuitofhappiness [*sic*]."[177] Olsen emphasizes the all-encompassing facade of capitalist ideology in her narrative by running words together to indicate their impenetrability from a working-class point of view. At the same time, working-class experience is prettily transformed into sentimental songs and iconographic images, which appeal to aesthetic and political sensibilities defined from a middle-class perspective. This mythology is ironically projected and subsequently integrated into working-class consciousness. Jim repeats the exclusive effects of this process in a speech where reality and representation become confused and equally insignificant:

feet slapping the pavement, digging humbly into carpets, squatting wide apart in front of chairs and the no job no job nothing doing today buzzing in his ears; eking out the coffee—and shuffling along, buddy (they made a song out of it) can you spare a dime, and the freights north east south west, getting vagged, keep movin, keep movin (the bulls dont need to tell ya, your own belly yells it out, your own idle hands), sing a song of hunger the weather four below holes in your pockets and nowhere to go, the flophouses, the slophouses, a bowl of misery and a last month's cruller and the crabs having a good time spreading and spreading (you didnt know hell would be this bad, did you?)[175]

Jim's humiliating capitulation to his economic situation is depicted in an image of a "drowned man who [has] no choice but to hang onto it [his job] for notso dear life."[176] Anna displays a similar tenacity, fighting waves of exhaustion and sickness and trying desperately to continue her motherly duties. In contrast to Jim, however, Anna's eventual submission to the defining power of capitalist economics is expressed as a psychological retreat inside her body, rather than as an aggressive physical explosion. Reflecting this gender opposition, directly after Jim's speech, Olsen presents an image of Anna that is described in stark contrast to his masculine power: "Momma was asleep again, falling asleep right in her chair like she was always doin now, with her mouth open, and cryin as if somebody was hitting her, turnin her head and cryin."[177]

Anna's acquiescence echoes her husband's surrender to the capitalist discourse that defines working-class identity in *Yonnondio*. However, Anna's subjection is enforced by an additional level of physical aggression that further circumscribes her self-identity. Thus, she sits in exhausted silence as if she were expecting Jim to hit her, and struggles to perform basic household tasks against a dualistic perspective that simultaneously depletes her energy and invades her consciousness. Her frustration and fear is projected onto her children—particularly Maizie—who rely on their mother to help them see beyond the physical immediacy of their material situation. Instead, Anna continues the malignant trajectory that Jim has transferred onto her body. When Maizie presents her with a failed report card, Anna does not have the energy to react constructively; instead she responds with a reflexive, physical threat: "You bring another one and I'll beat you to a pulp."[178]

In an expressive hierarchy formulated on physical strength, Anna is restrained and repressed within her body, a regressive process that confines her consciousness to maternal and sexual experience and subsequently prevents her from expressing herself as an individual working-class woman. Nonetheless, Olsen suggests that the continuum of physical violence that leads to Anna's silence is not simply the result of female victimization by men, but is the inevitable result of material exclusion from the ideological discourse of capitalist economics. This fundamental connection is made brutally clear when one evening Jim returns home drunk and rapes his pregnant wife.

Jim's violent assault, although reprehensible, is presented as an expression of his enforced capitulation to his economic status. Olsen's intentionally problematic empathy for Jim's tortured perspective is made clear after he discovers Anna unconscious on the floor and calls a doctor:

"Miscarriage. You didn't know she was pregnant—again?" (Damn fools they ought to sterilize the whole lot of them after the second kid.)

"Four months, mm. You remember how long your wife's been sick?" Of course not. These animals never notice but when they're hungry or want a drink or a woman.

"Hmmmmmm. Yes. . . . So it was intercourse before as well as the fall?" Pigsty the way these people live. "And she's been nursing all along? We'll have a look at the baby." Rickets, thrush, dehydrated. Dont' blame it trying to die. . . .

"Your wife's a sick woman. Needs all the rest she can get, fresh fruits, vegetables and liver. And medical attention."[179]

The doctor's speech reiterates the economic inequalities that have distorted and corrupted Jim's psyche, and eventually led to his terrible crime against his wife. Olsen writes the doctor's unspoken thoughts so as to reveal the subtextual meaning of his judgmental questions. His comments highlight the way social deprivation and institutionalized oppression are transformed into decontextualized personal responsibility by capitalist ideology. As a result, Jim expresses his guilt as an individual sense of inadequacy that ironically reinforces his feeling of economic failure: the doctor tells him "everything she [Anna] needs, but not how to get it."[180] Remorse finally silences Jim, temporarily repressing his physical outbursts into inarticulate frustration, which, Olsen concludes, "will never be spoken—till the day that hands will find a way to speak."[181]

Paula Rabinowitz suggests that Jim's frustration remains inexpressible in *Yonnondio* because Olsen is attempting to uncover a specifically female perspective in the narrative, which is spoken through women's bodies. Consequently, because "men's bodies are inscribed through their labor, they require a language of the hands."[182] This interpretation repeats the notion that language that is theoretically identified as being male is voiced only at the cost of female speech and in tandem with the rhetoric of institutionalized power. In Rabinowitz's view, Olsen has simply reversed the gender opposition so as to reveal a female point of view that is expressed through Anna's defiled body. Reflecting this assertion, the events that follow Jim's assault on his wife concentrate on the development of Anna's individual consciousness. Rather than being an extension or an expression of her bodily functions, however, Anna's individual identity depends on her being able to distance herself from the physical hardships and debilitating circumstances that overwhelm her body. Moreover, while Anna achieves a certain amount of psychological independence from the repressions of her traditional female role, that is, in opposition to Jim, and set apart from the demands of motherhood, her freedom to express herself as a (theoretically defined) woman is consistently balanced and fundamentally determined by her working-class identity. Consequently, Anna's capacity for self-expression is grounded in the same material circumstances as Jim's. Her "labor" as a woman is not presented in opposition to Jim's "labor" as a manual worker; rather, the Holbrooks are all ultimately defined by an economic process that silences both working-class women and men, in relation to a theoretical perspective that is clearly expressed from a middle-class standpoint.[183]

From this point of view, rather than being an unadulterated attack on female identity in general, the rape is presented by Olsen as a perversion of the basically loving relationship that Jim and Anna have struggled to maintain throughout the text. Ironically—in the same way that Sheen McEvoy was psychologically "freed" by the explosion at the mine—the attack temporarily allows Anna to extrapolate herself from the seemingly inescapable continuum of violence in *Yonnondio*. She turns away from Jim whenever he comes into her room: "[S]he never answered . . . or looked at him or questioned why it was that she was lying there." She speaks only to ask "Is Bess eating all right?" but does not wait for Jim's reply. She lies with "her head turned toward the window," focusing on the small space of light that might signify her personal freedom.[184]

The newly self-defining distance that emerges between Anna and the invasive demands of her husband is extended in relation to her role as a mother. When Anna turns away from the window and back toward the room, her sense of peace is disturbed by her aching swollen breasts. This physical reminder of her motherly responsibilities forces her out of her solitary bed and back to her household duties. At first, she asserts a sense of pride in her female role. She efficiently sorts out her children's clothes, makes a mental list of items to be mended, and tells her neighbor, Mrs. Kryckszi, that she no longer needs help around a house that she considers to be her exclusive domain.

Anna's temporary sense of pride and fulfillment is insidiously undermined as Olsen introduces the ideological tenets of middle-class discourse to the text. Anna attends the clinic where she sees posters that remind mothers that "Dirt Breeds Disease" and "Flies Spread Germs."[185] The phrases revolve around Anna's consciousness, reinscribing her working-class identity within the text, suggesting that she cannot properly protect her children, that she is an improper mother and an inadequate woman, proclaiming her sense of failure, and restricting her identity within her marginalized economic circumstances. The unremitting hardship of "being poor and a mother" destroys Anna's sense of personal empowerment, and saps her physical strength with an uncompromising recognition of the futility of her material situation:

It was all of these things that brought her now to swaying in the middle of the floor, twisting and twisting the rompers in soundless anguish. It was that she felt so worn, so helpless; that it loomed gigantic beyond her, impossible ever to achieve, beyond any effort or doing of hers: that task of making a better life for her children to which her being was bound.[186]

Despite this indisputable reality, Anna responds to the impossibilities of working-class motherhood by continuing the feminized narrative trajectory that began with her escape from the physical assaults made on her body. Rather than resuming the relentless labors of motherhood, she establishes a psychological separation between herself and her children: "[S]omething broken and new and tremulous—had been born in her."[187] Anna begins to assert her independence. She takes in laundry against Jim's wishes, hoping to earn enough money of her own to enable Will to finish high school. At the same time, she establishes her own physical space, taking her work outside and spending time weeding the garden instead of cleaning the house. In the open air, Anna can focus on the "boundless sky" that has signified unlimited possibility throughout *Yonnondio*. Her mind wanders beyond her physical being as she follows the mist out along the river and blows soap bubbles into the sun. Her freedom is projected onto her children, and she begins to imagine exciting futures for them again. She tells Benjy about the far-off places where her brother has sailed, and which he might also visit when he grows up.

The imaginative spaces that Anna creates for herself and her children are set in a wider, more physically constricting context that Olsen seems to present as being gender specific. Anna tells her sons about the "wonders of the world" they might travel to, but adds wistfully that the journey is something "boys get to do . . . not girls."[188] Similarly, Anna's sense of psychological freedom transgresses defined gender boundaries, confusing and scaring Benjy:

"Let's not go in. I declare I feel like a gypsy, wanderin and campin, doing everything outdoors, rolling up in the night too, sleepin out, never goin in."

"Let's go in, Momma," pulling at her in sudden fright. "We got to go in. Its suppertime. Don't talk goofy, Momma. Mommas always goes in."[189]

Maizie is also disturbed by her mother's new expressions of individuality and psychological freedom. As she watches her mother dancing around the garden with Benjy following, Maizie gradually becomes aware of an almost indiscernible space where she might be able to transcend the material circumstances of her working-class identity, and the physical constraints made on her female body. Anna seems to be leading Maizie away from the defining class and gender dialectic in Olsen's narrative and into a textual space that appears to connote a liberating perspective for working-class women. Not quite comprehending, Maizie stands "transfixed in wonder and fear," while Anna walks "dreamlike round and round the yard . . . disappearing in and out of the clutching mists; emerging and disappearing. . . . Her voice came dreamy and disembodied."[190]

The ethereal connection between Anna and Maizie is made temporarily concrete in Olsen's text, when Anna leads an almost allegorical journey through symbolically rendered manifestations of economic and engendered oppression, toward an idyllic place in the countryside. Significantly, the narrative trail begins negatively for Anna. She has set off with her children in search of dandelions that might comply with the "one serving: Green Leafy Vegetable Daily" instruction, pejoratively recommended by health authorities ignorant of working-class circumstances.[191] Nevertheless, as the family wanders further from their house, Anna becomes increasingly distracted from her motherly task and instead begins braiding the dandelion stems and starts looking for inedible clover. Mindful of the fleeting moment of personal freedom she experienced at the farm, Maizie becomes steadily more uncomfortable with her mother's actions. She rejects Anna's attempts to make a daisy chain and interrupts her esoteric musings with agitated demands. Maizie's discomfort is compounded as Anna leads the children through an affluent neighborhood. Her mother's apparent obliviousness to their shabby clothes and unhealthy appearance only serves to make Maizie more aware of her working-class status: "[A] vague shame, a weedy sense of not belonging, of something being wrong about them, stirred uneasy through [her]," as Anna carries on regardless.[192]

In response to Anna's detachment, Maizie takes on her mother's role. She keeps the younger children in order and protects them from the insidious sense of inadequacy felt as they confront a wealthy lady with a patronizing smile. As Anna leads them farther toward a fragrantly green riverbank, Maizie's defensive reserve is at last overwhelmed by her mother's beauty. Anna's individuality—separated from the children and set apart from her poverty—and her stories describe a positive, seemingly attainable future for Maizie to follow. The two women, no longer defined by their roles as mother and daughter or confined by their economic situation, sit together and create between them a utopian narrative space of "happiness and farness and selfness," which symbolizes and uniquely expresses a transcendent sense of possibility and independence for working-class women:

The fingers stroked, spun a web, cocooned Maizie into happiness and intactness and selfness. Soft wove the bliss round hurt and fear and want and shame—the old worn, fragile bliss, a new frail selfness bliss, healing, transforming. Up from the grasses, from the earth, from the broad tree trunk at their back. Latent life streamed and seeded. The air and self shone boundless. Absently, her mother stroked; stroked unfolding, wingedness, boundlessness.[193]

In 1984, Olsen was asked about "the relationship of a creative core of self to the social force of the times." Angrily, Olsen replied: "It is irrelevant to even talk of the core of self when circumstances do not sustain its expression or development, when life has tampered with it and harmed it."[194] The idyllic moment of stasis between Anna and Maizie in *Yonnondio* reflects Olsen's statement. The incessant demands of the younger children suddenly and inevitably return mother and daughter to the material context that defines their identities and silences their expressive powers.[195] Furthermore, the reconnection to their socially ascribed female role occurs as the elemental peace around them is disturbed by the wind blowing through the packing house, reminding Anna and Maize of the equally unremitting demands of their economic situation. The remainder of *Yonnondio* follows the familiar trajectories of economic and physical oppression that invaded and subsumed Anna and Maizie's consciousness at the riverbank. Nevertheless, the practical futility of that transcendent moment is not obviously overriding in *Yonnondio*. The Holbrook family continues to maintain a space for hope and possibility in their lives. At the end of the text, working-class identity—in particular female working-class identity—remains undefeated. The younger Holbrook daughter, Bess, expresses herself with force and personally defining power:

Bess who has been fingering a fruit-jar lid—absently, heedlessly drops it—aimlessly groping across the table, reclaims it again. Lightening in her brain. She releases, grabs, releases grabs. I can do. Bang! I did that. I can do. I! A look of Neanderthal concentration is on her face. That noise! In triumphant, astounded joy she clashes the lid down. Bang, slam, whack. Release, grab, slam, bang, bang. Centuries of human drive work in her; human ecstasy of achievement, satisfaction, deep and fundamental as sex: I can do, I use my powers; I! I![196]

Despite this final expression of individuality, spoken from a working-class and female point of view, the material circumstances that overwhelmed the Holbrooks in *Yonnondio* also prevented Tillie Olsen from continuing her work. Although she was able to animate, explain, and infuse the petrified body of the Korl Woman with life, by describing the experiences of working-class women in complicated, inspiring, and ultimately tragic detail, Olsen's own economically deprived and socially marginalized position meant that her work was destined to remain an outline; or, at the most, an artistic project that was necessarily unfinished, imperfect, and filled with empty spaces.[197] At the end of *Yonnondio,* Olsen explains why she considered her novel to be an unavoidably inadequate representation of working-class women:

Reader, it was not to have ended here, but it is nearly forty years since this book had to be set aside, never to come to completion.

These pages you have read are all that is deemed publishable of it. Only fragments, rough drafts, outlines, scraps remain—to tell what might have been, and never will be now.[198]

Contemporary feminist theory—postfeminist, even—posits that fragmentation, disruption, and distortion of predetermined conceptions of what constitutes a gender identity represent a radical progression from traditional feminist proclamations that all women are alike in their experience of patriarchal oppression. In the same way, cultural critics have tried to present a more diffuse idea of various ethnic or working-class experiences of racism or economic oppression. The evidence of *Yonnondio,* as an incomplete record of working-class women's lives, radically complicates this eminently accommodating progression from modernist unity to postmodern fluidity. How can a subject position—in this case one that is both working-class and female—be disrupted in a radical sense if it has only ever been represented, depicted, reported, made visible and made audible from a distance of economic privilege? Moreover, as Olsen's experience suggests, how can textual disunity and narrative fragmentation be construed as being politically subversive if—as is clear in *Yonnondio*—the fissions are reflections of material deprivation, and the silences are not manufactured but are manifestations of the ways economic and educational disadvantages, internalized inadequacy, and systematic social exclusion have prevented the author from completing her work.[199]

To read *Yonnondio* as a work that is positively incomplete—that is to say, its unfinished state is a deeply resonant reflection of Olsen's writing life and of working-class women's lives in general—is a devastatingly tragic conclusion to this book. Nevertheless, by examining how it might have been possible to represent economically and socially marginalized people in ways that allow them to speak for themselves could be considered an (immensely inadequate) position from which to overturn the circumstances that have ensured their silence: in literature, in art, in academic thought, in philosophical theory, and in political analyses of gender, race, and class identity. At the same time, however, to simply read and understand that silence is not enough: working-class women should not have to rely on twists of fate and singular successes in order to be able to express themselves as individuals. Olsen believes that the fact her work exists at all was dependent on a stroke of luck that was not so kind to other working-class women who never had the chance to write as she had done. Nevertheless, her lack of bitterness belies a deep-rooted anger that is evident in *Yonnondio*, and is an emotion that might serve as reminder of all the working-class women who became silent witnesses to American culture, history, and politics between 1933 and 1945. Moreover, anger—tempered with frustration that nothing much has changed—should be fundamental to any analysis of the individual lives and personal experiences of working-class women since then, and is echoed in Olsen's words:

How can I be personally bitter, when I have been able to do what so few of my sex and class have had the chance to do? But I am bitter, do not forgive, their silencing and the enormous loss of what they had to give.[200]

Notes

Introduction

1. Zandy 9.

2. Zandy 9.

3. One of the main reasons given for not writing about working-class identity in the United States is that most Americans consider themselves to be middle class, therefore there can be no such thing as working-class consciousness. On the contrary, Sennett and Cobb have suggested in *The Hidden Injuries of Class* that people from economically deprived backgrounds repress their pasts and measure their class identity according to the consumer items they are able to buy, or else they tend to project a potential for middle-classness onto their children. Finally, American culture ensures the capitulation of working-class people to an image of classlessness by presenting their marginalization as a matter of individual responsibility and personal failure.

4. Fussell 2-12.

5. For a comprehensive statistical investigation of the ways poverty is defined in the United States see Albelda et al.

6. Rogovin and Frisch 81-316.

7. Rogovin and Frisch 125.

8. Rogovin and Frisch 175.

9. Rogovin and Frisch 290.

10. Rogovin and Frisch 263.

11. Silverman 8.

12. Silverman 9.

13. Silverman 32.

14. Caldwell 51-54.

15. Silverman 180.

16. Rawlings xi.

17. Rawlings xii.

18. See Sennett and Cobb, *The Hidden Injuries of Class.*

19. Olsen, *Silences* 46.

20. Natanson 4.

21. Natanson 18

22. Esther Bubley: "The people in the darkroom were practically foaming at the mouth, they were so opposed to a black photographer. They sounded like a bunch of rednecks. It's amazing they didn't just destroy Parks' negatives" (Natanson 62).

23. Parks, *To Smile* and *Voices*.

24. Parks 1990: 83.

25. Moutassmy-Ashe 60.

26. Moutassmy-Ashe 74.

27. Moutassmy-Ashe 85.

28. Moutassmy-Ashe 98.

29. Moutassmy-Ashe 78.

30. Wright, *American Hunger*.

31. Carby, *Reconstructing Womanhood* 165.

32. Natanson 1992: 261.

33. Hurston 21.

34. Wright, *Native Son*.

35. If my book had continued beyond the 1930s and early 1940s, I could have included Olsen's later collection of short stories, *Tell Me a Riddle* published in 1964; and "Requa," published in *The Iowa Review*, 1.3 (1970) 54-74. I could have also included Anne Petry's novel *The Street* (1946), Louise Meriwether's *Daddy Was a Number Runner* (1970) and *This Child's Gonna Live* by Sarah E. Wright, first published in 1969.

36. Some critics have begun to investigate history and literature in ways that examine the intersections between class, gender, and race identity. For example: Roediger, *The Wages of Whiteness: Race and the Making of the American Working-Class*, and Morrison, *Playing in the Dark: Whiteness and the Literary Imagination*.

Introduction to Part I

1. Olsen, *Tell Me* 265.

2. Barthes 25-28.

3. Ohrn 25.

4. Barthes 66.

5. Barthes 73.

6. Olsen, *Tell Me* 271.

7. Stott 58.

8. Stange xiii.

9. Stein 3-10.

10. See Trachtenberg "From Image to Story: Reading the File," *Documenting America* 43-73.

11. Rosler 306.

12. Berger 284.

13. Olsen, *Tell Me* 190.

14. Schloss, 256.

15. Olsen, *Tell Me* 191.

16. Benjamin, Walter, "The Work of the Art in the Age of Merchanical Reproduction," *Photography in Print*, Vicki Goldberg, editor.

Chapter 1: Dorothea Lange: Representing Rural Poverty

1. Susman 9.

2. Susman xx.

3. Susman xix-xxx.

4. Information on Stryker can be found in Maren Stange's *Symbols of Ideal Life*, 89-131 and in F. Jack Hurley *Portrait of a Decade*, 15-16.

5. Stryker and Wood 9.

6. Stange, *Symbols* 130.

7. Trachtenberg 61.

8. Stange, *Symbols* 123.

9. Stryker and Wood 19.

10. FDR pledged to help "the forgotten man" when he accepted the nomination to run for President at the Democratic Convention, June 2, 1932. It is interesting to note that the policy platform that was drafted for Roosevelt was criticized for being too conservative. Senator Key Pittman protested that "the platform has the merit of being short, and the demerit of being cold. There is not a word in it with regard to the "forgotten man" (see Leuchtenberg 8-9).

11. Warren Susman suggests that despite the criticisms of capitalism in the 1930s, economic failure and social marginalization were still popularly represented as being personal, individualized character flaws, rather than as a result of an unfair and unequal social order. One of the examples given by Susman that reflects this popularly held notion was the proliferation of "how-to-do-it books" in the 1930s, i.e., Dale Carnegie's *How to Win Friends and Influence People* in 1936, a significant precursor of the self-help books and psychobabble chat shows prevalent today.

12. Quoted in Meltzer 84.

13. Meltzer 85.

14. Meltzer 84.

15. Meltzer 337.

16. Stryker and Wood 20.

17. Baldwin 190.

18. Baldwin 191. Participation in the agricultural future planned by the FSA had very basic economic and race requirements. Programs designed to help tenants buy their own land selected only those clients most likely to repay their loans. Consequently, selection procedures were intrinsically and exclusively racist. In Mississippi, only 2% of clients were black out of a population of tenant farmers that was 75% African American (see Baldwin 197).

19. Baldwin 107.

20. Baldwin 88.

21. Lange interview.

22. Ohrn 24.

23. Meltzer 82.

24. Trachtenberg 59.

25. Stryker Collection reel one.

26. Stryker Collection reel one.

27. Ohrn 197.

28. Lange 79.

29. Lang and Schuster 110.

30. Lange and Taylor 53.

31. Lange and Taylor 98.

32. Lange and Taylor 104.

33. Lange and Taylor 106.

34. Lange and Taylor 107.

35. Baldwin 107.

36. Baldwin 107.

37. Quoted in Meltzer 133.

38. Ohrn 79.

39. Stryker and Wood 9.

40. Curtis 47-67.

41. Curtis 50.

42. Curtis 50.

43. Curtis 67.

44. Curtis 58.

45. Fisher 131.

46. Ware 50.

47. Ware 40.

48. Curtis 62.

49. Janiewski 89.

50. Fertility, contraception, and sterilization were major issues of concern for women in the New Deal Government. The availability of birth control to working-class women was usually predicated on a moral bias where middle-class women assumed poor women to be licentious and unnaturally sexual. Such crusades often disregarded the cultural attitudes of working-class women toward family life and sexuality. At the same time, middle-class policy-makers often used their control over access to contraception to engineer the lifestyles of less well-educated women. (See Hagood *Mothers of the South*; Sanger *Margaret Sanger: An Autobiography*; and Le Sueur "Sequel to Love.")

51. Lange 105.

52. Ohrn 107.

53. Lange 110.

54. As a young girl traveling to school through the Lower East Side of New York, Lange practiced making herself "invisible." This was a description she gave to illustrate how she was able to observe experiences other than her own without feeling threatened, or that she was being intrusive or judgmental.

See Meltzer, Ohrn, and Schloss for the ways Lange used this talent in her FSA photography.

55. Curtis 57-58.

56. Curtis 67.

57. Mann 99-101.

58. Meltzer 98.

59. Ohrn 102.

60. Rosler 313.

61. Curtis 67.

62. Rosler 313.

63. Rosler also mentions an article in the *Sunday New York Times Magazine*, where the families visited by James Agee and Walker Evans in *Let Us Now Praise Famous Men* are rephotographed as if to reveal their "real" identities.

64. Rosler 317

Chapter 2: Marion Post Wolcott: The Economics of Deception

1. Hendrickson 154.

2. Hendrickson 222.

3. In Hendrickson's book, also in Sally Stein's introduction to *Marion Post Wolcott*, Fisher's *Let Us Now Praise Famous Women*, Julie Boddy's article in *Decades of Discontent* and F. Jack Hurley's *Marion Post Wolcott: A Photographic Journey*.

4. Hurley, *Marion Post Wolcott* xi-xii

5. Stein 3.

6. Stein 9.

7. Hendrickson 154.

8. Leuchtenberg 323.

9. Chamberlain 7.

10. Chamberlain 6.

11. For example, in an article for the Washington Post, Post Wolcott was headlined in a description: "Girl Photographer for FSA Travels 50,000 Miles in Search of Pictures. It take considerable courage, not to mention credentials galore, venture into the hinterlands with a camera these days—particularly when you are a comely young girl" (see Fisher 145).

12. Hendrickson 222.

13. Hendrickson 223.

14. Fisher 144.

15. Fisher 144.

16. Stein 9.

17. Hurley 42.

18. Stein 9.

19. Stein 45.

20. This essentializing interpretation of artistic work by women is evident in assessments of Laura Gilpin by Martha A. Sandweiss in "Laura Gilpin and the Tradition of American Landscape Photography" and "The Landscape (chosen by desire): Laura Gilpin Renegotiates Mother Nature" in which Karen Hurst mentions Post Wolcott as being comparative to what she perceives as being Gilpin's biological affiliation with the land.

21. Kolodny 145.

22. In this way, Post Wolcott's emotional responses to the landscape seem to be a reaction against her job as a documentary photographer. Her desire to become part of the landscape rather than just an observer of it, could be interpreted as a female connection that is set in opposition to the Western surveys of the nineteenth century which, some feminist critics have suggested, reflected an exclusively male reaction to the land, i.e., the need to quantify, measure, stabilize, and tame the landscape as an economic resource.

23. Hendrickson 158

24. Hendrickson 16.

25. Hendrickson 20. In an interview with Hendrickson, Post Wolcott recalled that her mother "used to design clothes for herself that everybody else would have thought almost risqué. They were something like gypsy clothes. And she would sew things for me that were something like bloomers that were for backyard play. Which of course Daddy didn't approve of."

26. Hendrickson 20 .

27. Boddy 153-76. Boddy notes that Post Wolcott's desire to study with Mary Wigman extended from the dancer's reputation for revealing "an intense awareness of social grief and a commitment to do her utmost through dance to provide people with relief from the pangs of grief" (157).

28. Hendrickson 33. Fleischmann was a well-known portrait photographer in Austria at that time. Her studio in center of Vienna was a focal point for radical political activity and Bohemian gatherings.

29. Hendrickson 35.

30. Hendrickson 35.

31. Hendrickson 34.

32. Hurley 13.

33. Stein 44.

34. Hendrickson 31.

35. Hurley 9.

36. Stein 5.

37. Hurley 9.

38. By 1936, the ideological transformation of the Communist Party into the Popular Front had signalled the emergence of a distinctively American form of political radicalism. The international imperatives of class war had been replaced by more patriotic concerns, such as antifascism. The Popular Front

broadened definitions of radical cultural expression to include the mythology of an heroic American past that stressed American traditions and values. For a comprehensive analysis of this transition see Ottanelli, *The Communist Party of the United States*.

39. Campbell 94.

40. Lyons 156.

41. Campbell 93.

42. Steiner occasionally offered his studio to the Group for rehearsal purposes, and both Steiner and Strand visited the Group's retreat in Bridgeport, Connecticut.

43. Hendrickson 38.

44. Clurman 140.

45. On June 20, 1938, Paul Strand wrote to Stryker: "Dear Roy, It gives me great pleasure to give this note of introduction to Marion Post because I know her work well. She is a young photographer of considerable experience who has made a number of very good photographs on social themes in the South and elsewhere. . . . I feel that if you have any place for a conscientious and talented photographer you will do well to give her an opportunity."

46. Strand's focus on the radical potential he considered to be implicit in traditional American landscapes is particularly clear in his documentary book *Time in New England*, published in association with Nancy Newhall in 1954. The book was intended to symbolically reconstruct the revolutionary foundations of the American Dream; to reclaim the historical roots of a radical American past, where communities flourished by equally sharing resource and labor; and consequently to provide a photographic model for a more socialistic United States. For a criticism of Strand's approach see Stange, Maren, ed., *Paul Strand: Essays on His Life and Work* (New York: Aperture, 1990).

47. In an essay "Winter Landscape in the Early Republic: Survival and Sentimentality" Bernard Mergen suggests that in images of the New England winter, early settlers could claim that "their ability to survive was proof of their moral as well as physical superiority [over Europeans]. Moreover, the long winters provided a time of freedom and recreation in the fullest sense." See Gidley, Mick and Lawson, Robert Peebles, eds., *Views of American Landscapes* (Cambridge: Cambridge University Press, 1989). Mergen's analysis is made clear, also, in relation to descriptions of the winter landscape in New England in Crevecoeur's *Letters from an American Farmer* and Thoreau's *Walden; or, Life in the Woods*.

48. Hendrickson 260.

49. Hendrickson 71.

50. Hendrickson 71.

51. Hendrickson 71.

52. Hendrickson 166.

53. Fisher 153.

54. Stein 7.

55. Hendrickson 82.

56. Stein 8.

57. Fisher 153.

58. Stein 8.

59. Lerner 475.

60. Lerner 476.

61. Stein notices that there are "a number of figures" in the image, but only discusses the two black men who are walking in the opposite direction to the white woman. Fisher—whose analysis is culled directly from Stein—does not even acknowledge the presence of the third black man.

62. Hendrickson 261.

63. Brannan and Fleishhauer 176.

64. This conclusion is central to William Stott's analysis of *Let Us Now Praise Famous Men* where, he suggests, Evans and Agee reverse the traditional dynamic of documentary photography and, instead of valorizing the viewer's moral superiority over the subject, they present the tenant farmers' lives as being socially legitimate and equal to the viewer's experience. According to Stott, this depiction of the basic humanity of the rural poor provoked middle-class viewers to question the desirability of their point of view which, in the light of Agee's and Evans' text, was "attenuated . . . through many possessions." In contrast, the tenant farmers and sharecroppers displayed a spiritual core, "uncovered to view" to reveal "the essentials of the human condition." See Stott 274-75.

65. Hendrickson 140.

66. Hendrickson 145.

67. Hendrickson 145.

68. Brannan and Fleishhauer 176.

69. Brannan and Fleishhauer 176.

70. The artificiality of the woman's demeanor before she adjusted herself for the camera is clear in comparison with another of Post Wolcott's Miami Beach images, where a woman is pictured sunbathing: the sun is shining down directly on her body to create an unrealistically bright shot, and her face is covered with sunglasses which emphasize her mask-like expression.

71. Stein 6.

72. The difference between nudity and nakedness is central to John Berger's analysis of paintings of female nudes where, he suggests: "to be nude is to be seen as naked by others and yet not recognized for oneself. A naked body has to be seen as an object in order to become nude. . . .

"Nakedness reveals itself. Nudity is placed on display. To be naked is to be without disguise. To be on display is to have the surface of one's own skin, the hairs of one's own body, turned into a disguise, which in that situation can never be discarded. The nude is condemned to never being naked. Nudity is a form of dress."

See Berger 54.

Chapter 3: Esther Bubley: Revolutionary Spaces

1. "Washington in Wartime" 44-48.

2. "Washington in Wartime" 47.

3. Blum 48.

4. In this way, the arrangement of photographs reflects the purposes of FSA images. See the example given in Stange, *Symbols* 102.

5. Field et al 23.

6. Field et al. 39.

7. Field et al. 55.

8. Field et al. 63.

9. Field et al. 43.

10. Archibald 11.

11. Archibald 63.

12. Archibald 64.

13. Archibald 150.

14. Details on Bubley's early life are scant. Brief biographies appear in Plattner 55, and in Fisher 121-29.

15. All of the images from Bubley's Greyhound Bus series are reprinted in *Documenting America*, one photograph in particular gives an idea of her point of view: directed from a position in the aisle through the windscreen and focused on the road ahead.

16. Dieckmann 56.

17. Dieckmann 56.

18. Hurley 170.

19. As the founder of *Look!* magazine in 1934, Cowles would certainly have been familiar with the work of the FSA. Nevertheless, his views about the power of images in relation to expansive texts were forthright, particularly in one comment: "The public generally speaking won't read long columns of type in any newspaper or magazine explaining heavyweight important issues." See Winkler 40.

20. Winkler 62.

21. Winkler 65 .

22. Hurley 164.

23. Fisher 121.

24. Fisher 121.

25. Dieckmann 61.

26. Plattner 55.

27. Dieckmann 56.

28. Dieckmann 59.

29. See Brannan and Fleishhauer.

30. Fisher 128.

31. Anderson 62.

32. Wartime publicity campaigns concentrated almost exclusively on white middle-class women to the detriment of working-class women who were often portrayed as fatalistic, reactionary, and somewhat simple in relation to dependable, resourceful, and capable middle-class women. This difference in representation was especially ironic given that working-class women had been employed before the war, and were more likely to continue working—albeit in low-paid, low-status jobs—after 1945. For a comparison of popular images of middle-class and working-class women during the 1940, see Honey, *Creating Rosie the Riveter*. For an analysis of how this marginalization affected white working-class women in the post-war period see Kennedy, *If All We Did Was Weep at Home*.

33. Rupp 145.

34. Dieckmann 57.

35. Dieckmann 56.

36. For example in "Life Goes Boating with Sailors and Their Girls," June 7, 1943.

37. Architecture in Washington, DC, was intended to reflect the democratic ideals imagined by Thomas Jefferson symbolically rendered in Greek style monuments. He also wanted the capital city to represent the spirit of Republicanism in its use of Romanesque designs. The National Gallery of Art, opened in 1941, was the latest building to reflect Jefferson's architectural ideals. This construction became especially pertinent as America entered the War. See Green, *Washington, Capital City 1879-1950*.

38. Anderson 140.

39. Anderson 104.

40. Anderson 105.

41. Anderson 105.

42. Anderson 104.

43. Anderson 103.

44. Sutterfield 196.

45. Sutterfield 196

46. Fisher 95.

47. Fisher 97.

48. The obvious example is Lange's "Migrant Mother."

49. Doane 1.

50. Title given by Bubley, 1943.

51. Bubley's photograph is comparable to a similar image by Marjory Collins, where the focus is entirely on a shop mannequin and the people outside

the window are barely visible. See "R. H. Macy & Co department store during the week before Christmas. New York, New York" in Fisher 122.

52. Fisher 60.

53. Fisher 102.

54. Keim, *Washington and Its Environs* 64.

55. Green 172.

Introduction to Part II

1. Le Sueur, "Our Fathers," *Ripening* 116.

2. Morris 6.

3. Le Sueur, *Ripening* 119.

4. Le Sueur, *Ripening* 120.

5. Le Sueur, *Ripening* 116.

6. Le Sueur, *The Girl* 148.

7. Bakhtin, *The Dialogic Imagination.* See Bakhtin's "Discourse in the Novel" in *The Dialogic Imagination* 259-422.

8. Holquist 34.

9. Le Sueur 123.

10. Rabinowitz 21.

11. Rabinowitz 4

12. Nekola and Rabinowitz 3.

13. Rabinowitz 127.

14. Rabinowitz 84.

15. Rabinowitz 83.

16. Rabinowitz 71.

17. Rabinowitz 139.

18. Rabinowitz 15.

19. Rabinowitz 181.

20. Rabinowitz 98.

21. Olsen 137.

Chapter 4: Meridel Le Sueur: Sexual Revolution

1. Ross 49.

2. Ross 49.

3. Pells 52.

4. Pells 52.

5. Pells 97.

6. Pells 180.

7. Blake 123.

8. Blare 124.

9. Chambers 171.

10. Coiner 168.

11. Coiner 169-71.

12. Pratt 261.

13. Hedges 2.

14. Le Sueur, *Collected* 4.

15. Hedges, Elaine, Introduction, *Ripening*, Meridel Le Sueur (New York: Feminine P, 1990) 8.

16. Le Sueur, "I Was Marching," *Ripening* 158.

17. Le Sueur, *Collected* 158.

18. Le Sueur, "The Fetish of Being Outside," *Collected* 202.

19. Le Sueur, *Collected* 199.

20. Le Sueur, *Collected* 200.

21. Le Sueur, *Collected* 203.

22. Le Sueur, *Collected* 200.

23. Le Sueur, *Collected* 202.

24. Le Sueur, *Collected* 199.

25. Le Sueur, *Collected* 202.

26. Le Sueur, *Collected* 158.

27. Le Sueur, *Collected* 161.

28. Le Sueur, *Collected* 161.

29. Le Sueur, *Collected* 162.

30. Le Sueur, *Collected* 162.

31. Le Sueur, *Collected* 160.

32. Le Sueur, *Collected* 160.

33. Le Sueur, *Collected* 160.

34. Le Sueur, *Collected* 160.

35. Le Sueur, *Collected* 161.

36. Le Sueur, *Collected* 164.

37. Le Sueur, *Collected* 165.

38. Le Sueur, "What Happens in a Strike," *Collected* 185.

39. Le Sueur, *Collected* 185.

40. Le Sueur, *Collected* 185.

41. Le Sueur, *Collected* 185.

42. Le Sueur, *Collected* 185.

43. Le Sueur, *Collected* 185.

44. Le Sueur, *Collected* 186.

45. Le Sueur, *Collected* 186.

46. Le Sueur, *Collected* 190.

47. Le Sueur, *Collected* 191.

48. Le Sueur, *Collected* 191.

49. Le Sueur, *Collected* 190.

50. Le Sueur, *Collected* 191.

51. Le Sueur, *Collected* 192.

52. Le Sueur, *Collected* 191.

53. Le Sueur, *Collected* 191.

54. Le Sueur, *Collected* 191.

55. Le Sueur, "The Ancient People and the Newly Come," *Ripening* 43.

56. Le Sueur, *Ripening* 43.

57. Le Sueur, *Ripening* 65.

58. Duncan 66.

59. Le Sueur, "Crusaders," *Ripening* 48.

60. Le Sueur, *Ripening* 49.

61. Le Sueur, *Ripening* 49.

62. Le Sueur, *Ripening* 49.

63. Le Sueur, *Ripening* 49.

64. Le Sueur, *Ripening* 50.

65. Le Sueur, *Ripening* 50.

66. Le Sueur, *Ripening* 115.

67. Le Sueur, *Ripening* 115.

68. Le Sueur, *Ripening* 115.

69. Le Sueur, *Ripening* 115.

70. Le Sueur, "The Laundress," *Ripening* 109.

71. Le Sueur, *Ripening* 111.

72. Le Sueur, *Ripening* 5.

73. Le Sueur, *Ripening* 108.

74. Le Sueur, *Ripening* 111.

75. Le Sueur, *Ripening* 111.

76. Le Sueur, *Ripening* 111.

77. Le Sueur, *Ripening* 111.

78. Le Sueur, *Ripening* 5.

79. Le Sueur, *Ripening* 113.

80. Le Sueur, "Eroded Woman," *Ripening* 225.

81. Le Sueur, *Ripening* 226.

82. Le Sueur, *Ripening* 227.

83. Le Sueur, *Ripening* 227.

84. Le Sueur, *Ripening* 226.

85. Le Sueur, *Ripening* 226.

86. Le Sueur, *Ripening* 226.

87. Le Sueur, "Women Know a Lot of Things," *Ripening* 172.

88. Le Sueur, *Ripening* 174.

89. Le Sueur, "The Dark of the Time," *Ripening* 232.

90. Le Sueur, *Ripening* 173.

91. Le Sueur "Women on the Breadlines," *Ripening* 141.

92. Le Sueur, *Ripening* 137.

93. Le Sueur, *Ripening* 138.

94. Le Sueur, *Ripening* 138.

95. Le Sueur, *Ripening* 139.

96. Le Sueur, *Ripening* 139.

97. Le Sueur, *Ripening* 139.

98. Le Sueur, *Ripening* 139.

99. Le Sueur, *Ripening* 139.

100. Le Sueur, "Women Are Hungry," *Ripening* 152.

101. Le Sueur, *Ripening* 152.

102. Le Sueur, *Ripening* 153.

103. Le Sueur, *Ripening* 154.

104. Le Sueur, *Ripening* 154.

105. Le Sueur, *Ripening* 141.

106. Le Sueur, *Ripening* 119.

107. Le Sueur, *Ripening* 150.

108. Le Sueur, *Ripening* 150.

109. Le Sueur, *Ripening* 140.

110. Le Sueur, *Ripening* 141.

111. Le Sueur, *Ripening* 139.

112. Le Sueur, *Ripening* 139.

113. Sipple 138.

114. Sipple 144.

115. Le Sueur, *Girl* 9.

116. Le Sueur, *Ripening* 138.

117. Le Sueur, *Ripening* 138.

118. Le Sueur, *Ripening* 138.

119. Le Sueur, *Ripening* 140.

120. Le Sueur, *Ripening* 141.

121. Le Sueur, *Ripening* 141.

122. Le Sueur, *Ripening* 141.

123. Le Sueur, *Ripening* 142.

124. Le Sueur, *Ripening* 142.

125. Le Sueur, *Ripening* 143.

126. Le Sueur, "Spring Story," *Ripening* 85.

127. Le Sueur, *Ripening* 85.

128. Le Sueur, *Ripening* 96.

129. Le Sueur, *Ripening* 94.

130. Le Sueur, *Ripening* 95.

131. Le Sueur, *Ripening* 96.

132. Le Sueur, "Holiday," *Ripening* 20.

133. Le Sueur, *Ripening* 20.

134. Le Sueur, *Ripening* 20.

135. Le Sueur, *Ripening* 20.

136. Le Sueur, *Ripening* 28.
137. Le Sueur, *Ripening* 24.
138. Le Sueur, *Ripening* 24.
139. Le Sueur, "Harvest," *Ripening* 17.
140. Le Sueur, *Ripening* 11.
141. Le Sueur, *Ripening* 15.
142. Le Sueur, *Ripening* 15.
143. Le Sueur, *Ripening* 16.
144. Le Sueur, *Ripening* 15.
145. Le Sueur, *Ripening* 18.

Chapter 5: Tillie Olsen: An Arduous Partnership

1. Olsen, "A Biographical Interpretation" 158.
2. Olsen, "Biographical" 54.
3. Olsen, "Biographical" 154.
4. Olsen, "Biographical" 158.
5. Olsen, "Biographical" 76.
6. Olsen, "Biographical" 72.
7. Olsen, "Biographical" 76.
8. Olsen, "Biographical" 80.
9. Davis 12.
10. Davis 15.
11. Davis 15.
12. Davis 24.
13. Olsen, "Biographical" 75.
14. Olsen, "Biographical" 76.
15. Davis 3.
16. Davis 64.
17. Olsen surveys all of Davis's published work in her biographical inter-pretation, some of which, she suggests, shows the kind of promise that was evi-dent in "Life in the Iron Mills." However, most was of an inferior standard and was marked by sentimentality, occasional melodrama, and moral didacticism. See Olsen, "Biographical" 69-170.
18. Olsen, "Biographical" 156.
19. Davis 64.
20. Davis 11.
21. Davis 26.
22. Rabinowitz 175-82.
23. Olsen, *Tell Me* 173.
24. Olsen, *Tell Me* 173.
25. Olsen, *Tell Me* 173.
26. Olsen, *Tell Me* 172.

27. In an introduction to *Yonnondio*, Olsen describes the process of editing and reconstructing the original manuscripts from 1932 into what she considered to be a publishable form in 1973: "The first four chapters, in final or near-final form when fitted together, presented only minor problems. The succeeding pages were increasingly difficult to reclaim. There were usually two to fourteen versions to work from 38 to 41 year old pencilled-over scrawls and fragments to decipher and piece together. Judgment had to be exercised as to which version, revision or draft to choose or combine; decisions made whether to include or omit certain first drafts and notes; and guessing had to be done as to where several scenes belonged."

See Olsen, *Tell Me* 135-36.

28. Biographical details from Rosenfelt, and Duncan 31-57.

29. Duncan 36.

30. Duncan 36.

31. Rosenfelt 378.

32. Rosenfelt 379.

33. Rosenfelt 383.

34. Duncan 37.

35. Duncan 37.

36. Duncan notes that Olsen's disagreement with her teacher occurred after a "misunderstanding around the meaning of Hamlet's talking to his dead father," when the teacher hit Olsen in the forehead with a book. See Duncan 37.

37. Expanding on her experiences at Central High School, Olsen refers to Sennett and Cobb *The Hidden Injuries of Class*.

38. Rosenfelt 376.

39. Rosenfelt 376.

40. Olsen, "The Strike" 245-51.

41. Olsen, "The Strike" 249.

42. Olsen, "The Strike" 245.

43. Olsen, "The Strike" 245.

44. Olsen, "The Strike" 246.

45. Olsen, "The Strike" 246.

46. Olsen, "The Strike" 247.

47. Olsen, "The Strike" 247.

48. Olsen, "The Strike" 247.

49. Olsen, "The Strike" 248.

50. Olsen, "The Strike" 248.

51. Olsen, "The Strike" 248.

52. Olsen, "The Strike" 248.

53. Olsen, "The Strike" 249.

54. Olsen, "The Strike" 251.

55. Rosenfelt 385.

56. Olsen, "The Strike" 245.

57. Olsen, "The Strike" 245.

58. Olsen, "The Strike" 250.

59. Olsen, "The Strike" 250.

60. Olsen, "The Strike" 250.

61. Olsen, "Thousand-Dollar Vagrant" 67.

62. Olsen, "Thousand-Dollar Vagrant" 67.

63. Olsen, "Thousand-Dollar Vagrant" 68.

64. Olsen, "Thousand-Dollar Vagrant" 67.

65. Olsen, "Thousand-Dollar Vagrant" 68.

66. Olsen, "Thousand-Dollar Vagrant" 68.

67. Olsen, "Thousand-Dollar Vagrant" 68.

68. Olsen, "Thousand-Dollar Vagrant" 68.

69. Olsen, "Thousand-Dollar Vagrant" 68.

70. Olsen, "Thousand-Dollar Vagrant" 68.

71. Olsen, "Thousand-Dollar Vagrant" 68.

72. Olsen, "Thousand-Dollar Vagrant" 68.

73. Olsen, "I Want" 179-81.

74. Olsen, "I Want" 179.

75. Olsen, "I Want" 179.

76. Olsen, "I Want" 179.

77. Olsen, "I Want" 179.

78. Olsen, "I Want" 179.

79. Olsen, "I Want" 179.

80. Olsen, "I Want" 180.

81. Olsen, "I Want" 181.

82. Olsen, "I Want" 180.

83. Olsen, "I Want" 180.

84. Olsen, "I Want" 180.

85. Olsen, "I Want" 180.

86. Rabinowitz 125.

87. Duncan 39.

88. Duncan 53.

89. Rosenfelt 394.

90. Duncan 55.

91. Olsen's proposals for the continuation of *Yonnondio* are discussed in Duncan 51-52.

92. Rosenfelt 394.

93. Rosenfelt 391.

94. Yalom 58.

95. Orr 21.

96. Duncan 44.

97. Rosenfelt 404.
98. Olsen, *Tell Me* 149.
99. Olsen, *Tell Me* 147.
100. Olsen, *Tell Me* 149.
101. Olsen, *Tell Me* 157.
102. Olsen, *Tell Me* 149.
103. Olsen, *Tell Me* 149.
104. Olsen, *Tell Me* 150.
105. Olsen, *Tell Me* 146.
106. Olsen, *Tell Me* 150.
107. Olsen, *Tell Me* 150.
108. Olsen, *Tell Me* 153.
109. Olsen, *Tell Me* 146.
110. Olsen, *Tell Me* 147.
111. Olsen, *Tell Me* 157.

112. I am thinking particularly of assertions made by French feminists such as Julia Kristeva and Luce Irigary, who use Lacanian psychology to show how women might undermine the masculine "symbolic order" and speak from a perspective that is multi-faceted and diffuse, and is an expression of female sexuality in opposition to male phallic power. For example, in "Women's Exile," Irigary describes her feminist project as an attempt to articulate women's speech as a radical force: "I am trying first of all . . . to reexamine the masculine imaginary, to interpret how it has reduced us to silence, to unitism, and I am trying, from that perspective, at the same time to find a possible space for the feminine imaginary." See Moi, *Sexual/Textual Politics*, and Marks and Courtivron, *New French Feminisms*.

113. More recently, feminist theoreticians have criticized Irigary and Kristeva for accepting Lacanian gender oppositions. For example, in *Gender Trouble* Judith Butler argues that rather than accepting the "symbolic order" as being exclusively male, women should subvert that institutionalized power from within, by disrupting and confusing gender identities. Here, she utilizes Bakhtinian notions of the masquerade, where women can adopt "masculine" attributes (and vice versa) and thus subvert the symbolically constructed, institutionalized facade of gender identity. To a certain extent, Olsen allows this to happen in *Yonnondio*, as Jim and Anna exchange their masculine and feminine "guises." Nevertheless, Olsen challenges Butler's theory by showing how the power of masquerade is at best fleeting (and in Sheen McEvoy's case, is dependent on madness) in an economically deprived material context. See Butler, *Gender Trouble*.

114. Olsen, *Tell Me* 147.
115. Olsen, *Tell Me* 158.
116. Olsen, *Tell Me* 159.

117. Olsen, *Tell Me* 169.
118. Olsen, *Tell Me* 159.
119. Olsen, *Tell Me* 160.
120. Olsen, *Tell Me* 160.
121. Olsen, *Tell Me* 161.
122. Olsen, *Tell Me* 165.
123. Olsen, *Tell Me* 166.
124. Olsen, *Tell Me* 179.
125. Olsen, *Tell Me* 177.
126. Olsen, *Tell Me* 183.
127. Olsen, *Tell Me* 186.
128. Olsen, *Tell Me* 187.
129. Olsen, *Tell Me* 192.
130. Olsen, *Tell Me* 186.
131. Olsen, *Tell Me* 186.
132. Olsen, *Tell Me* 197.
133. Olsen, *Tell Me* 191.
134. Olsen, *Tell Me* 197.
135. Olsen, *Tell Me* 192.
136. Olsen, *Tell Me* 198.
137. Olsen, *Tell Me* 189.
138. Olsen, *Tell Me* 198.
139. Olsen, *Tell Me* 198.
140. Olsen, *Tell Me* 199.
141. Olsen, *Tell Me* 200.
142. Olsen, *Tell Me* 200.
143. Olsen, *Tell Me* 202.
144. Olsen, *Tell Me* 203.
145. Olsen, *Tell Me* 204.
146. Olsen, *Tell Me* 205.
147. Olsen, *Tell Me* 205.
148. Olsen, *Tell Me* 205. Again, male and female experiences are connected inexorably to the mine as a symbol of working-class identity. See page 41.
149. Olsen, *Tell Me* 205.
150. Olsen, *Tell Me* 209.
151. Olsen, *Tell Me* 207.
152. Olsen, *Tell Me* 209.
153. Olsen, *Tell Me* 213.
154. Olsen, *Tell Me* 267.
155. Olsen, *Tell Me* 214.
156. Olsen, *Tell Me* 214.
157. Olsen, *Tell Me* 213.

158. Olsen, *Tell Me* 213.
159. Olsen, *Tell Me* 213.
160. Olsen, *Tell Me* 293.
161. Olsen, *Tell Me* 300.
162. Olsen, *Tell Me* 326.
163. Olsen, *Tell Me* 302.
164. Olsen, *Tell Me* 302.
165. Olsen, *Tell Me* 328.
166. Olsen, *Tell Me* 328.
167. Olsen, *Tell Me* 303.
168. Olsen, *Tell Me* 303.
169. Olsen, *Tell Me* 303.
170. Olsen, *Tell Me* 303.
171. Olsen, *Tell Me* 230.
172. Olsen, *Tell Me* 230.
173. Olsen, *Tell Me* 232.
174. Olsen, *Tell Me* 233.
175. Olsen, *Tell Me* 234.
173. Olsen, *Tell Me* 233.
177. Olsen, *Tell Me* 236.
178. Olsen, *Tell Me* 240.
179. Olsen, *Tell Me* 254.
180. Olsen, *Tell Me* 256.
181. Olsen, *Tell Me* 257.
182. Rabinowitz 133.
183. This opposition is at the crux of Rabinowitz's analysis. She contends that male and female labor are separated in radical texts, and represented as industrial/manual work defined as male; and female emotionality, reproductivity, and sexuality work for which Rabinowitz uses the term "desire."
184. Olsen, *Tell Me* 261.
185. Olsen, *Tell Me* 262.
186. Olsen, *Tell Me* 271.
187. Olsen, *Tell Me* 278.
188. Olsen, *Tell Me* 282.
189. Olsen, *Tell Me* 283.
190. Olsen, *Tell Me* 281.
191. Olsen, *Tell Me* 283.
192. Olsen, *Tell Me* 285.
193. Olsen, *Tell Me* 49.
194. Duncan 39.
195. Rabinowitz suggests that "the bodies of mother and daughter fuse . . . only to be called back . . . by the voices of Anna's insistent sons," further

emphasizing what she portrays as the fundamental gender division in *Yonnondio*. This assertion is somewhat reductive, however, since Anna and Maizie are accompanied by all the Holbrook children—boys and girls—and also it does not acknowledge the interruption of "the wind through the packing house," which reminds the two women of their economic identities as well as their gender status.

196. Olsen, *Tell Me* 334.

197. Olsen began her writing career again in 1962, with the publication of a collection of short stories: *Tell Me a Riddle*. Besides *Yonnondio*, Olsen's only other published work of fiction has been a single short story "Requa" in the *Iowa Review*. In this respect, her writing life has echoed the prophecy of her analytical work *Silences* (1978), where she suggested that the psychological effects of her economic situation were probably irrevocable: "This most harmful of all my silences has ended, but I am not yet recovered; may still be a one-book silence." See Olsen, *Silences*.

198. Olsen, *Tell Me* 336.

199. In *Calling Home*, Janet Zandy suggests that as a woman from a working-class background, her connection to her past and her aspirations as an academic working in an middle-class environment have resulted in a feeling of personal fragmentation. She states that "there were always divisions, separations, not neat ones either—raw, and ragged, holes." Zandy's testimony reflects Olsen's experience in that a sense of individuality is difficult, if not impossible, to attain for working-class women if individuality is always defined from a middle-class perspective. Consequently, as Zandy concludes, "For writers who were born into the working-class and aspire out of it through education or professional jobs, the connecting link back to a community is tangled or even lost."

200. Kaplan 4.

Bibliography

Agee, James, and Walker Evans. *Let Us Now Praise Famous Men.* Boston: Houghton, 1960.

Albelda, Randy, and Nancy Folbre. *The War on the Poor: A Defense Manual.* New York: New P, 1996.

Anderson, Karen. *Wartime Women: Sex Roles, Family Relations and the Status of Women During World War II.* Westport: Greenwood, 1981.

Archibald, Katherine. *Wartime Shipyard: A Study in Social Disunity.* Berkeley: U of California P, 1947.

Bakhtin, M. M. *The Dialogic Imagination: Four Essays.* Austin: U of Texas P, 1981.

Baldwin, Sidney. *Poverty and Politics: The Rise and Decline of the Farm Security Administration.* Chapel Hill: U of North Carolina P, 1968.

Barthes, Roland. *Camera Lucida: Reflections on Photography.* London: Flamingo, 1984.

Benjamin, Walter. "The Work of Art in the Age of Mechanical Reproduction." *Photography in Print: Writings from 1816-Present.* Ed. Vicki Goldberg. Albuquerque: U of New Mexico P, 1988. 319-34.

Berger, John. *Ways of Seeing.* London: Penguin, 1972.

Berger, John, and Jean Mohr. *Another Way of Telling.* New York: Pantheon, 1982.

Blake, Fay M. *The Strike in the American Novel.* Metuchen: Scarecrow, 1972.

Blum, John Morton. *V Was for Victory: Politics and American Culture During World War II.* New York: Harcourt, 1976.

Boddy, Julie. "Photographing Women: The Farm Security Administration Work of Marion Post Wolcott." *Decades of Discontent: The Women's Movement, 1920-1940.* Ed. Lois Scharf and Joan M. Jenson. Boston: Northeastern UP, 1987. 153-66.

Brannan, Beverly W., and Carl Fleischhauer, eds. *Documenting America 1935-1943.* Berkeley: U of California P, 1988.

Butler, Judith. *Gender Trouble: Feminism and the Subversion of Identity.* New York: Routledge, 1990.

Caldwell, Erskine, and Margaret Bourke-White. *You Have Seen Their Faces.* New York: Modern Age, 1937.

Campbell, Russell. "America: (The Workers') Film and Photo-League." *Photography/Politics: One* London: Photography Workshop, 1979.

Carby, Hazel V. *Reconstructing Womanhood: The Emergence of the Afro-American Woman Novelist.* New York: Oxford UP, 1987.

Chamberlain, Samuel, ed. *Fair Is Our Land.* New York: Hastings, 1942.

Chambers, Whittaker. Editor's Note. *Harvest Song: Collected Essays and Stories.* By Meridel Le Sueur. Albuquerque: West End P, 1990.

Clurman, Harold. *The Fervent Years: The Story of the Group Theatre and the Thirties.* London: Dennis Dobson, 1946.

Coiner, Constance. "Literature of Resistance: The Intersection of Feminism and the Communist Left in Meridel Le Sueur and Tillie Olsen." *Left Politics and the Literary Profession.* Ed. Lennard J. Davis and M. Bella Mirabella. New York: Columbia UP, 1990. 162-85.

Curtis, James. *Mind's Eye Mind's Truth: FSA Photography Reconsidered.* Philadelphia: Temple UP, 1989.

Davis, Rebecca Harding. *Life in the Iron Mills Or, the Korl Woman.* New York: Feminist P, 1972.

Dieckmann, Katherine. "A Nation of Zombies: Government files contain the extraordinary unpublished photographs that Esther Bubley took on one long bus ride across America." *Art in America* Nov. 1989: 55-70.

Doane, Mary Ann. *Femmes Fatales: Feminism, Film Theory, Psychoanalysis.* New York: Routledge, 1991.

Duncan, Erika. *Unless Soul Clap Its Hands: Portraits and Passages.* New York: Shocken, 1984.

Fisher, Andrea. *Let Us Now Praise Famous Women: Women Photographers for the U.S. Government 1935 to 1945.* London: Pandora, 1987.

Frank, Miriam, Marilyn Ziebarth, and Connie Field, eds. *The Life and Times of Rosie the Riveter: The Story of Three Million Working Women During World War II.* Emeryville: Clarity Educational Productions, 1982.

Fussell, Paul. *Class.* New York: Ballantine, 1983.

Green, Constance McLaughlin. *Washington: Capital City 1879-1959, Volume Two.* Princeton: Princeton UP, 1963.

Hagood, Margaret Jarman. *Mothers of the South: Portraiture of the White Tenant Farm Woman.* Chapel Hill: U of North Carolina P, 1939.

Hedges, Elaine. Introduction. *Ripening.* By Meridel Le Sueur. New York. Feminist P, 1990. 1-28.

Hendrickson, Paul. *Looking for the Light: The Hidden Life and Art of Marion Post Wolcott.* New York: Knopf, 1992.

Holquist, Michael. *Dialogism: Bakhtin and His World.* London: Routledge, 1990.

Honey, Maureen. *Creating Rosie the Riveter: Class, Gender, and Propaganda During World War II.* Amherst: U of Massachusetts P, 1984.

Hurley, F. Jack. *Marion Post Wolcott: A Photographic Journey.* Albuquerque: U of New Mexico P, 1989.

——. *Portrait of a Decade: Roy Stryker and the Development of Documentary Photography in the Thirties*. Baton Rouge: Louisiana State UP, 1972.

Hurston, Zora Neale. *Their Eyes Were Watching God*. Urbana: U of Illinois P, 1978.

Hust, Karen. "The Landscape (chosen by desire): Laura Gilpin Renegotiates Mother Nature" *Genders* 6 (Fall 1989): 20-48.

Janiewski, Dolores. "Flawed Victories: The Experience of Black and White Women Workers in Durham during the 1930s." Scharf and Jensen 85-109.

Kaplan, Cora. Introduction. *Tell Me a Riddle*. By Tillie Olsen. London: Virago, 1980. 4-14.

Keim, De B. Randolph. *Washington and Its Environs: An Illustrated Descriptive and Historical Hand-Book to the Capital of the United States of America*. Washington City: Keim, 1874.

Kennedy, Susan Eastabrook. *If All We Did Was to Weep at Home: A History of White Working-class Women in America*. Bloomington: U of Indiana P, 1979.

Kolodny, Annette. *The Lay of the Land: Metaphor as Experience and History in American Life and Letters*. Chapel Hill: U of North Carolina P, 1975.

Lange, Dorothea. *Dorothea Lange: The Making of a Documentary Photographer; An Interview Conducted by Suzanne Riess*. Berkeley:U of California Regional Oral History Office, 1968.

——, and Paul Schuster Taylor. *An American Exodus: A Record of Human Erosion in the Thirties*. New Haven: Yale UP, 1969.

Le Sueur, Meridel. *The Girl*. London: Women's P, 1986. Rev. ed. Albuquerque: West End P, 1990.

——. *Harvest Song: Collected Essays and Stories*. Albuquerque: West End P, 1990.

——. *Ripening: Selected Work*. New York: Feminist P, 1990.

——. "Sequel to Love." Nekola and Rabinowitz 36-38.

Lerner, Gerda, ed. *Black Women in White America: A Documentary History*. New York: Vintage, 1992.

Leuchtenberg, William E. *Franklin D. Roosevelt and the New Deal, 1932-1940*. New York: Harper Torchbooks, 1990.

"*Life* Goes Boating with Sailors and Their Girls." *Life* 7 June 1943: 98-1001.

Lyons, Nathan, ed. *Photo-Notes: February 1938-Spring 1950* Rochester: Visual Studies Workshop, 1977.

Mann, Marjory "Dorothea Lange." *Popular Photography* March 1970: 84-85, 99-101.

Marks, Elaine, and Isabelle de Courtivron, eds. *New French Feminisms: An Anthology*. Amherst: U of Massachusetts P, 1980.

Meltzer, Milton. *Dorothea Lange: A Photographer's Life*. New York: Farrar Straus Giroux, 1978.

Mergen, Bernard. "Winter Landscapes in the Early Republic: Survival and Sentimentality." *Views of American Landscapes*. Ed. Mick Gidley and Robert Lawson-Peebles. Cambridge: Cambridge UP, 1989. 27-43.

Meriwether, Louise. *Daddy Was a Number Runner.* New York: Feminist P, 1970.

Moi, Toril. *Sexual/Textual Politics: A Feminist Literary Theory*. London: Methuen, 1985.

Morris, Pam, ed. *The Bakhtin Reader: Selected Writings of Bakhtin, Medvedev, and Voloshinov*. London: Arnold, 1994.

Morrison, Toni. *Playing in the Dark: Whiteness and the Literary Imagination.* Cambridge: Harvard UP, 1992.

Moutassamy-Ashe, Jeanne. *Viewfinders: Black Women Photographers.* New York: Dodd, 1986.

Natanson, Nicholas. *The Black Image in the New Deal: The Politics of FSA Photography.* Knoxville: U of Tennessee P, 1992.

Nekola, Charlotte, and Paula Rabinowitz, eds. *Writing Red: An Anthology of America Women Writers, 1930-1940.* New York: Feminist P, 1987.

Ohrn, Karin Becker. *Dorothea Lange and the Documentary Tradition.* Baton Rouge: Louisiana State UP, 1980.

Olsen, Tillie. "A Biographical Interpretation." Davis 69-156.

——. "I Want You Women Up North to Know." Nekola and Rabinowitz 179-81.

——. *Silences.* New York: Delta/Seymour, 1978.

——. "The Strike." Nekola and Rabinowitz 245-51.

——. *Tell Me a Riddle and Yonnondio.* London: Virago, 1980.

——. "Thousand-Dollar Vagrant." *New Republic* 29 Aug. 1934: 67-69.

Orr, Elaine."On the Side of the Mother: *Yonnondio* and *Call It Sleep." Studies in American Fiction* 21.2: 209-30.

Ottanelli, Fraser M. *The Communist Party of the United States: From the Depression to World War II.* New Brunswick: Rutgers UP, 1991.

Parks, Gordon. *To Smile in Autumn: A Memoir.* New York: Norton, 1979.

——. *Voices in the Mirror: An Autobiography.* New York: Doubleday, 1990.

Pells, Richard H. *Radical Visions and American Dreams: Culture and Social Thought in the Depression Years.* New York: Harper, 1973.

Petry, Ann. *The Street.* Boston: Houghton Miflin, 1956.

Plattner, Steven W. *Roy Stryker, U.S.A., 1943-1950: The Standard Oil (New Jersey) Photography Project.* Austin: U of Texas, 1983.

Pratt, Linda Ray "Woman Writer in the CP: The Case of Meridel Le Sueur." *Women's Studies: An Interdisciplinary Journal* 14.3 (1988): 247-64.

Rabinowitz, Paula. *Labor and Desire: Women's Revolutionary Fiction in Depression America.* Chapel Hill: U of North Carolina P, 1991.

Rawlings, Marjory Kinnan. *The Marjory Kinnan Rawlings Reader.* New York: Scribner, 1956.

Roediger, David R. *The Wages of Whiteness: Race and the Making of the American Working Class.* London: Verso, 1991.

Rogovin, Milton, and Michael Frisch. *Portraits in Steel.* Ithaca: Cornell UP, 1993.

Rosenfelt, Deborah. "From the Thirties: Tillie Olsen and the Radical Tradition." *Feminist Studies* 7.3 (1981): 371-406.

Rosler, Martha. "In, around, and afterthoughts (on documentary photography)." *The Contest of Meaning: Critical Histories of Photography.* Ed. Richard Bolton. Cambridge: MIT, 1989.

Ross, Andrew. *No Respect: Intellectuals and Popular Culture.* New York: Routledge, 1989.

Rupp, Leila J. *Mobilizing Women for War: German and American Propaganda, 1939-1945.* Princeton: Princeton UP, 1978.

Sandweiss, Martha A. "Laura Gilpin and the Tradition of American Landscape Photography." *The Desert Is No Lady: Southwestern Landscapes in Women's Writing and Art.* Ed. Vera Norwood and Janice Monk. New Haven: Yale UP, 1987.

Sanger, Margaret. *Margaret Sanger: An Autobiography.* New York: Norton, 1938.

Satterfield, Archie. *The Home Front: An Oral History of the War Years in America, 1941-1945.* New York: Playboy, 1981.

Scharf, Lois, and Joan M. Jensen. *Decades of Discontent: The Women's Movement,1920-1940.* Boston: Northeastern U P, 1987.

Sennett, Richard, and Jonathan Cobb. *The Hidden Injuries of Class.* London: Faber, 1993.

Shloss, Carol. *In Visible Light: Photography and the American Writer, 1840-1940.* New York: Oxford UP, 1987.

Silverman, Jonathan, ed. *For the World to See: The Life of Margaret Bourke-White.* New York: Viking. 1983.

Sipple, Susan. "Witness (to) the Suffering of Women: Poverty and Sexual Transgression in Meridel Le Sueur's 'Women on the Breadlines.'" *Feminism, Bakhtin, and the Dialogic.* Ed. Dale M. Bauer and Susan Jaret McKinstry. Albany: SUNY, 1991. 135-53.

St. John de Crevecoeur, J. Hector. *Letters from an American Farmer.* London: Dent, 1937.

Stange, Maren. *Symbols of Ideal Life: Social Documentary Photography in America, 1890-1950.* New York: Cambridge UP, 1992.

——, ed. *Paul Strand: Essays on His Life and Work.* New York: Aperture, 1990.

Stein, Sally. "Marion Post Wolcott: Some Thoughts on Some Lesser Known FSA Photographs." *Marion Post Wolcott, FSA Photographs.* By Marion Post Wolcott. Carmel: Friends of Photography, 1983.

Stott, William. *Documentary Expression and Thirties America.* Chicago: U of Chicago P, 1986.

Strand, Paul, and Nancy Newhall. *Time in New England.* New York: Aperture, 1980.

Stryker, Roy. The Roy Stryker Collection. University of Louisville Photographic Archives, Louisville, KY.

Stryker, Roy Emerson, and Nancy Wood. *In This Proud Land: America 1935-1943, As Seen in the FSA Photographs.* New York: New York Graphic Society, 1973. Greenwich: New York Graphic Society, 1973.

Susman, Warren I. *Culture As History: The Transformation of American Society in the Twentieth Century.* New York: Pantheon, 1984.

Thoreau, Henry David. *Walden; Or, Life in the Woods.* New York: Holt, 1961.

Tockarczyk, Michelle M., and Elizabeth A. Fay, eds. *Working-Class Women in the Academy: Laborers in the Knowledge Factory.* Amherst: U of Massachusetts P, 1993.

Trachtenberg, Alan. "From Image to Story: Reading the File." *Documenting America, 1935-1943.* Ed. Carl Fleischauer and Beverly Brannon. Berkeley: U of California P, 1988.

Ware, Susan. *Beyond Suffrage: Women in the New Deal.* Cambridge: Harvard U P, 1981.

"Washington in Wartime." *Life* 4 Jan. 1943: 47-51.

Winkler, Allan M. *The Politics of Propaganda: The Office of War Information, 1942-1945.* New Haven: Yale UP, 1978.

Wright, Richard. *American Hunger.* New York: Harper, 1977.

——. *Native Son.* New York: Modern Library, 1940.

Yalom, Marilyn, ed. *Women Writers of the West Coast: Speaking of Their Lives and Careers.* Santa Barbara: Capra, 1983.

Zandy, Janet ed. *Calling Home: Working-Class Women's Writings.* New Brunswick: Rutgers UP, 1990.

Index